Coin Collecting For Dummies®

W9-BAA-097

Cheat Sheet

Auction Houses, Coin Clubs, and Organizations

Buy, sell, or join — you can do it all with the companies and organizations listed here. This is a condensed listing (in alphabetical order) of what I consider to be the biggest and best companies and organizations within their respective fields. If you have access to the Internet, visit www.CoinLink.com for an extensive listing of numismatic Web sites.

Auction houses

Auctions by Bowers and Merena, Inc.
P.O. Box 1224
Wolfeboro, NH 03894-1224
Phone: 800-458-4646
www.bowersandmerena.com

Early American History Auctions, Inc.
P.O. Box 3341
La Jolla, CA 92038
Phone: 858-459-4159
www.earlyamerican.com

Heritage Numismatic Auctions, Inc.
Highland Plaza
100 Highland Park Village, Second Floor
Dallas, TX 75205-2788
Phone: 800-872-6467
www.heritagecoin.com

Ira & Larry Goldberg Coins & Collectibles, Inc.
350 S. Beverly Drive, Suite 350
Beverly Hills, CA 90212
Phone: 310-551-2646
www.goldbergcoins.com

Ponterio & Associates, Inc.
1818 Robinson Avenue
San Diego, CA 92103
Phone: 619-299-0400
www.ponterio.com

Sotheby's
1334 York Avenue
New York, NY 10021
Phone: 212-606-7000
www.sothebys.com

Stack's
123 West 57th Street
New York, NY 10019
Phone: 212-582-2580
www.stacks.com

Superior Galleries
9478 West Olympic Boulevard
Beverly Hills, CA 90212-4246
Phone: 310-203-9855
www.superiorgalleries.com

Specialty coin clubs

Bust Half Nut Club (Half Dollars from 1794 to1839)
P.O. Box 87641
Canton, MI 48187

Colonial Coin Collectors Club (U.S. colonial coins)
c/o Angel Pietri
1560 Manchester Boulevard
Fort Myers, FL 33919

Early American Coppers Club (U.S. Half Cents and Large Cents)
P.O. Box 15782
Cincinnati, OH 45215
www.eacs.org

Liberty Seated Collectors Club (Liberty Seated Coins from 1836 to 1891)
P.O. Box 776
Crystal Lake, IL 60039-0776
www.numismalink.com/lscc.html

Numismatic Bibliomania Society (coin books)
5911 Quinn Orchard Road
Frederick, MD 21701
www.coinbooks.org

For Dummies: Bestselling Book Series for Beginners

Coin Collecting For Dummies®

Specialty coin clubs (continued)

John Reich Collectors Society (early American gold and silver coins)
P.O. Box 135
Harrison, OH 45030-0135
http://rob.com/jrcs

Collector and dealer organizations

American Numismatic Association
818 North Cascade Avenue
Colorado Springs, CO 80903-3279
Phone: 719-632-2646
www.money.org

American Numismatic Society
Broadway at 155th Street
New York, NY 10032
Phone: 212-234-3130
www.amnumsoc.org

Professional Numismatists Guild (dealers)
3950 Concordia Lane
Fallbrook, CA 92028
Phone: 760-728-1300
www.pngdealers.com

Numismatic Periodicals

Buy and read the following periodicals to keep up with the latest news and information about numismatics.

Coin World
P.O. Box 150
Sidney, OH 45365-0150
Phone: 800-253-4555
www.coinworld.com

COINage Magazine
4880 Market Street
Ventura, CA 93003-7783
Phone: 805-644-3824
www.coinagemag.com

Coins Magazine, Numismatic News, and World Coin News
700 E. State Street
Iola, WI 54990
Phone: 800-258-0929
www.krause.com/coins

The Numismatist
818 North Cascade Avenue
Colorado Springs, CO 80903-3279
Phone: 719-632-2646
www.money.org

Book and Supply Dealers

Books about coins are one of the best numismatic investments you can make. In terms of knowledge and utility, these books pay for themselves many times over. In addition, using the proper supplies with your coin collection will help them retain — or increase — their value over time. Check with the following companies for a wide variety of books and supplies.

CoinFacts.com, Inc.
P.O. Box 90037
Pacific Beach, CA 92169
www.CoinFacts.com

Stanton Books & Supplies
P.O. Box 15477
Savannah, GA 31416-2187
Phone: 800-828-8306
www.stantonbooks.com

For Dummies: Bestselling Book Series for Beginners

Coin Collecting

FOR

DUMMIES®

Coin Collecting

FOR

DUMMIES®

by Ron Guth

Wiley Publishing, Inc.

Coin Collecting For Dummies®

Published by
Wiley Publishing, Inc.
909 Third Avenue
New York, NY 10022
www.wiley.com

Copyright © 2001 by Wiley Publishing, Inc., Indianapolis, Indiana

Published simultaneously in Canada

For general information on our other products and services or to obtain technical support, please contact our Customer Care Department within the U.S. at 800-762-2974, outside the U.S. at 317-572-3993, or fax 317-572-4002.

Wiley also publishes its books in a variety of electronic formats. Some content that appears in print may not be available in electronic books.

Library of Congress Cataloging-in-Publication Data:

Library of Congress Control Number: 2001092752

ISBN: 0-7645-5389-5

Manufactured in the United States of America

10 9

1B/QT/QZ/QS/IN

About the Author

Ron Guth is a jack-of-all-trades and master of one — numismatics. Ron is a Certified Public Accountant (CPA), a licensed auctioneer, and a writer, but the bulk of his time is spent on his true love — coin collecting and dealing. Ron's battle with coin fever began when he was 12 years old (roughly 35 years ago), and he's never gotten over it. After a decade of collecting, Ron went professional in 1976 when he began working for a local coin shop in Tampa, Florida. In 1978, he partnered with David Goldsmith and purchased the Bay Area Coin Exchange in Tampa. Ron and Dave blasted through the silver boom, and then split up in 1981, when Ron moved to Evansville, Indiana (his wife's hometown) where he set up shop on First Avenue. In 1984, Ron formed Mid-American Rare Coin Auctions with Jeff Garrett of Lexington, Kentucky. The company quickly established itself as an innovative leader in the industry and, within the first year, became the fifth largest rare coin auction company in America. In 1988, Ron sold his interest in the company, went back to school to finish his Bachelor's degree in accounting and finance, and has since become a numismatic consultant and a major dealer in German coins.

In 1984, Ron won the American Numismatic Association's Wayte and Olga Raymond and Heath Literary awards. He has written many coin-related articles and is listed as a contributor to several books, including Walter Breen's *Encyclopedia of United States Coins,* Krause Publication's *Standard Catalog of German Coins,* Roger Cohen's *American Half Cents,* Walter Breen's *Encyclopedia of United States Half Cents,* and others. Ron has served as a numismatic consultant for many rare coin companies, including major firms such as the Professional Coin Grading Service, Heritage Numismatic Auctions, and Early American History Auctions.

As a rare coin auctioneer, Ron has sold over $100 million in rare coins, including the $1.84 million 1913 Liberty Head Nickel (tied for the second most valuable coin ever sold at auction). His chant has been heard at auctions conducted by just about every major name in the business, including R.M. Smythe, Heritage Numismatic Auctions, Kagin's, Lyn Knight, David Akers, Currency Auctions of America, Ponterio & Associates, Early American History Auctions, Mid-American Rare Coin Auctions, and Superior Galleries.

Ron's professional affiliations include Life Membership in the American Numismatic Association and memberships in the Rittenhouse Society, Early American Coppers Club, Colonial Coin Collectors Club, Civil War Token Society, and numerous regional and state organizations.

In 1999, Ron formed CoinFacts.com, Inc., a Web site that provides free, indepth information about U.S. coins to anyone with Internet access. In 2000, he launched PaperMoneyFacts.com to provide a similar service for paper money collectors.

You can visit Ron on his Web sites at www.coinfacts.com or www.papermoneyfacts.com or contact him at ron@coinfacts.com.

Dedication

This book is dedicated to my family: Jana the jungle babe, Mookus, Crusty, and Oosa Boosa. Thanks for all your love and support — and for doing the dishes so that I could write.

Author's Acknowledgments

Someone once said that a person is the sum of their experiences and the people they've known. Certainly, in my years of dealing and collecting, I've come across many individuals who have played an important part in making me who I am today. Now is my chance to thank them. In no particular order, they are as follows:

- **Kim and Karl Biltz:** For turning me on to coins

- **Marc Earle:** My first real coin buddy

- **Joe Person** (deceased): A world-class coin dealer who had plenty of time for a young kid

- **Walter Breen** (deceased): A true numismatic genius with a fatal flaw

- **Dana Linett:** Thanks for introducing me to California, historical documents, and the ultimate in marketing techniques

- **Jeff Garrett:** A great friend and one of the sharpest eyes and minds in the coin business

- **Barbara Talbot:** My mom and the best cheering section a son could ever have

- **Tom Mulvaney:** *The* best coin photographer in the business

- **Jim Halperin:** Thank you for all your support and the annual subscription to *Prevention* magazine

- **Larry Hanks:** A coin dealer with that rare combination of a soul and a faith that can move mountains

Special thanks go to Richard Doty for serving as technical reviewer for this book.

In the non-numismatic world, I owe a debt of gratitude to Michael Cunningham and Tonya Maddox at Hungry Minds, Inc. for pulling me into and guiding me through one of the most exhilarating rides of my life. I never knew that writing a book could be so exhausting, fun, demanding, fun, time-consuming, and (did I mention?) fun.

Last, but not least, there's Tere Drenth — a powerhouse editor who packs 30 hours into every day. This incredible lady is going to be famous one day — I just know it!

Publisher's Acknowledgments

We're proud of this book; please send us your comments through our online registration form located at www.dummies.com/register.

Some of the people who helped bring this book to market include the following:

Acquisitions, Editorial, and Media Development

Project Editors: Tere Drenth, Tonya Maddox

Acquisitions Editor: Michael Cunningham

Acquisitions Manager: Tracy Boggier

Copy Editor: Greg Pearson

Technical Reviewer: Richard G. Doty

Editorial Managers: Jennifer Ehrlich

Editorial Administrator: Michelle Hacker

Editorial Assistant: Carol Strickland

Cover Photos: Dan McGarrah\
Stock Connection\PictureQuest

Production

Project Coordinator: Bill Ramsey

Layout and Graphics: Amy Adrian, Jacque Schneider, Brian Torwelle, Jeremey Unger

Special Art: Photos by Tom Mulvaney, Ron Guth, and Early American History Auctions, Inc.

Proofreaders: Angel Perez, Marianne Santy, TECHBOOKS Production Services

Indexer: TECHBOOKS Production Services

Publishing and Editorial for Consumer Dummies

Diane Graves Steele, Vice President and Publisher, Consumer Dummies
Joyce Pepple, Acquisitions Director, Consumer Dummies
Kristin A. Cocks, Product Development Director, Consumer Dummies
Michael Spring, Vice President and Publisher, Travel
Brice Gosnell, Publishing Director, Travel
Suzanne Jannetta, Editorial Director, Travel

Publishing for Technology Dummies

Andy Cummings, Acquisitions Director

Composition Services

Gerry Fahey, Executive Director of Production Services
Debbie Stailey, Director of Composition Services

Contents at a Glance

Cartoons at a Glance

By Rich Tennant

"Check it out, Wendel — six Liberty Nickels! I found them behind the cushion when I was having the furniture wrapped in plastic covering."

page 323

"I hear he's uncirculated and in AVF condition, but he has also been struck twice and is definitely off center."

page 5

"That's right! A 1943 bronze Cent in a pair of penny loafers. Denise is checking it out now."

page 177

"Get coins! Preferably graded!"

page 61

"Along with my Franklin Nickels and Roosevelt Dimes, I've collected several McDonald's Quarter Pounders. Many of them are missing a pickle and show an off-center patty."

page 143

"This is probably the rarest coin in my collection. It's the one that stayed in my pocket during a three-day slot machine competition in Las Vegas."

page 295

Cartoon Information:
Fax: 978-546-7747
E-Mail: richtennant@the5thwave.com
World Wide Web: www.the5thwave.com

Table of Contents

Introduction

Welcome to *Coin Collecting For Dummies*. You may have just discovered coin collecting for the first time and want to find out more. Or perhaps you've collected coins for a while and want to take your hobby to the next level.

Coin collecting is a hobby you can share with family and friends. It's relaxing and inexpensive (although it can be very expensive!). Coin collecting teaches history, geography, observational skills, organizational skills, and analytical tools — all without your knowing it. If you buy properly, coins can be an excellent place to park your money for a rainy day, and if you buy the right coins and the market improves, you may even be able to make a profit on your collection.

About This Book

The purpose of this book is to turn you into a world-class numismatist in as short a period of time as possible. The chapters are laid out in parts that focus on particular areas of numismatics, including everything from getting involved in coin collecting to deciding what to collect, to protecting yourself and your coins, to grading, buying, and selling coins.

This book is designed to appeal to collectors at every level, from beginner to advanced. I wrote it in everyday English without overloading you with a bunch of coin terms. (However, if you run across a term you don't understand, you can find a great numismatic glossary in the Appendix). This is not a hardcore coin book. Rather, this book is a great general reference that points you in different directions for further investigation. You can always come back to this book to regroup, resupply, and ready yourself for something new.

Perhaps the most important goal of this book is to get you excited — and to keep you excited — about coin collecting. Coin collecting has been an important part of my life for many years and I hope you'll develop a sense of appreciation for the hobby, as well.

Why You Need This Book

No one needs coins, but if you decide to collect them, you certainly need this book. I wish I'd had one like it in my collecting career. Coin collecting can sometimes be a confusing maze of choices sprinkled with little traps along the way. Sure, you can go it alone, but why not make your journey into numismatics a lot easier by picking my brain and learning from the mistakes I've made over the past 30-something years?

Numismatics is a huge, wide-open field. Think of this book as a road map to help you navigate your way. Different issues may become important to you as your collecting evolves, so keep this book handy and refer to it often.

How This Book Is Organized

This book is organized into six parts that provide you with a concise introduction and overview, involve you in starting your collection, and take you deeper and deeper into the world of numismatics. Each chapter is designed to stand on its own, so you can start reading wherever you choose and jump from chapter to chapter with ease.

Part I: Numismatics: Easier Done Than Said

Don't be intimidated by the word *numismatics* — it's just a big word for coin collecting. In this part, I give you plenty of reasons to fall in love with coin collecting. I also stress the importance of doing a little homework before you jump in with both feet, and I steer you into some areas in which you want to become knowledgeable about coins. Finally, I show you how to store coins properly so that you and future generations can enjoy them to their fullest.

Part II: Buying Coins the Safe Way

You buy coins with the money left over after paying all your living expenses, so make those purchases count. That can be difficult because it's a jungle out there! In this part, I alert you to some of the scams less-than-reputable dealers use to separate you from your hard-earned money. I discuss the various numismatic price guides that help value your collection and buy and sell coins. I also introduce you to the bane of coin collecting — counterfeit and altered coins — and show you how not to fear them. Where you buy your coins can be just as important as what coins you buy, so this part presents an in-depth look at working with dealers and buying coins at auction.

A coin's condition (also known as the *grade*) is the single most important factor that affects its value. Learning to grade takes time, patience, and practice. In this part, I introduce you to some of the concepts behind grading, explain how to learn to grade coins, and show you how to use third-party grading services to your benefit.

Part III: Choosing Coins for Your Collection

Coins have been made for thousands of years by hundreds of different countries, so you have a lot to work with. Where to start? What to collect? This part takes a look at ancient coins, U.S. coins, world coins, and the wild and wooly stuff that will really get your numismatic juices pumping. By the time you're done with these chapters, you'll have a good idea of what you want to collect.

Part IV: Focusing on U.S. Coins

The U.S. has a rich and varied numismatic history that includes some of the greatest coins in the world. In this part, I present more than just a peek at most of them. My goal in these chapters is to present you with choices and then let you decide which ones are for you.

Part V: Selling (Sob!) Your Numismatic Treasures

You can't take your coins with you when you die. So what's the best way to sell them before you do? In this part, I present the three main options: selling your collection by yourself, selling to or through a dealer, and selling at auction. Each method has its pros and cons, all of which are outlined here.

Part VI: The Part of Tens

My editors said to have fun with this part — so I did! In this part, you meet the 10 most valuable U.S. coins (wait until you see the prices), my 10 favorite coin designs (what a bevy of beauties), and my 10 favorite numismatic Web sites (great places to buy, sell, and browse).

Icons Used in This Book

Throughout this book are handy road signs — called *icons* — that point you toward valuable advice and away from potential hazards.

Heeding the advice next to these icons helps you spend wisely and, therefore, have additional pennies for the stuff you really can use.

An old, old hobby that continues to evolve has developed many shortcuts to help its participants have more fun. This icon highlights some of the most important tips.

This is the type of information you want at your fingertips. Consider marking these pages for quick reference.

This icon points out specific coins or types of coins that you may want to add to your collection.

This icon highlights deeper, more technical information that may come in handy as you pursue coin collecting. Feel free to read or skip these mini-lectures!

Part I

Numismatics: Easier Done Than Said

The 5th Wave   By Rich Tennant

"I hear he's uncirculated and in AVF condition, but he has also been struck twice and is definitely off center."

In this part . . .

If you're new to *numismatics* (coin collecting), this part is an important one to get you started on the right foot.

In this part, I explain why coin collecting is such a fun and exciting hobby and why millions of people now call themselves numismatists. I also show you the importance of finding out as much as you can about numismatics, not just to protect yourself as a consumer, but also to give you a big advantage over other collectors. I save you money right off the bat by showing you how to take advantage of the wholesale pricing that's available to the smart collector.

I also discuss buying strategies and how to plan your collection so that you maximize the money you spend on, well, money! The right strategy saves you time and money and increases your enjoyment of the hobby.

Finally, I jump into the nitty-gritty of collecting coins, presenting a number of options for storing your coins so that they remain as beautiful and as valuable as they are today. I also discuss security issues and how to best protect your coins from theft and harm, both at home and on the road.

Chapter 1

Understanding (and Pronouncing) Numismatics

In This Chapter

▶ Beating the intimidation the word "numismatics" instills
▶ Collecting coins from Silver Dollars to 50 States Quarters

I'll bet you have a jar at home into that you throw your loose change into at the end of each day. At some point, the jar gets so full (or, if you're like me, you get so broke) that you have to roll up the coins, take them to the bank, and exchange them for paper money. As you separate the coins, are you ever distracted (even for a short moment) by the coins themselves, suddenly intrigued by the very fact that these small pieces of metal represent value, history, and your hard labor? Have you ever had the desire to sort the coins by date, trying to see how many different ones you can find? Have you ever picked through the dates trying to find the best-looking coin?

If you have, you've experienced a small taste of what it is to be a coin collector. Coin collecting refines a person's natural desire to accumulate. Coin collecting teaches about organization, classification, preservation, authentication, verification, and all sorts of other "-ations." Coins humble collectors with their ancient stories. The coin you hold in your hand may have seen the fall of Rome, it may have been carried by a king, it may have endured the Black Plague, it may have been carried by a G.I. on D-Day, or it may simply be a brand new coin just about to begin its own journey.

The fact that you're reading this book is a good sign that you've already been bitten by the collecting bug. Coin collecting is a great disease whose treatment is to find out as much as you can about the hobby and make yourself feel better with an occasional addition to your growing collection. This chapter helps you get started.

Admitting Your Numismatism

Numismatics is the study or collecting of coins, medals, tokens, and the like. Therefore, a *numismatist* is someone who studies or collects coins.

Go on, you can say them: new-miz-*mat*-ics. New-*miz*-ma-tist. Good!

No, you don't have to know how to pronounce or spell these words to be a coin collector, but sooner or later you'll be wearing them like badges of honor. After all, you'll be joining a rich company of kings and queens, presidents, industrialists, robber barons, brewers, and millions of other folks who have been proud to be known as numismatists.

Discovering How Cool Coin Collecting Can Be

People love money. People love people who have money. Numismatists have money. Therefore, people love numismatists.

Don't believe me? Try this test. Go down to your local coin store and buy a Morgan Silver Dollar dated anywhere from 1878 to 1921. Pick out a nice one, but don't pay more than ten dollars. Put it in your pocket the next time you go to a party. At the party, casually pull the coin from your pocket and show it to your friends. You'll probably get comments like

- "Where in the world did you get that?"
- "I haven't seen one of those for years."
- "My Dad used to give me one of those every year for my birthday."
- "Is that a real Silver Dollar?"
- "Wow, those things have got to be worth a hundred bucks nowadays!"
- "Can you get me one?"

Return the coin to your pocket and pull out a picture of your kid. Big deal. Everyone has a kid. The party returns to normal — boring!

Face it, numismatists are cool.

What makes a collection complete?

Completion is in the eye of the beholder. Many years ago, collectors were interested only in collecting by date. Therefore, in order to be complete, a collection had to include one coin from every year that coin was minted. Later, collectors developed an interest in *mintmarks* (the tiny letters that indicate where a coin was minted). Suddenly, to be complete, a collection now had to include a coin from every year and every mint. Then came collecting by variety (major or minor changes in the design of a coin) and the definition of completion expanded even further.

Obviously, completion is an ever-changing standard. Taken to the extreme, the only complete collection of coins is one that includes every coin ever made! Striving for completion will drive you nuts, especially if you allow others to define completion for you. Therefore, decide your own goals and set your own standards for completion. When you've completed that collection, consider a new definition of completion and go for it!

Collecting versus Accumulating

The collecting instinct is a common trait among people; it shows up in many ways. You'll discover that many of your friends are collectors of something. Who do you know collects baseball cards, Hummel figurines, beer cans, Coca-Cola memorabilia, books, or dolls? Even people who claim to collect nothing probably have accumulations of some *thing* they haven't even realized they're collecting — tools, newspapers, shoes, you name it. There's a special comfort in collecting, in surrounding yourself with familiar objects and building a store of assets — perhaps in response to some primeval instinct that prepares you for a rainy day.

The allure of money is especially strong. Coins represent real value. They can be exchanged for other objects we desire. The warmth of silver and the weight of gold are irresistible to some. Coins travel throughout the world and through time itself, representing and absorbing history as they pass from one person to the next. Oh the stories coins could tell if they only had voices.

Pull a dime out of your pocket and what do you see? If you see only ten cents to spend, we've got a lot of work to do. But, if you look at your dime and wonder at the artistic work of the engraver and the meaning of the symbols and the words, or if you see Franklin Roosevelt, the Great Depression, and the New Deal, man, you're hooked. You're going to make a great numismatist!

Here's a great way to find out whether you're an accumulator or whether you have the potential to become a coin collector: Visit your local coin store and purchase a folder made for the Pennies from the '70s, '80s, and '90s. (A *folder* is a cardboard holder with holes for every different date.) Raid your change jar or go to the bank and buy $20 worth of Pennies. Sort the coins out and fill as many different holes as you can. If possible, find the best-looking coin to place in the folder. After you've gone through all the coins, sit back and take a look at your work. Do you wonder why some coins were harder to find than others? Do you wonder why you couldn't find even a single example of some coins? Are you interested in completing the set? Did you have fun searching through the coins?

If you answered, "yes" to any of these questions, you've discovered the difference between being a collector and an accumulator.

Collecting Various Types of Coins

Throughout the years, people all around the world have experimented with a variety of items used to denote value. The natives of Papua New Guinea valued the dried carcasses of the beautiful Bird of Paradise. The Yap Islanders valued huge, round stones. The early Chinese created copper money in the shape of knives. Native Americans used wampum (*cowries*, small shells or beads strung on strands of leather) as a medium of exchange. All sorts of innovative methods have been used to facilitate trading, but none of them enjoyed the characteristic so important to those round little pieces of metal we call coins — convenience.

Making the first coins

The first coins appeared around 600 B.C. in Lydia, a tiny state in Asia Minor. The Lydians were blessed with quantities of *electrum,* a naturally occurring mixture of gold and silver found in the rivers of the area. The Lydians fashioned the electrum into lumps of equal weight and stamped them with crude punches. The marks on the earliest coins were basic shapes, mostly squares and triangles, but these quickly gave way to fancier designs such as images of animals or letters.

Lydia became a very wealthy state through trade and the efficiencies provided by its new coinage. One of the richest Lydians of them all was its last ruler, King Croesus, who some believe was the model for the greedy King Midas of fairy-tale fame. (However, I doubt whether Croesus ever turned his daughter into a golden statue.) Croesus also made coins of silver, valued at 1/20 of the electrum coins, which tells us that he loved gold 20 times as much as he loved silver. (So do I.)

The rest of the world noticed the Lydian coinage experiment and soon every city, state, nation, and empire was producing coins of their own. Today, collectors can choose between coins from Greece, Rome, Persia, Egypt, and many other places in the ancient world. Some of the designs on these ancient coins are incredibly beautiful. In fact, when Teddy Roosevelt became President, one of the first things he did was improve the designs on our coins using the classical designs of ancient Greek and Roman coins as a basis. Visit Chapter 11 to find out more about ancient coins.

Pining away for paper money

Coins have been around for thousands of years, but paper money is a fairly recent invention. Paper money offers several advantages over coins:

- Paper money is cheaper to produce than coins.

- Paper money is easier to transport than coins.

- Paper money production is virtually unlimited.

Despite these advantages, the first paper money didn't appear until around 700 A.D. in China. Several centuries passed before paper money appeared in Europe. Why the big delay?

The answer lies in people's mistrust of government. A five dollar bill is worth five dollars as long as the government agrees to honor the agreement printed on the paper. The old saying, "It isn't worth the paper it's printed on," expresses the value of paper money that lacks any backing. The United States has been blessed with a fairly stable currency for over 100 years, but look back a bit further and you'll find lots of people who lost all their money because they trusted the paper money the U.S. government or private banks gave them. "It isn't worth a Continental" refers to the worthless paper money paid to soldiers in the Revolutionary War. Banknotes of the early to mid-1850s are known as *Broken Bank* notes for good reason — the banks that issued them went broke.

Knowing this, would you rather have a $10 bill or a $10 Gold piece? See, you don't like paper money either!

Gold and silver coins

Look at the history of coins and you'll notice two metals that have played a critical part in the development of money: gold and silver. These two metals formed the basis for every great civilization's system of money. Greece, Rome, Egypt, Spain, England, the United States, and others all based their monetary systems on gold and silver. When you hear of the great treasures of the world, you imagine piles of gold and silver, not piles of tin and copper. Why have people throughout the ages been so in love with gold and silver when there are plenty of other metals from which to choose?

Gold is popular because it is

- **Rare.** Gold is one of those metals that is recognized as being rare and desirable, but it is not so rare that it is too expensive or difficult to find.

- **A naturally occurring element.** Gold is found in nature as flakes or nuggets on the surface of the earth, or in thin veins buried deep within the earth. The purity of natural gold may vary from location to location, but it requires little processing to achieve a uniform quality.

✔ **Malleable.** Pure gold is soft and can be beaten into extremely thin sheets or pulled into long wires or strips. Because it is so soft, gold takes good impressions from dies (the steel cylinders used to strike coins) and it won't wear them out as fast as a harder metal may.

✔ **Reasonably inert.** Except for some acids, most chemicals have little or no effect on gold. In normal use, gold will not react with moisture or oxygen, meaning that coins made of gold will last virtually forever.

✔ **Beautiful.** Pure gold has a soft yellow color and a gorgeous sheen that appeals to our visual senses. Mix gold with certain metals, and you'll come up with an interesting range of color. The colors that come up most frequently on U.S. gold coins are reds, greens, and soft pinks.

Silver is popular because it is

✔ **Common.** Vast quantities of silver have been found in various parts of the world, including the United States and Mexico. Because it is more common than gold, silver is perfect for creating coins for use by the general population.

✔ **A naturally occurring element.** Found deep within the earth, silver is usually mixed with another great coinage metal — gold. While native silver is perfectly good for casting into ingots and making into coins, most of it is processed to purify the silver and to separate out the more valuable gold.

✔ **Beautiful.** Pure silver has a bright, white luster and a deep brilliance. As it tarnishes, silver can acquire some lovely colors, including blues, reds, and purples. This is especially true for coins that have been stored near a source of sulfur, such as paper albums.

Faking us out

Prior to 1933, U.S. gold and silver coins contained their full value in metal. After the Great Depression, Roosevelt recalled all U.S. gold coins, except those of numismatic value. No more gold coins were produced after 1933. Nevertheless, the U.S. Mints at Philadelpia, Denver, and San Francisco continued producing silver coins through 1964. Today, none of our circulating coins contain even a whisper of gold or silver. Dimes, Quarters, Half Dollars, and Dollars are made of base metals, and even the "copper" Cent is made of copper-plated zinc.

As long as economies are strong and inflation is low, people accept coins that have no intrinsic value. People are perfectly happy to rely on the good faith and credit of their countries to support their money. However, if the economy goes sour, wars erupt, or inflation hits, people always return to real money made of gold and silver. Why did so many people buy $1,000 bags of old silver coins at a huge premium in the months leading up to Y2K? Because they wanted real money that would buy real things if the Y2K disaster turned out to be as bad as everyone feared.

Many collectors prefer coins that are white and untarnished, but other collectors will pay huge premiums for coins with bright rainbow-colored tarnish (known to collectors as *toning*). However, be aware that toning can often hide flaws and defects that could lower the value of the coin.

Commemorative coins

In the 1930s, numerous proposals for commemorative coins (see Figure 1-1) appeared before the U.S. Congress. Although many of the coinage bills had narrow appeal, they made it into law and the U.S. Mint dutifully struck the coins, which were then sold through distributors who added a premium above the face value of the coins. The collecting public paid its premium for the coins and were happy to add them to its collections. But, the U.S. Mint seemed to be saying, "Here's the latest commemorative, please send your money and oh, by the way, there's another commemorative coin coming out next month, so please be ready to send your money for that one as well."

Figure 1-1:
Commemorative coins.

Collectors complained that too many different coins were being produced and that speculators were manipulating the markets and prices. The U.S. Mint got the hint, the flood of commemoratives slowed to a trickle, and collectors were happy. Nevertheless, many new people were attracted to coin collecting by the often beautiful commemorative coins, just as they are by today's commemorative coins. In Chapter 19, I tell you more about these interesting coins.

BU Rolls

In the 1960s, collectors went nuts for *BU Rolls,* those original, bank-wrapped rolls of Brilliant Uncirculated coins (see Figure 1-2). Collectors tried to obtain rolls of as many different dates, denominations, and mintmarks as they could. Certain issues, like the 1950-D Nickel, were promoted as being rare (there go the speculators again) and prices shot up. One day, the public woke up and realized that coins with mintages in the millions are not rare. Today, the BU 1950-D Nickel Roll remains cheaper than it was 35 years ago and new collectors can't understand why BU Penny Rolls from the 1950s are so inexpensive. Like all good fads, the BU Roll craze created lots of new collectors.

A *mintmark* is a tiny letter (or letters) that indicates where the coin was minted. U.S. Mints include Philadelphia (P or no letter), Denver (D), Dahlonega, GA (D), Carson City, NV (CC), New Orleans (O), San Francisco (S), and West Point (W), and Charlotte, NC (C). Notice that two mints (Dahlonega and Denver) use the same letter. However, these two mints made coins during completely different time periods, so there's no need to worry about telling them apart!

Figure 1-2:
BU Rolls.

Silver Certificates

The front of old Silver Certificates (see Figure 1-3) state that they are redeemable on demand for One Silver Dollar (or later, for silver). That ended in 1968, when the United States discontinued the redemption of Silver Certificates. For a short while, the U.S. government allowed the public to redeem Silver Certificates, in person, for a fixed amount of silver per note, either in granules or bars. Happily, the market value of the silver exceeded the value of the note itself, so coin dealers found themselves the enviable recipients of another windfall. Suddenly, everyone began looking through their wallets for Silver Certificates to sell to coin dealers. You can bet that many new collectors were created among the thousands of people who visited coin shops to sell their Silver Certificates.

Figure 1-3:
Silver
Certificates.

Silver Bars

Silver popped up again in the early 1970s when one-ounce silver art bars (see Figure 1-4) became the rage. *Art bars* are thin, rectangular affairs with polished surfaces and designs that commemorate just about everything imaginable — weddings, birthdays, a new year, Thanksgiving, trains, hearts, cats — you name it. Mintages were limited, unusual varieties appeared, and some rather deliberate errors showed up. In short, a flood of new and unusual art bars overwhelmed the market and quickly killed it. However, while it was alive, the art bar craze introduced thousands of people to coin collecting, many of whom stayed.

Figure 1-4:
Silver bars.

Getting Excited about Collecting Today

When I was a kid, a friend and I rode our bikes to the bank each Saturday morning and swapped our allowance for rolls of coins. We ran to a bench outside the bank, unwrapped the rolls, and pulled out all the old coins we could find. Then, we filled the rolls up with replacement coins, ran back inside to the teller, and swapped the picked-over rolls for new ones, repeating the process until we ran out of money or time. At the end of the morning, we had piles of Indian Cents, Buffalo Nickels, Mercury Dimes, Standing Liberty Quarters, Walking Liberty Half Dollars, and plenty of the more modern silver coins that had been discontinued a few years earlier. We spent the next week trading our treasures with other kids, and we even sold some of the coins to local coin dealers — at a profit. Man, did we have fun.

Sadly, in the year 2000, a kid wastes his time trying to find anything rare or unusual in today's change. Occasionally, a *Wheatie* (the Lincoln Cents with wheat ears on the back, struck prior to 1959) shows up, but all the silver coins have disappeared and the modern clad coins have huge mintages and no collector value. No wonder kids have migrated away from coins to baseball cards, comic books, and other collectibles.

However, all is not lost. Recent developments have brought millions of new collectors back to coin collecting, many of whom are kids. People are looking at their change to see whether any treasures await them. Here are a couple of the reasons people are getting excited about coin collecting again.

50 States Quarters

In 1999, the U.S. Mint began the 50 States Quarters program, a series of 50 special Quarter Dollars, each one representing an individual state. The new coins share a common *obverse* (coin front); the *reverses* (coin back) are chosen from designs submitted by each state. Each year, five new Quarters are issued, thus spreading the program over a total of 10 years. The United States Treasury reports that over 100 million Americans are collecting the State Quarters, many of them completely new to collecting.

Figure 1-5:
The Delaware Quarter — first of the 50 States Quarters.

To find out more about the 50 States Quarters, visit Chapter 19 or the U.S. Mint Web site at www.usmint.gov.

Sacagawea Dollar

In what was perhaps the biggest and most expensive advertising campaign ever seen for a new coin, the U.S. Mint introduced a new One Dollar coin in 2000 (see Figure 1-6). The new Dollar featured the Native American guide Sacagawea (and her infant son) on the front and an eagle on the back. In order to make the coin distinctive, the edge was left flat and plain, and the entire coin was given a coating the color of gold. In a stroke of genius, the U.S. Mint contracted with Wal-Mart stores throughout the country to distribute the new coins in limited quantities. Banks received very few of the coins, creating the false impression that the new coins were rare. In fact, billions of the Sacagawea Dollars have been produced and they will never be rare, but try to find one at your local bank or store. On top of that, many people thought the coins were made of real gold!

Figure 1-6:
The 2000
Sacagawea
Dollar.

The public has gobbled these coins up like crazy and locked them away in their sock drawers and safe deposit boxes. Many of these hoarders have discovered the joys of numismatics and are now actively involved in collecting other coins as well.

New commemorative issues

I mentioned earlier the abuses in the commemorative coin programs in the 1930s. Collectors in the 1940s and 1950s had a few commemorative coins to choose from, but collectors in the 1960s and 1970s were left high and dry. In 1982, the Mints began issuing commemorative coins again on a tentative basis. Today, the U.S. Mint has hit its stride, issuing one or more commemorative coins each year in a variety of metals, set combinations, and price levels. New commemorative coins are available in gold, silver, and copper-nickel on subjects that appeal to a broad audience. Each new issue creates excitement among existing collectors and brings new collectors into the hobby.

See Chapter 19 to find out more about the many interesting commemorative coins issued by the U.S. government.

Error coins

I give the U.S. Mints a lot of credit for a job well done. They've reintroduced the Susan B. Anthony Dollar, they created and marketed the incredibly popular Sacagawea Dollar, they came up with 10 new Quarter Dollar designs in two years, and they worked round-the-clock to strike billions and billions of coins so that we can go out and spend them. As coin collectors and dealers, we owe a debt of gratitude to the Mints for doing something we've been trying to do for decades — getting new people interested in numismatics.

I don't say that mints are perfect. In fact, I acknowledge that U.S. Mints are far from it. However, as far as numismatics goes, that's a good thing. Few industries have product lines in which the rejected items are more valuable than the perfect ones. Bad light bulbs get thrown away, imperfect clothing is sold as seconds, and defective washing machines sell in classified ads. None of them fetch a premium — certainly not the tens of thousands of dollars that some coin errors have brought.

In 2000, a number of spectacular error coins stunned the numismatic world. One such error was a coin with the front of a 50 States Quarter and the back of a Sacagawea Dollar. This was the first U.S. coin ever to bear two denominations. Because the two dies differ in diameter, no one believed it was even possible for such an error to exist. This error received tremendous publicity in the national media, causing millions of noncollectors to begin examining their change. You can bet that many of them have become coin collectors. By the way, only seven of these errors had been found as of July 2001!

Chapter 2

Arming Yourself with Knowledge

*O*n one hand, becoming a coin collector is easy. On the other hand, becoming a great collector requires effort, study, and planning. New collectors are often overwhelmed with words they've never heard before, concerns about counterfeit coins, grading issues, storage techniques, and so on. Unfortunately, there's no Coin Collecting University . . . unless you count the School of Hard Knocks, where the tuition is high and the classes are really tough. However, you can study on your own and become quite a coin expert in your own right. In this chapter, I show you the importance of finding out whatever you can about coins, knowing where to go for advice, and figuring out how to establish long-term collecting goals.

Gaining Knowledge Before You Buy

They say that if you give a person a fish, you feed him or her for a day. But, if you teach a person to fish, you feed the person for a lifetime. You must learn the basics of fishing (how to collect coins) before you make your first cast (your first coin purchase). That way, you'll know why you're "fishing," what you're "fishing" for, and what you're going to do after you catch your first "fish!"

Understanding the parts of a coin

Before you start collecting coins, it helps to know what a coin is!

Coins have three sides. We call the front the *obverse*, the back the *reverse*, and the edge, well . . . the edge. Coins are usually stamped (or *struck*) from *dies*, which are pieces of metal (usually round steel) with designs on them. *Engravers* (people with engraving tools) create the designs on the dies — in the past, this was done by hand, but today much of this process has been automated. *Legends* and *mottoes* are the wording that you see on either side of a coin. Many of the designs and wording are required by law — others are at the discretion of the designer. Coins are struck at a *mint,* usually a government-run operation. The number of coins struck is called the *mintage.* Coins are struck for either use in general *circulation* (pocket-change) or as *Proofs* (specially made for collectors). The quality of Proof coins is substantially higher than that of coins struck for circulation.

Believe it or not, you now know as much about coins as do most beginning collectors, but there's a lot more to master. So . . . let's go!

Putting the book before the coin

Numismatic book purveyor Aaron Feldman used to place a slogan in each of his advertisements that read, "Buy the book before the coin" (see Figure 2-1). His advice became increasingly important as the prices of coins rose to dizzying heights over the years. Apart from wanting you to buy his books, Feldman gave some pretty good advice.

The best way to find out about coins is to read about them (so pat yourself on your back for making the effort to educate yourself). Many wonderful reference books await the coin collector, ranging from general works to highly specialized books dealing with die varieties, obsolete types, error coins, and much more of that wild and woolly stuff that only serious collectors can love.

Unfortunately, you may have trouble finding some of these books. Try these spots:

- **Libraries:** Most have very few books on coins. The books that are available are usually only basic reference books.
- **Bookstores:** You're lucky to find anything beyond basic price guides and general reference works.
- **Numismatic book and supply dealers:** Most are ready to satisfy your needs and help you locate those hard-to-find reference books — when you're ready.

For new collectors, I recommend the following resources.

Trade papers

For the latest numismatic headlines, I recommend subscribing to one or more of the excellent weekly coin papers or monthly numismatic magazines. Trade papers offer a combination of general numismatic information for beginning collectors, in-depth articles for advanced collectors, and price guides, not to mention access to the numerous advertisers with whom you can do business. Many of the larger numismatic organizations and clubs produce their own publications. My favorites include *The Numismatist* by the American Numismatic Association and *Fun-Topics* by the Florida United Numismatists.

Numismatic books

How can you collect coins when you don't even know what's available to collect? This is where general numismatic books come in. A coffee-table coin book makes a great starting point because you can see a large variety of different coins in full, dazzling color.

Eventually, you will want a book that lists and describes all U.S. coins by date and mint, preferably with pricing information for a variety of grades. With this information, you can decide which coins appear interesting to you and you can set collecting goals that are achievable and within your budget.

Price guides

Price guides contain listings of coins along with their values in different levels of condition. Different types of price guides address different areas of the market, such as wholesale and retail (see below). You can purchase numismatic price guides at your local book store or they are often included in trade papers such as *Coin World* and *Numismatic News*. I discuss price guides in much greater detail in Chapter 5.

- **Wholesale price guides:** Satisfy the needs of dealers who buy and sell from each other
- **Retail price guides:** Help dealers and collectors assign sell prices to their coins
- **Certified price guides:** Record the often close buy and sell spreads for coins that have been graded and certified by independent services

Grading guides

Learning to grade coins may be the most important aspect of numismatics, so I recommend taking a look at the various grading guides to learn which approach works best for you. *Photograde* uses photographs — all you do is match your coin to the picture in order to figure out the grade. Other grading guides use line drawings or written descriptions. Whichever guide you choose, the closer you align your eyes to the rest of the market, the more successful you will be as a collector. When you know how to grade coins properly, you can spot overgraded and overpriced coins. More importantly, you can spot undergraded and underpriced coins. Check out Chapters 9 and 10 for more information about grading.

What would you do?

Are you obligated to tell someone when they have underpriced or undergraded a coin or missed a valuable variety? The answer is No. Sort of. If someone, especially a dealer who is supposed to know better, offers to sell you a coin at an incorrectly low price, good for you. But, if someone asks for your opinion about a variety, grade, or value, be honest. You can always try to carve out a commission for yourself or work out a deal to handle the sale of the coin, but always tell the truth. You'll develop a wonderful reputation as an honest numismatist and you'll be able to sleep soundly at night.

Embracing your inner grasshopper

So David Carradine didn't collect coins, but he did know what value a mentor holds. One of the best things you can do as a beginning collector is hook up with someone who is already involved in numismatics as a dealer or collector. A good advisor can demonstrate to you the fine points of coin collecting and show you coins that you may not otherwise see. Many old-time collectors have plenty of great stories about the coins they've owned, the coins they regret not buying, the wonderful people they've met along the way, and their experiences at coin shows and in coin shops. What most old-time collectors don't have is someone willing to sit down and listen to them; so your desire to find out more may be rewarded with some eager mentoring.

Where can you meet other numismatists?

- ✔ **Coin clubs:** Attend your local coin club meetings to get together with other collectors in your area.

- ✔ **Coin shops:** Visit all the coin dealers in your area at least once to see how they deal with you on a personal level. Stick with the ones you like.

- ✔ **Coin shows:** Take a day off to go to local coin shows. Meet new collectors and dealers from outside your area, and choose from lots of interesting coins (see Figure 2-1). Don't forget to bring your kid(s).

- ✔ **Educational seminars:** Most major coin shows host educational seminars, presented by expert numismatists, on a wide range of subjects. Learn about pioneer gold, U.S. fiscal paper, Civil War tokens, the history of the U.S. Mint, and much more. Use the question-and-answer period to get to know the experts and to pick their brains.

- ✔ **ANA Summer Seminar:** Attend the American Numismatic Association's Summer Seminar at their headquarters in Colorado Springs. Each year the ANA offers week-long courses in a variety of useful subjects, including "Grading U.S. Coins," "Coin Photography," "Detection of Counterfeit and

Altered U.S. Coins," "Rarities From Shipwrecks," and others. Class sizes are limited and attendees have full access to the instructors. You can't get any closer to the experts than this!

✔ **Specialty clubs:** Join a specialty club. Meet collectors who share your collecting interest by joining specialty clubs, such as the Bust Half Nut Club, the Early American Coppers Club, the Colonial Coin Collectors Club, and many others. Also, be sure to attend their annual meetings (usually in conjunction with the ANA's annual convention).

Figure 2-1:
A coin show.

Sense for cents

I wish I could tell you how to find such an advisor, but as I think back on my years as a coin collector and dealer, no one person stands out in the role I describe. But I can think of many people who gave unselfishly of their time and knowledge to help make me a better numismatist. I met them at coin club meetings, in their shops, at shows, and in their homes. One dealer gave me access to his inventory of over 200 Half Cents. In return for assigning variety numbers to each coin, I got to hone my attribution skills, plus I received a few of the coins as a reward for my work. Two collectors took me to their respective bank vaults for private showings of some of the finest collections of U.S. colonial coins ever assembled. I've seen countless presentations, at coin club meetings, by collectors and dealers who have put a lot of time and effort into teaching the audience.

Don't be afraid to ask questions. Most coin dealers and collectors are extremely helpful people who are willing to answer your questions. Don't be shy. In my opinion, there's no such thing as a stupid question in numismatics — we were all beginners at one time.

Going online with the Internet

How did we ever get along without the Internet? The amount of information now available to collectors on the World Wide Web is staggering. With a few mouse clicks and keyboard entries you can find information on any U.S. coin, gain access to thousands of dealers, search for coins for your collection, buy books and coins online, set up your own virtual coin shop, and communicate with collectors and dealers around the world.

Even if you don't have a computer, please don't skip this section. There's a world of information out there that's simply too valuable to pass up.

- ✔ **Library:** Most libraries offer Internet access to their members free of charge (sign up in advance to reserve a slot of time).

- ✔ **College:** If you live in a university town, check to see if your local college offers Internet access.

- ✔ **Internet café:** You can always pay for access — even some of the major printing chains (Kinko's comes to mind) allow you to surf for a fee.

If you're not familiar with the Internet and how it works, take a break, buy and read *The Internet For Dummies* by John R. Levine, Carol Baroudi, Jordan M. Young, and Margaret Levine Young (Hungry Minds, Inc.), and come right back here. Meanwhile, consider the following ways to get information online.

- ✔ **Go to any search engine (I like** www.goto.com **and** www.google.com**) and type in a word or phrase that interests you.** To give you an example of what's out there, I typed the word **coin** into the Google.com search engine on January 14, 2001. In .17 seconds, the search engine found roughly 1,450,000 pages that contained the word "coin." None of us will live long enough to visit that many pages!

- ✔ **Bookmark the sites you find useful or interesting.** Many numismatic sites offer links to other sites, so don't be afraid to take a side trip. Everyone has his favorite Web sites (I list mine in Chapter 26), and soon you'll develop your own stable of favorites.

- ✔ **To communicate with other collectors and find out what topics are hot in today's market, subscribe to the rec.collecting.coins newsgroup through your e-mail program.** Newsgroup members post messages or respond to those that have already been posted. Sometimes the back-and-forth gets pretty intense, but it's always interesting and often quite informative.

Affecting a Coin's Value

One of the greatest misconceptions about coins concerns their value. Given a choice, most non-numismatists will pick a 2,000 year old Roman denarius over a U.S. $20 Gold piece any day, even though the denarius is worth $50 compared to $400 for the $20 Gold piece (see Figure 2-2). Age seems to be an important factor to non-numismatists — in their minds, the older a coin is, the more valuable it becomes. Therefore, a 2,000-year-old coin must be worth a million bucks! Nothing could be further from the truth.

Figure 2-2:
Roman denarius (left) or $20 Gold piece (right) — which do you prefer?

Several factors affect the value of a coin: rarity, demand, supply, age, condition, and external factors. Any one of these factors can be significant by itself, or it may require some help from one of the other factors. For example, a coin may be common in low grades, indicating a low rarity, but in high grade, the same coin may be very rare, making it what is known as a *condition rarity*. In such a case, the value of the coin makes a huge jump in price as it moves from a lower grade to a higher grade.

Age: Good for wine . . . good for coins?

Age has little or no effect on the value of a coin. There are many coins from the last 20 years that are much more valuable than coins from 2,000 years ago. Certainly, time allows for coins to become better dispersed throughout the collecting community and the world, making them a little more difficult to find. But just because a coin is old does not mean that it is rare or valuable.

The hoard factor

A *hoard* is a large grouping of the same (or similar) coins, usually discovered many years after they were made.

In the 1960s, the 1903-O Silver Dollar (struck at the New Orleans Mint) was considered one of the great rarities of the Morgan Dollar series, despite a mintage of 4,450,000 pieces. For some reason, there were simply not enough coins to supply the collector demand. Then, one day, the Treasury Department discovered a hoard of 1903-O Silver Dollars while cleaning out its vaults. Overnight, the price of a 1903-O Silver Dollar plunged, as the supply increased to satisfy the existing collector demand.

The recent recovery of gold coins from the *S.S. Brother Jonathan* and the *S.S. Central America* shipwrecks dramatically affected prices of certain dates in the Double Eagle denomination. Once considered a rarity in high grade, the 1857-S $20 is now one of the most common early gold coins, thanks to the hoard found on the *Central America.* Hoards account for the low prices of many ancient Roman and Greek coins, as metal detectors and construction projects continue to turn up clay jars filled with old coins.

The size of a hoard and the way the coins are sold into the coin market determine the effect on prices. In the 1970s, a vast hoard of over 600,000 U.S. Silver Dollars, once owned by the eccentric LaVere Redfield, began filtering into the market. The sheer size of the hoard threatened to kill prices because there was simply not enough money in the coin market to absorb all the coins at once. But shrewd control of the pricing and distribution of the hoard kept prices from falling. In fact, some experts argue that interest in Silver Dollar collecting actually increased because of the way the hoard was handled.

Condition: Pumping them up

The condition of a coin is a hugely important factor in determining its price. The difference in a single point on the grading scale can equate to a difference of thousands of dollars in value. Because of the intense competition to own the finest example known of a given date, a large premium is attached to the very best coins. Take the 1953-S Franklin Half Dollar as an example. This is a very common coin in low grades, worth only the value of the silver it contains. Even in Uncirculated condition, you can buy a nice-looking example for around $20. But well-struck, high-grade examples are extremely rare and valuable. How valuable? In January 2001 the finest certified 1953-S Franklin Half Dollar came on the market and sold at auction for a whopping $69,000! If you think that's a crazy price, remember that there was at least one underbidder who wanted the coin almost as badly as the winner did.

When Dr. Sheldon devised his 70-point pricing scale in the 1940s, he noticed that price and condition followed each other rather closely (at least they did in the Large Cents he collected and studied). Sheldon noticed that collectors considered the finest example of any date to be worth seventy times the value of the worst example. A Very Fine example may be worth 20 to 30 times the value of the worst example and an About Uncirculated coin may be worth 50 to 55 times as much. Using this information, he created a scale to show the relationship between the grades and prices of Large Cents. Later, the coin market morphed Sheldon's pricing scale into a grading system that was applied to other series of U.S. coins, even though inflation had already destroyed the relationship between price and condition. Today, the Sheldon grading scale is the bedrock of U.S. numismatics and the number 70 is universally recognized (at least, in numismatics) as the pinnacle of quality.

Demand: Demanding high dollar

Demand is an important factor in determining the value of a coin. High demand increases values and low demand hurts values. Two coins of identical rarity may enjoy wildly different values, depending on the demand for each coin. A common coin in a series where there are many active collectors (such as Silver Dollars) is always more valuable than a common coin in a series that is largely ignored by collectors (such as Jefferson Head Nickels).

Demand is fickle. A series that is in demand today may be out of favor tomorrow. Beware of fads and take a contrarian approach when buying coins. In other words, stay away from the *hot* areas and concentrate on the *cool* areas, remembering that every dog has its day. Demand may be artificial. With rare coins, it doesn't take much to run up the price. Before buying a particular coin, do a little research to see how the price has trended over the past year or two. Has there been an unusual spike in the price or has the price remained fairly stable?

Rarity: Hunting for treasures

The *rarity* of a coin relates to the number of examples that have survived through time. A *high mintage figure* (meaning that lots of a coin were made) doesn't necessarily mean low rarity — or vice versa. For example, the reported mintage figure for a 1927-D $20 Gold piece is 180,000 pieces, which is fairly high, but this coin ranks as one of the all-time great rarities in the series. Why? Experts suspect that most examples of this date were destroyed before they were released into circulation. On the other hand, a 1913-S $20 has a reported mintage of only 34,000 pieces (small by any standard), yet there is little or no premium attached to this coin in circulated condition. Why? Because almost the entire mintage survived. In some cases, mintage figures may be incorrect or include coins from an earlier or later year.

Do not rely on mintage figures alone to determine the rarity of a particular coin.

Hoarding Washington Carver

One of my favorite coins is the 1951 Washington Carver Commemorative Half Dollar (see the following figure). In MS-65 condition, PCGS has certified only 78 examples, yet the current bid price is only $270. Theoretically, I could buy up every PCGS MS-65 example for $21,000. But I know from experience how hard it is to find this coin at coin shows and in other dealers' inventories. If I bought up only 10 or 20 pieces, the price would start going up. Just a small increase in the demand for this coin would translate into a big jump in price. Should I do it? Would you?

Supply: Giving them what they want

If too many coins are made each year and not enough people want them, prices remain low. On the other hand, if a coin's supply falls short of the demand, prices rise.

Back in 1986, when the Professional Coin Grading Service (PCGS) began certifying U.S. coins, demand for their product was huge and the supply was low, even though PCGS did its best to grade as efficiently as possible. I remember seeing my first PCGS certified MS-65 common date Morgan Silver Dollar. 'Twas a thing of beauty, all bright, shiny, and nearly perfect — it was also priced at $600! Now, 15 years later, hundreds of thousands of Morgan Dollars have been certified by PCGS. Because the supply is large enough to satisfy the demand of most collectors, the price of a common date PCGS certified MS-65 Morgan Dollar has dropped to under $100. A similar situation occurs each year as the new government-issued Proof sets hit the market. The collectors lucky enough to receive the first sets often sell them for a nice profit, because everyone wants to own one. Later, as the U.S. Mint releases more and more sets, the price drops because the supply rises to meet the demand.

Buy Proof sets directly from the U.S. Mint each year. If you miss out for some reason, wait until the market has cooled down a bit and prices stabilize. It may take some months, but be patient. In most cases, you'll have to pay more than the issue price, but in general, you'll avoid the hefty premiums charged when the supply is low.

Supply and demand work opposite each other. Just as demand can be manipulated to raise prices, so can supply. Again, become aware of any funny business in the market by carefully researching potential purchases. Ask your advisor if she knows of any behind-the-scenes activity that may affect the supply of the coin in which you're interested.

Buying Strategies

Anyone can go to a coin show, spend lots of money, and have little to show except a meaningless accumulation of stuff. You can do the same thing at a stamp show, or an antique show, or a car show — you name it. Half the fun of coin collecting is developing a plan and seeing it through. You won't believe the thrills of your first coin purchase, of finally locating a rare and elusive coin after months of searching, and of ultimately completing your collection.

Accumulating versus collecting

There's a fine line between an accumulation and a collection of coins. Say, for example, your grandfather gave you a cigar box full of coins he picked up when he was overseas in the service. All the coins are loose, unorganized, and unidentified — the definition of an *accumulation*.

With a little bit of time, effort, and study, you can turn that same group of coins, that accumulation, into a fine collection of coins. First, sort the coins out by country. Because many of the *legends* (letters or wording) on the coins are in a foreign language, a good reference book is necessary. After you've identified all the coins by country, sort by denomination and then by date. Weed out any duplicates, saving the best for your collection, and set aside the lesser-quality pieces to trade or sell later. Place each coin in a protective holder and include some descriptive information. During this entire process, you discover a little something about history, geography, foreign language, metallurgy, and organizational techniques.

I promise that after you understand what coin collecting is about, no cigar box full of coins will ever look the same.

Pacing yourself

Consider this: Based on prices in today's market, you would need roughly $75–100 million to assemble a complete collection of U.S. coins. A few years ago, you could have assembled a complete collection for less. The point I'm trying to make is that you will simply run out of money before you run out of coins to buy, so there's no reason to go on a spending spree.

You can't always get what you want. Even if you had all the money in the world, some coins may not be available in your lifetime. If a great rarity does become available, you still have to compete against other buyers, which is a whole different issue. I've seen people freeze during auctions or chicken out at the last minute, only to have the coin sell to another bidder. Minutes later, they realize their error and wish they could relive the moment. Unfortunately, by that time, the opportunity has been lost. Sometimes, when the opportunity arises, you may not be ready financially or otherwise. A lot of collection-building is based on luck, perseverance, determination, and timing.

In Chapters 15 to 20, I offer suggestions for collecting various U.S. coins along with comments about rarity, cost, and the chances of completing the collection. Look over each section, see what possibilities exist for you, choose an area that interests you, and then have fun!

Deciding What to Collect

Because money is a limiting factor, figure out how much you want to budget for your collection, and then decide where to spend it. Here are some suggestions for interesting and challenging ways to collect coins:

- **Denomination:** Try putting together a complete set of all the different denominations issued by the United States. Start with the coins in circulation and then include obsolete coins like a Half Cent, a three-cent piece, a 20-cent piece — coins that most people have never heard of.

- **Type:** You'll find a number of different types within each denomination. For example, Half Dollars include the Flowing Hair, Draped Bust, Capped Bust, Seated Liberty, Barber, Walking Liberty, Franklin Head, and Kennedy types. You can collect by type within a denomination, or you can expand into other denominations.

- **Date:** Collecting by date is a fun and affordable way to obtain every date for a particular series. For example, you could easily collect a Half Dollar from every year they were minted since 1900. There's no reason to pay extra for a rare mintmark — just pick the least expensive coin for the year and add it to your collection. Not only will you have one coin from every year, but you will have added several different types along the way.

✔ **Date and mintmark combination:** Collecting every date and mintmark combination becomes a bit more challenging and expensive. Most series have what I call a *stopper* — a rare mintmark that can sometimes be prohibitively expensive. Believe me, you don't want to attempt to collect a set of Barber Dimes unless you have a lot of money. You may find and be able to afford every date in the series except for the extremely rare 1894-S — you'll need $100,000 or more for a nice one! On the other hand, there are several series that you can complete without breaking the bank. If you can't afford the Barber Dime set, try the Barber Half Dollars instead. The coins are bigger and every date and mintmark in the set is affordable.

Keep in mind that until recently, coins minted in Philadelphia had no mintmark.

✔ **Year:** Many people attempt to buy every coin issued in the year of their birth. If you're under 50 years old, all you have to do is buy the Mint Sets and Proof Sets issued by the government in the year of your birth, plus any commemorative coins issued that year. If you're older than 50, you may have to search a little harder — but that's half the fun of collecting coins, isn't it? If you really want to go all out, try collecting coins issued in your birth year by other countries!

Staying focused

After you decide on a collecting plan, stick with it. Focus on your goals and remain immune to the siren call of other coins. I know it's hard to resist, but in order to conserve your resources and be ready when buying opportunities arise, you must remain strong.

While I recommend sticking with your game plan, I don't want to say that you can never change your mind. But, there's an important reason not to get distracted — a little thing called transaction costs.

Transaction costs are the fees you pay to get in and out of the coin market. If you're familiar with the stock market, you know their name for transaction costs: *commissions.* When you buy a stock, you are charged a commission based on the price of the stock; when you sell a stock, you are charged a commission again. Because the commissions come out of your pocket, you must figure them into your cost of the stock and the amount of any profits or losses that you make when you sell the stock. In many cases, commissions can eat up all of your profits or enlarge your losses.

Transactions costs are also a part of numismatics, but not in such an obvious way. In numismatics, transaction costs are baked into the *buy/sell spreads* (the difference between what a dealer will pay for a coin and how much he will sell it for). Buy/sell spreads are much wider than they are in stocks. For example, the buy/sell spread on a $100 stock may be 50 cents, but on a $100 coin the buy/sell spread may be as wide as $30. Here's an example: Say you buy a coin for $100. Ask the dealer what he would pay to buy the coin back in a week. If the buy-back price is $90, you're facing a potential loss of $10. Therefore, the market has to go up $10 just for you to break even on the coin.

Every time you buy a coin that is not a part of your collecting plan, you face unnecessary transaction costs — one more reason not to buy any unplanned coins.

Need new glasses?

Here's my out-of-focus story. Fifteen years ago, I purchased a 1757 Bavarian Thaler (a Thaler is a large, silver German coin about the size of a U.S. Silver Dollar). The back of the Bavarian Thaler features a Madonna and Child because the area is predominantly Catholic and the Virgin Mary is the Patroness Saint of Bavaria. I liked the coin, shown in the following figure, because it was an inexpensive way to own a Thaler from that time period and because I still have family members on my father's side in the part of Bavaria around Munich. Bavaria issued the Madonna Thaler from 1753 to 1799, so I decided to collect one coin from each year.

I should have left it at that, but I soon found out that some years come with both a Madonna reverse and a lions and shield reverse. Sure enough, I got distracted and started collecting those, too. Some Madonna Thalers come with an A mintmark, so I had to have those, as well. Then, I really went goofy. Some Madonna Thalers are minutely different from others. Even though they may be from the same year, the letters may be in a different position, the design may be slightly different, or the die may have broken and cracked during the minting process. I started collecting Madonna Thalers by die variety, something no person in history has ever attempted — certainly no sane person. Today, I have a collection of over 300 different die varieties of the Madonna Thalers.

How out-of-focus have I become? Well, I've never completed the date set . . . I still need the 1753 Thaler! Got one?

Thinking long-term

Most big-name coin collections were formed over a long period of time by people who had a clear vision of what they wanted to accomplish. By approaching coin collecting with the same attitude, your experience with numismatics can be just as enjoyable and just as successful as anyone else's.

Two areas are of primary importance when developing your long-term view. If nothing else, these two areas offer hope for the collector who may otherwise decide that finding certain coins seems impossible. Patience may be its own reward, but a long-term view in coin collecting can make or save you money and open opportunities that are most certainly real and possible.

✔ **Long-term price trends:** Looking back at the history of coin collecting, you'll see a general upward trend in coin prices. Just like everything else in the world, coins cost more today than they did 50 years ago. Down the road, you can expect higher prices than today. As you set your collecting goals, plan for future price increases and determine whether you can afford to finish what you've started. Keep in mind that there may be some wild swings along the way — hot markets, where the coins you seek will seem out of reach, followed by cool markets, where the coins you collect will seem like bargains.

✔ **Long-term opportunities:** The longer you're active in collecting, the better your chances are of acquiring the rare coins you need. Sometimes the opportunity to purchase a coin is rarer than the coin itself, so you must be patient and ready to pounce when your coin finally appears. Never assume that a coin is locked away forever. Who ever thought that Johns Hopkins University would sell off the Garrett collection? Who suspected that we'd ever have a chance to bid on coins from Byron Reed's collection or from the Joseph C. Mitchelson collection? We simply don't know what neat collections lurk around the corner. But the fact that strong hands have sold their coins in the past gives us hope that others will do the same in the future.

Chapter 3

Storing Your Collection Correctly

● ●

In This Chapter

▶ Displaying your collection

▶ Handling and cleaning your coins

▶ Avoiding moisture

▶ Securing and insuring your collection

● ●

Assuming it stays in circulation, a coin lasts roughly 30 years during a regular journey from the time it is minted to the day it wears out completely. Just check the change in your pocket to see how much money you have dated before 1970. You won't find very much, if any. Over the years, coins are damaged, lost, worn out, burnt up, corroded, dirty, or they end up in piggy banks and coin collections.

Given proper protection, coins last much longer than 30 years, and even longer than our lifetimes. A coin may last forever under perfect conditions. So, while you may think you own the coins in your collection, you're really just taking care of them for the next owner. By protecting your coins today, you benefit from the preservation of their value for yourself and future generations, just as you have benefited from the efforts of collectors who have come before. Your coins are safe and sound — all because of the care you've given them. Wow, you're pretty important, aren't you?

The three most important things you can do to preserve your coins?

✔ Protect them.

✔ Keep them safe.

✔ Keep them dry.

Holdering Them the Right Way

Choosing the right holder is an important first step in your collecting plan because the cost of holders can sometimes be quite high, especially if your collection is large. There are many types of holders and accessories for protecting, storing, and displaying your collection. Some holders are meant only for short-term storage and may actually harm your coins over long periods of time. Surprisingly, some holders (the ones supposed to protect your coins) are made of chemicals that may attack and damage your coins. Others are perfect for long-term storage and the careful preservation of your numismatic lovelies.

- ✔ **Cigar box (stogie storer):** Inexpensive (unless you smoke high-priced stogies) and great for beginners. Lacks a certain level of sophistication and panache.

- ✔ **Paper envelope:** Inexpensive. A variety of sizes are available at your local stationery or office supply stores. Most coin dealers sell small 2"×2" paper envelopes made specially for coin collectors (see Figure 3-1). You can write lots of information about the coin on the outside of the envelope. Colors allow you to code your collection. Sulfur-free versions are excellent for long-term storage.

The sulfur used to manufacture paper causes coins to tarnish (most of the envelopes targeted to the coin market are sulfur-free) and you can't see the actual coin without opening the holder and disturbing the coin.

Figure 3-1:
Paper
envelope.

✔ **Cardboard 2×2s:** Inexpensive. These start out as 2"×4" sheets of *Mylar* (clear plastic film) glued to card stock containing two holes of identical size (see Figure 3-2). The coin is placed on the Mylar, and then the holder is folded over and then stapled together. Some cardboard 2×2s have a layer of adhesive that seals the holder shut and eliminates the need for staples. Coins are easily viewed through the Mylar windows. Excellent for long-term storage (except in areas of high humidity) and as long as the Mylar film remains intact.

Crimp the staples to make sure that they don't damage the coins in other holders. Removing coins from cardboard 2×2s must be done carefully, so as not to scratch the coin. Even when stapled shut, the outer edges leak air, allowing *toning* (tarnish) to develop on the rims of the coin. Depending on the manufacturer, some cardboard 2×2s contain tiny paper particles from the cutting and punching process. If not removed fully from the holder, these tiny particles can migrate to the surface of your coin where they trap moisture and begin oxidizing the surface of your coin. Cracks in the thin Mylar film may allow a localized toning spot to develop where air and moisture seep through.

✔ **Vinyl 2×2s:** Inexpensive and great for handling and viewing of coins. Also known as *flips*, these 2"×4" holders have two pockets that fold over to a convenient 2"×2" size (see Figure 3-3). One side holds your coin, the other a card upon which you may place a description.

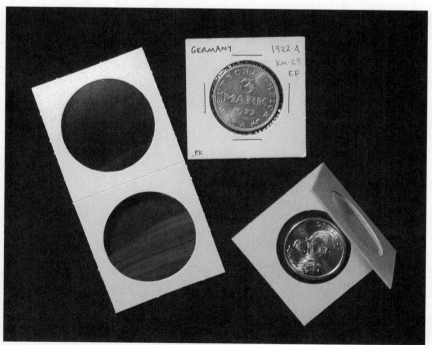

Figure 3-2: Cardboard 2×2s.

I have a difficult time getting the harder flips to stand up in a row inside a box. The softer, vinyl flips don't seem to have this problem. Excellent for short-term storage. Used by most dealers and auction houses as a convenient method of displaying, protecting, and shipping coins.

Some vinyl flips are made with PVC, a chemical that can leach out over time and damage your coins. Therefore, these are not recommended for long-term storage. Certain brands are made without PVC, but this causes them to become brittle and crack.

✔ **Hard plastic holders:** Expensive. These consist of three layers of hard plastic — one to hold the coin plus two outer layers for protection — all screwed together (see Figure 3-4). Often custom made, these holders are available in a variety of sizes and colors for individual and multiple coins. Custom printing may be added to these holders to identify the coin(s). The plastic layers are essentially *inert* (they don't react chemically with the coins), so they are perfect for long-term storage. Hard plastic holders are attractive and offer clear views of both sides of the coin.

If the diameter of the hole is not perfect, the coin may shift around in the holder, thereby exposing it to possible abrasive action. If the hole is too small, it must be enlarged by hand, often resulting in an amateurish look. Some air and moisture may seep in through the sides.

These are among the bulkiest of all coin holders, so storage can become a problem. In order to hold the coin itself or examine the edge of the coin, the holder must be destroyed.

Figure 3-3:
Vinyl 2×2s.

Figure 3-4:
Hard plastic
holders.

✔ **Slabs:** Expensive — the cost of *slabbing* a coin can range from $10 to over $100 each, depending on the company used and the level of service chosen. *Slabs* are the hard plastic cases used to encapsulate coins graded by independent certification companies (see Figure 3-5). A small slip of paper, sealed in the holder, identifies the coin and shows the grade assigned to it. Excellent for long-term storage. These offer the tightest seals of any holders and some are claimed to be watertight and airtight. Some slabs include bar codes on the internal labels for convenient inventory control using a bar-code reader, a database, and a computer.

Figure 3-5:
Slabs.

✔ **Coin album:** A broad range of prices, quality, and levels of protection. A variety are available for the coin collector (see Figure 3-6), including basic albums with holes into which the coins are pushed, albums with vinyl pages, and albums in which coins are placed into holes that are protected on both sides with plastic slides. Most albums and folders are designed for specific collections (for example, Lincoln Head Cents, Peace Dollars, and so on). Albums and folders are especially suited for *lower-grade circulated coins* (worn coins). The empty holes urge you to continue collecting. Albums and folders make organizing and displaying your collection a cinch.

Paper folders will eventually tone your coins, plus only one side of the coin is visible. Vinyl albums may leak PVC. Improper use of the slide-type albums can leave damaging *slidemarks* (hairline scratches) on the surface of your coins.

✔ **Tube:** Very convenient and relatively inexpensive way to store and protect large quantities of coins. Coin tubes are used to store rolls of coins of various denominations (see Figure 3-7). Some tubes are round and clear, others are square and opaque. All of the tubes being manufactured today are made of inert materials. Each coin in a tube stays in contact with another coin, possibly leading to surface damage, nicks, and dings, especially as the coins are inserted into and removed from the tube.

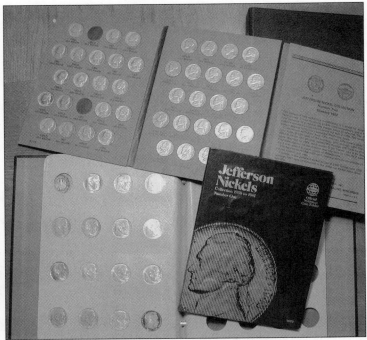

Figure 3-6:
Coin
albums.

Figure 3-7:
Tubes.

Keeping Away from the Cleaning Products?

I remember the day a nicely dressed man in his mid-forties came into my coin shop with a complete set of Peace Dollars he wished to sell. He explained how his father had painstakingly built the collection over many years. He had inherited the coins after his father died. Now, many years later, he was curious to find out how much more valuable his coins had become.

Before I opened the album, he pointed out that some of the coins had become tarnished over the years, so he had cleaned them to make it easier for me to see what they looked like. Hearing that, my heart sank. Sure enough, when I opened up the album, I saw rows and rows of bright, shiny Peace Dollars. But, they were too bright, too shiny, and too unnatural; all were obviously scrubbed and cleaned. Once beautiful, high-grade coins, they were now polished pieces of junk worth a fraction of their former value. A very disappointed person left my store that day.

Leave coin cleaning to the experts, or at least never clean a coin until you master proper cleaning techniques.

Most coins should be left alone, but some coins cry out to be cleaned. The following coins could benefit from a cleaning, but they all need to be treated differently:

- Coins found by metal detectors
- Coins that are extremely dark with tarnish
- Coins that have begun to tone at the edges, but are untoned at the centers
- Coins that have developed a film from spending too much time in a vinyl flip (coin holder)
- Coins with tape residue or some other localized problem

I know you have coins that need to be cleaned, and I know you're dying to clean them. So, because you're going to do it anyway, I may as well give you some safe-cleaning tips. (Abstinence seems to be out of the question.) Please practice these techniques on inexpensive coins until you feel comfortable cleaning coins that are more valuable. Finally, if you don't feel comfortable cleaning coins, don't do it. There's an old saying: "'Tis better to have never cleaned at all than to have cleaned and lost."

Removing dirt

Dirt is an abrasive that will scratch the heck out of a coin if you're not careful. Never rub, never scrub, never polish — always use a light touch.

1. **Use an artist's paintbrush to lightly whisk off any surface dirt.**

   Be careful not to exert any pressure.

2. **Rinse the coin under warm water to remove additional surface dirt.**

   Don't rub the coin between your thumb and forefinger.

3. **After rinsing the coin, pat it dry with a soft towel.**

   Avoid pressure and any rubbing motions.

Do not use paper towels to dry a coin, as the wood fibers in the paper may leave hairline scratches on fine surfaces.

For really crusty and dirty coins, soak them in olive oil for a couple of days and try picking the dirt off with a toothpick (see Figure 3-8). Again, be careful not to exert too much pressure or the toothpick may scratch your coin.

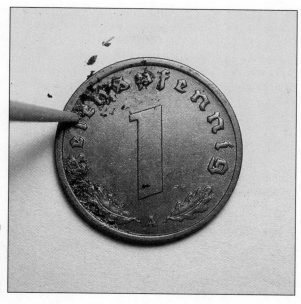

Figure 3-8:
Using a
toothpick.

Removing PVC film

PVC softens hard plastic into vinyl, a popular material in coin holders. Unfortunately, PVC can leach out of the vinyl and onto your coins, causing a light haze, green spots, or an oily film. Over time, PVC attacks the surface of a coin, dulling the luster and etching the metal. PVC contamination is so serious that the major companies that grade and certify coins (see Chapter 10) refuse to grade any coin with visible traces of PVC.

Removing PVC contamination is easy, but it must be done with care. Acetone, the chemical used in nail polish remover, works very well at removing PVC film and spots, but be careful to use it only in a well-ventilated area away from any flames. You can find pure acetone (the only kind I recommend) in the cosmetics section at your local drug store or in the paint section at your local hardware store. You may find it necessary to repeat the process with a clean swab until all of the PVC is removed (see Figure 3-9). The first swab will be green in color; the last swab should be clear.

Acetone is a dangerous chemical, so here's the warning on the bottle I'm holding: "Warning: Keep away from heat and flame. Keep away from small children. In case of accidental ingestion, induce vomiting and consult a physician. Harmful to synthetic fabrics, wood finishes and plastics." Kinda makes you think twice, doesn't it?

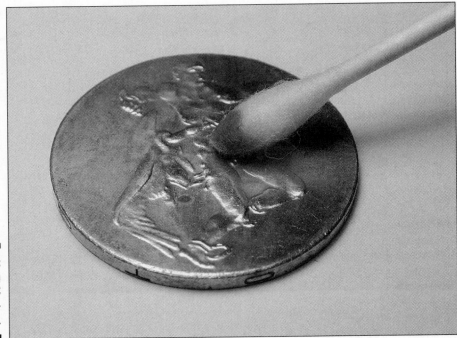

Figure 3-9:
Removing
PVC
contam-
ination.

Removing tarnish or toning

If your silver coin has light toning around the edges, if the toning is attractive, or if the toning is *iridescent* (showing shifting changes of color), consider leaving it alone. Many collectors pay huge premiums for nicely toned coins (see Figure 3-10). Nevertheless, if you absolutely hate the toning, try dipping your coin in a chemical bath specially formulated for removing tarnish (see Figure 3-11). Your local coin dealer probably carries Jeweluster, popularly known as Dip and widely used by collectors and dealers alike. In my opinion, pure Dip is too harsh, so I mix it with equal parts water to make a softer solution.

You may use Dip to clean nickel coins, but never copper coins. Never dip coins of different metals in the same solution because sometimes one metal will *plate out* onto the other coin. Instead of cleaning your coin, you'll be adding an extra layer of metal. Follow these steps for lightly tarnished coins:

1. **A quick in and out is all your coin needs.**

2. **Immediately rinse in warm water.**

3. **Use a soft cloth towel to dry your coin.**

    Pat, don't rub the coin dry.

Figure 3-10:
Toned coins:
nice on the
left, not so
nice on the
right.

Heavy toning becomes a problem for two reasons:

- The surfaces may have faint hairline scratches and/or marks that are difficult to detect beneath the toning. Before dipping the coin, be sure to examine it carefully to prevent any surprises.

- If the surfaces are too heavily tarnished, Dip will remove the tarnish but the result will be a coin with an unattractive, dull, flat luster.

Practice with a variety of inexpensive, toned coins to figure out what can be fixed and what can't. Again, when in doubt, leave the coin alone.

Removing lacquer

Some collectors attempt to preserve the quality of their coins by applying a thin coat of lacquer. Generally, this method works well to preserve coins as long as the layer of lacquer remains unbroken. However, spots and toned areas can result if the lacquer becomes damaged or if it begins to peel off the coin. Also, no certification service will grade a coin that has lacquer remaining on the surfaces.

As with PVC, acetone remains the chemical of choice for removing lacquer. A short bath in acetone will remove most of the lacquer on a coin, although additional baths may be necessary to remove all traces. Be patient, and above all, be careful. Acetone is a dangerous chemical even when used properly.

Figure 3-11:
Dipping.

Handling with Kid Gloves

Several years back, a dealer friend of mine handed me a *well-struck* (nearly perfect) 1913 Indian Head Nickel with full, complete details and he asked whether I thought it was a coin made for circulation or a coin that had been specially prepared for collectors (referred to as a *Proof*). We were standing at the reception desk of a hotel, and as I turned the coin over to examine the other side, it flipped out of my fingers and fell about four feet onto the hard tile floor. Besides feeling like a fool, I was even more upset to discover a big bruise on one of the rims of the coin. The bruise destroyed much of the coin's value and desirability. Suddenly, the coin was most certainly a Proof in my friend's eyes. I was forced (shamed, actually) into buying the coin for a lot more than it was worth — especially for a coin that no self-respecting collector would buy. I found out a lot about handling coins from that lesson.

Proper handling techniques fulfill our obligation to future collectors by preventing any further damage to the coins we handle. The following techniques prevent embarrassing and costly damage.

Washing your hands before touching

Whatever is on your fingers will be transferred to the edge of the coin you are handling. Coins hate doughnut glaze, potato chip salt, hamburger grease, and just about everything else, so wash your hands before you handle those beautiful coins.

Asking before removing a coin from a holder

Different dealers use different holders, often in different ways. For example, many collectors keep their copper coins in felt-lined pouches inside a small paper envelope. The pouches have a single opening. Some collectors place the pouch into the envelope so that the coin slides right out of the pouch when the flap of the envelope is opened (I call this the *straight-on method*). Others turn the pouch so that the coin is *locked in,* even when the envelope is opened. Here's where the problem lies. Some collectors turn the pouch to the left, others to the right. I had always preferred the straight-on method, so I was somewhat puzzled the first time I encountered a locked-in coin. The collector had turned the pouch to the right and when I pulled the pouch out of the envelope, the opening was facing down. Unexpectedly, the coin fell out of the pouch and plopped onto the pad on the table. Of course, I pretended that this was the most natural thing in the world, but I could tell by the look in his eye that the collector was getting a little worried.

Watching out for the holder

Without proper care, even the simple act of removing a coin from a holder carries the potential risk of damage. The term *flip rub* refers to wear or damage caused by rubbing a coin against the surfaces of a vinyl or plastic holder. Any dirt or contamination that comes between a coin and a holder acts as an abrasive, and any movement of the coin against the holder may cause damage to the surfaces of the coin. Therefore, the less often a coin is removed or inserted into a holder, the better.

That's why it's always a good idea to ask permission to remove a coin from a holder to examine it. The dealer may prefer to remove or insert the coin by himself, or simply refuse your request. Don't be offended — the dealer may simply want to protect the coin. On the other hand, be prepared to make a purchase decision under less than optimal conditions.

Handling a coin by the edges

The surfaces of a coin, especially those on *high-grade* (new or nearly new) examples, are very sensitive and vulnerable to even the slightest damage. I mentioned earlier how the wood fibers in paper towels can actually scratch the surfaces of a coin. Fingers and thumbs can damage the surfaces of a coin just as easily. A single grain of sand stuck between the ridges of a fingerprint can scratch a coin. The salty oils from fingers often interact chemically with the metal of a coin, leaving damage that may not appear right away, but could show up later and last forever. Handling a coin by the edges (see Figure 3-12) eliminates any possibility of surface contact and surface damage. Some collectors wear thin cotton gloves when handling their coins, but if your hands are clean and dry, gloves are unnecessary.

Figure 3-12:
The proper way to hold a coin.

Keeping your mouth shut

Each time you breathe, moisture-laden air escapes from your lungs. Each time you speak, tiny droplets of spittle fly from your mouth. Sounds disgusting, doesn't it? Well, imagine what happens to a coin that has been moisturized in this manner. Virtually all of the spots you see on copper coins (see Figure 3-13), regardless of the size of the spots, were caused by moisture of some sort. Therefore, it's best to hold your breath and not speak when examining an unprotected coin. Most of the time you won't have a problem keeping this rule, because nice coins tend to leave you speechless anyway! So far, we haven't gotten to the point of wearing masks over our mouths, but if coin prices go much higher, we may all start looking like Michael Jackson.

Figure 3-13:
A single spot of moisture can hurt a coin.

Holding a coin over a soft surface

A soft felt pad or a folded piece of cloth ensures that a dropped coin remains an undamaged coin. Be prepared to drop many coins in your lifetime — every coin dealer and collector I know has a story similar to mine (see Figure 3-14).

Figure 3-14:
This can happen when you drop a coin.

Keeping Them High and Dry

Moisture is a coin's worst enemy. Coins are made of metal, some of which is very chemically active. According to the laws of chemistry and physics, your coins will most certainly deteriorate over time unless you protect them.

A coin begins reacting with its environment as soon as a coin is *struck* (made). Any changes are subtle for the most part, but in some cases the changes may be significant. A copper coin's color changes; it may *corrode* or *oxidize*. This often starts as a tiny spot that grows until it eventually eats into the coin's surface. A single spot is bad enough, but poorly preserved coins may end up covered with spots and/or green corrosion. Naturally, collectors hate spots, corrosion, and coins with pitted surfaces (referred to as *pitting*). Unless the coin is a great rarity, such damage destroys any collector value.

Silver and gold coins are just as susceptible to chemical reactions. Over time, silver will tarnish or tone, resulting in a film of color that can range from light and subtle to dark and unattractive. Gold is relatively inert, but most gold coins include a small percentage of copper, which is a very sensitive metal.

Many of the chemical reactions that occur on the surface of a coin require, or are accelerated by, water. Simply put, water kills coins. Moisture of any kind should be avoided at all cost. If you live in an area of high humidity or ocean spray, protecting your coins becomes more difficult and important. However, there are several things you can do to ensure that your coins remain as pristine and as beautiful as they were the day you bought them.

Keeping 'em dry

Most holders are not meant to be watertight or airtight. Others claim to be so. However, I suggest erring on the side of caution by assuming that every holder leaks air or water. Take the same precautions with all holders, regardless of the claims made by the manufacturers. Remember, the changes that occur on the surface of a coin are at the chemical or molecular level, so you won't always be able to see it. All it takes is a tiny hole for air and moisture to seep in.

Store your coins in watertight containers. (Tupperware containers are good examples.) You never know when your water heater will break, the river will overflow its banks, or a hurricane will hit. Don't assume that the container you buy is actually watertight. Close the container (without your coins in it!), immerse it in water for several minutes, remove it, dry off the outside, and then inspect the inside to see whether any water seeped in.

Using a desiccant

A *desiccant* is a drying agent available at your local hardware store. You've probably seen small packets of desiccant in leather goods such as shoes and bags. Desiccants do a fabulous job of removing moisture from the air, and in some cases they may be reused simply by drying them out in an oven under low heat.

Why are desiccants necessary in a watertight holder? Because when you seal a coin in a watertight container, you're also sealing in any moisture in the atmosphere around it. A desiccant absorbs the moisture from the air, binds it, and keeps it away from your coin. In areas susceptible to moisture or humidity, desiccants are essential. In open containers, like safe-deposit boxes, check your desiccant every month and either re-dry it or replace it. In closed containers, you need only check the desiccant once every six months.

Securing Your Stash: At Home and on the Road

One of the most dramatic posters from World War II shows a sailor slipping beneath the waves for the last time, his ship destroyed and sinking in the background. The words, "Loose lips sink ships" jump from the poster, emphasizing the importance of discretion during times of war. The same is true for coin collectors.

Coins are thief magnets. Coins are valuable, portable, and easily sold. Thieves know that, but why help them out? Even without knowing it, you may be giving out hints that you're a coin collector or that you've got coins with you or at home. A little discretion and common sense can keep you and your coins safe.

The following are some tips for keeping your hobby secret:

- **Avoid discussing your collection in public.** I know you're proud of your collection and the neat new coins you just purchased, but be careful about how and where you discuss them.

- **Remove all hints of numismatics from your correspondence.** Placing the words "coin," "coin collector," "numismatist," or any other coin-related words on the return address of your envelopes is dangerous. Be sure to instruct anyone sending coins to you through the mail to remove any coin-related wording from their envelope or package, as well. Have your numismatic publications sent to a post office box and not your home.

✔ **Be careful whom you tell.** You may trust someone enough to let them know that you're a coin collector and you may even show them some of your goodies, but can you trust them never to tell anyone, who in turn, may tell someone else? An old adage in sales is that everyone knows a hundred people. Therefore, if you tell one person, you're telling a hundred, and each of them can tell a hundred . . . you get the picture. So be careful who you tell.

✔ **Hide your coins.** Don't leave your coins out for the cleaning lady, or anyone who may peek in your window, to see. Coin calendars are nice, but I guarantee you that someday one of your visitors will ask you, "Oh, are you a coin collector?"

Deciding between a home safe and a safe-deposit box

Should you store your coins at home or in a safe-deposit box in a bank? The answer depends on how comfortable you feel about keeping your coins at home, the value of your collection, and the importance of having your coins close by. Some collectors love to fiddle with their coins every chance they get. You may be in a situation where your collection is rapidly growing and changing, thereby requiring constant access to the coins. Other collectors are perfectly happy with an occasional trip to the bank to view their numismatic treasures. Ultimately, you must determine the amount of risk involved in keeping your coins at home, whether or not you can protect against those risks, and whether or not you can afford the loss in a worst-case scenario.

Home safes come in a variety of sizes and types, as follows:

✔ **Floor safes:** Embedded in the concrete floor of your home and the easiest to hide. However, they offer limited space and you may get tired of pulling the rug back and getting on your hands and knees just to open the safe.

✔ **Wall safes:** You've seen the movies: A figure clad in a black leather bodysuit moves stealthily across the room, swings the picture frame away from the wall, carefully fingers the dial of the wall safe, opens it, and then runs off with strings of pearls, bearer bonds, and wads of cash. In real life, thieves come in with crowbars, pop the safe out of the wall, and then scurry off to their lair where they can open the safe at their convenience. Unless your wall safe is embedded in concrete, don't bother getting one.

✔ **Regular safes:** Safes can protect your coins against fire, burglary, or both, and with regular safes you have many more options concerning size and weight. The main thing safes buy you is time, something burglars don't have a lot of. Small safes — no problem, the thieves will just cart them away. Cheap safes — no problem, they'll just pop them open on the spot. Large safes — if they can't cart them away, burglars will at least attempt to break into them on the spot.

✔ **Fire safes:** These types of safes are more for protection against fire than they are against burglars. Choose this type if you live in an area of high risk for fires and you feel relatively safe from theft. I've seen some neat coin collections reduced to melted lumps of metal because they weren't properly protected. Fire safes are rated by the length of protection they offer at a certain temperature. The higher the temperature and the longer the protection, the better for your coins.

Just as there are different choices in safes, there are multiple options in safe-deposit boxes. Things to consider are size, bank hours, access restrictions, terms of the agreement, the climate inside the vault, and insurance. You can read more about insurance in the "Insuring Your Investment" section, later in this chapter.

TIP

How alarming: A home system

Hard to believe, but there are still parts of the United States where you can leave your windows open and your doors unlocked without worrying about anyone breaking into your house or car. However, the rest of us need deadbolts on the doors, bars on the windows, alarm systems on our cars, and, sadly, alarm systems in our homes — and that's with nothing valuable inside! If you bring coins into the mix, having a home alarm system is not only a good idea, but it's essential. If you can't afford an alarm system, take your coins to the bank and lock them in a safe-deposit box.

Home alarm systems range from simple sensors on your doors and windows to sophisticated infrared, laser, and sound detectors. Check out your local vendors to find out which system is best for you. Consider the following when evaluating a system:

✔ Balance your need for security against the cost of the system.

✔ Ask yourself, "Do I want to live in an impenetrable fortress?"

✔ If you install a system, make sure that you have trusted friends, neighbors, or family in place for emergency contacts.

✔ Excessive false alarms may be costly. Many police forces start charging for any responses, above a certain number, to false alarms.

✔ Get a dog. Not a vicious dog, but one that barks whenever a stranger comes near your house. The right dog can be an excellent alarm and a good companion.

✔ Install motion sensors on your outside lighting so that any unusual movement turns the lights on. Thieves shun lighted areas.

Carrying coins in your car

Most thieves avoid confrontations, preferring instead simple break-ins when their victim is not around. Many coin thefts occur on the road, when for some reason, people let down their guard, become complacent, and enjoy a false sense of security and anonymity. If you read the trade papers long enough, you'll notice coin-theft reports with common themes.

Most car break-ins occur after a coin show. At the show, thieves notice who is buying and selling coins, who is carrying a large inventory, and who may be traveling alone. They watch as cars are being unloaded and loaded to see who is wary and who is complacent. The thieves may have watched you at a previous show to see how you behave on the road.

Dealers and attendees at coin shows receive identification badges and/or stick-on name tags. In the trade, we call these *rob me badges* (see Figure 3-15). If you walk out of a coin show wearing your badge or name tag, you advertise to the world (and the thief watching you) that you are a coin collector or dealer. Take the badge off before you walk out the door, and never wear it out in public.

Figure 3-15:
What you
see (left);
what the
thief sees
(right).

Carrying coins on a plane

Flying with coins presents special problems for the dealer and collector. First, you have the logistical problems. Coins add to the list of stuff you must carry and watch out for. Coins can be heavy and must be handled carefully on flights so that other passengers are not injured. Some airlines may charge extra fees for excess baggage weight, and in extreme cases, you may not be allowed to bring the extra weight at all!

Consider yourself vulnerable every step of the way, from the time you leave your home until the time you arrive at your hotel at the other end of your trip.

- ✔ **If you have a lot of luggage, enlist the aid of a skycap.** Make sure you keep your hands and eyes on your coins at all times. Don't turn your back on your coins, even for a second, and maintain physical contact with them at all times.

- ✔ **Be careful at the airport security checkpoint, where you are most vulnerable to coin theft.** After you make it through the metal detector, security guards will probably ask to search your coin bag (rows of coins form suspicious-looking metal rods in an x-ray). Ask for a private search so the whole world doesn't see what you have in your bag. Never allow the security guards (who may be imposters, for all you know) to take your coins out of your sight.

- ✔ **Try to board the airplane early so that you can stow your coins as close as possible to your seat.** If you can't find a compartment near your seat, stow your coins in the rows behind you, never ahead of you. In the crowded interior of an airplane, it's easier to stop someone behind you than it is to chase after someone ahead of you. Don't let anyone know what you're carrying. On long flights, check on your bag from time to time, just to make sure it's still safe and secure, especially if you've dozed off during the flight.

- ✔ **Don't allow your coins to be placed in the trunk of a cab or limousine, or you may end up watching helplessly as they are driven off without you.** You are much better off bringing the coins with you into the cab.

How comforting is your inn?

Security at hotels ranges from not-so-hot to nonexistent. Smaller motel chains and independent operators offer few options for the traveler with coins, in which case, you're pretty much relegated to baby-sitting your coins. Larger chains offer safe-deposit boxes in the main lobby office. Many hotels now offer small safes right in your own room. Nevertheless, if you're carrying very valuable coins or a lot of bulky coins, I recommend staying with them at all times. Never, ever leave your coins unattended in your room.

When you travel to a coin show, you have a choice of staying at the official convention hotels or at any other hotel in the city. Most coin shows are held at the official hotel or very close nearby, perhaps in an adjoining convention center.

As an alternative to hotel security, most major coin shows offer security rooms manned by the same staff that protects the show or by outside security firms (often off-duty police officers) hired for just that purpose. Many times, security rooms are open well before and after the actual coin show, giving dealers time to enjoy the sights and sounds of the city.

Dealing with a robbery

I hope that none of my readers ever need this advice, but I offer it nonetheless.

Just because you've been the victim of a coin robbery doesn't mean that it's the end of the world. You have a much better chance at recovering your coins today than you did 10 or 20 years ago. New technologies make it easier for you to send information about your robbery to those people who are most likely to recover your coins for you — coin dealers and law enforcement authorities.

✔ **Keep good records.** This way you can supply a list of the missing coins to law enforcement authorities. If you own a computer, just about any database or spreadsheet program will work perfectly. Be sure to include as much information as possible:

- A description of the coin, including any identifying marks

- Serial numbers (if the coins have been encapsulated by an outside grading company)

- Catalog identification numbers

- The current value of the coin

- The date you purchased the coin

- From whom you purchased the coin

✔ **Have your best coins photographed to help make positive identifications.** Several digital cameras on the market today make coin photography easy and inexpensive.

✔ **Begin locally and end globally.** Most criminals get caught because they're a few coins shy of a complete set (that's my one and only joke in this section). Assume that your coins will end up somewhere close by. Contact every dealer in the town where your coins were stolen, and then target dealers in the surrounding towns, dealers in the major cities in your state, and dealers in the major cities throughout the United States.

✔ **Provide every contact with as much information as possible, including inventory listings and photographs.** Be sure to include contact information for yourself and any law enforcement officials involved with your case.

✔ **Go online.** Publish a listing of your missing coins on the Internet. You may already have your own Website or access to one.

✔ **Use e-mail.** E-mail allows you to send the same message to a large number of recipients at the same time. When I say "large," I'm talking about the potential to contact hundreds and thousands of dealers. Assuming you have a computer and the proper connection, e-mail is free and can be used as often as you like. For example, you could send an e-mail message each week just as a friendly reminder for dealers to keep an eye open for your missing coins. Be sensitive to spamming issues (the sending of unsolicited e-mails). While most dealers are anxious to help people recover their stolen coins, others may find your e-mails a nuisance. If someone asks you to stop sending them e-mails, honor their request quickly and politely. Balance your desire to find your coins against the possibility of violating spam rules.

Insuring Your Investment

Insurance is a risk-based business, sort of a bet between you and the insurance company that something will or won't go wrong. The bet includes odds that affect the size of the bet (the premium you pay to the insurance company) and the size of the payoff (the amount the insurance company pays you after a loss). In other words, the more risk you are willing to live with, the less your insurance will cost and vice versa. For example, a higher deductible may reduce your annual premiums, but you receive less in the event of a loss.

Every insurance company treats coins differently, so be sure to discuss your needs with a professional insurance agent. Make sure you understand what you're buying and how your coin collection will be protected.

When you sit down with your insurance agent, ask the following questions:

✔ **Will my insurance policy cover my coin collection?** You may be shocked to discover that unless you purchase special coverage, your coin collection will only be insured for its face value. In other words, you get a buck for that Silver Dollar you purchased last year for $3,000! You may as well not even have insurance.

✔ **Am I required to get an appraisal of my collection?** You may be required to have an outside, independent appraiser prepare an official evaluation of your collection. This can get expensive, so find out what kind of information the insurance company requires, who they'll accept as an appraiser, and how additions and subtractions from your collection will be treated.

✔ **Will I be required to protect my collection?** Your insurance company may require you to install a home security system, a safe, or some other security device. You may already have such things in place, and, if you do, ask if they will help reduce your premiums.

✔ **Are the coins in my safe-deposit box covered?** Don't assume that insurance covers your collection down at the local bank. You may think your coins are perfectly safe, but your insurance company may think otherwise. Be sure to ask whether special coverage is required.

✔ **What about transporting my coins?** Are you covered when you bring coins from your home to your bank's vault? How about when you bring coins to and from a coin show? Your insurance company may place limits on the value of the coins you transport, and they may place restrictions on how they are transported.

✔ **What will the insurance cost?** Every insurance company is different, but expect to pay based on a cost-per-value basis. For example, you may be charged an annual premium of $1.50 for every $100 worth of value. In other words, if your collection was appraised at $10,000, your annual insurance premium would be $125.

✔ **What about deductibles?** A deductible reduces the amount of money you receive in the event of a claim. For example, if you have a deductible of $500 and your loss was $3,000, you receive $2,500. Sure, you can get a non-deductible policy, but those are the most expensive kind. Generally, the higher the deductible, the lower your annual premium. Your job is to find a balance between the two that makes you comfortable.

Don't be afraid to shop around. Expect to find a wide range of pricing and coverage options. Choose the company and policy that are right for you and you'll sleep better, knowing that if anything happens to your collection, you'll be covered.

Part II
Buying Coins the Safe Way

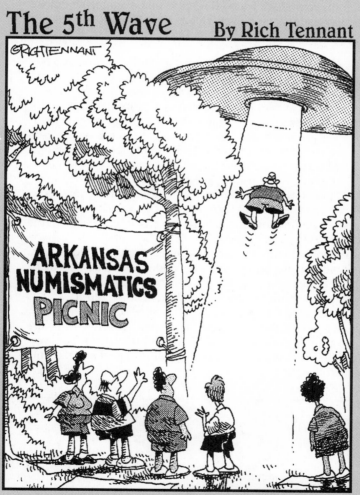

The 5th Wave   By Rich Tennant

ARKANSAS NUMISMATICS PICNIC

"Get coins! Preferably graded!"

In this part . . .

*L*ike most other collectibles, numismatics has its pot-holes in the road. However, if you know where they are, you can steer clear of them. In this part, I give you the tools to protect yourself from scams, counterfeit coins, altered coins, and overpriced coins. The money you save from these tips will more than cover the cost of this book.

I also show you how to use price guides to value your coins and to determine whether to buy a coin that's being offered to you. Most importantly, I show you where to look for coins and how to negotiate with dealers and buy coins from auctions. You may be surprised at how many good deals are just waiting to be discovered out there — you simply need the skills and confidence to go out and find them.

This part also introduces you to coin grading and shows you why improving your skills in this area can not only save you money, but also make you money. I explain the important elements of today's grading methods. I share the information you need to protect yourself from over-graded coins and to discover undergraded coins. I also introduce you to grading and certification services if you want to submit coins for grading. Grading requires patience, good working conditions, practice and skill. I give you all the ingredients you need to be a world-class grader. All you need to do is get out there and hone your skills. Remember that every grading expert started out just like you!

Chapter 4

Foiling the Fakes

. . . .

. . . .

"**I**mitation is the sincerest form of flattery." Except in numismatics, that is, where imitation becomes the sincerest form of deception.

Even the best dealers are fooled sometimes by counterfeit and doctored coins, so you are well served if you arm yourself with as much knowledge as possible. There's no reason you can't be just as knowledgeable as anyone else in your area of numismatic interest. In the meantime, heed the advice offered here until you are confident in your own abilities at detecting problem coins.

Any complete discussion of coin collecting requires a look at one of numismatics' dirty little secrets — that of counterfeiting, restoration, repairing, recoloring, and any of the many ways in which coins are either copied or doctored in an attempt to deceive the buyer. Counterfeiting came on the heels of the first coins and continues today. Coin doctoring sprang up more recently, when coin prices began to shoot through the roof and condition became a major factor in coin pricing.

Resisting Temptation

When someone offers to sell me a coin for $50, and I know that it is worth $100, I am sorely tempted to buy it on the spot. But over the years, my temptation has yielded to caution and suspicion. Except in rare and unusual circumstances, there has always been a good reason why the coin was priced so cheaply. Usually, it's because the coin had a problem — or two or more! Sometimes the problem can be very subtle, which means you must make a careful examination of any coin you consider buying, no matter how nice the coin looks. It's too easy to use a good light and a magnifying glass to check out any potential purchases. And, because it's too easy to make a mistake, let your common sense be your guide.

In Chapter 2, I talk about the importance of developing a good, strong relationship with a numismatic adviser. A large part of such a relationship revolves around trust. In other words, you trust your adviser to give you the straight story and to show you right from wrong. When you ask a question, you expect a correct and appropriate answer. But how do you know whether the information you're receiving is correct or whether the coins you are buying are genuine and graded properly, especially when there's money involved?

The answer is, "you don't." To borrow a phrase, the price of confidence in coin buying is eternal vigilance. Seek out good advice, take it with a grain of salt, verify it by checking with different sources, and keep a wary eye. Use the knowledge and experience you gain over time to not only uncover buying opportunities and rare varieties, but also to protect yourself against fraud and deception.

Knowing their motives

A quick look at any numismatic price guide reveals the profit opportunities for a person skilled in finely detailed metalworking. Look at the price difference between the common 1927 $20 Gold piece and the extremely rare 1927-D. Although the price difference is huge, the only actual difference between these two coins is a tiny mintmark above the date. All anyone needs to do to create a $400,000 rarity is spend $500–$750 for a common 1927 and add a small D to the front of the coin. However, most of the time, an added mintmark is detected easily, and you can bet that any 1927-D Double Eagle is scrutinized carefully whenever it comes on the market. Even so, the price difference is a huge

incentive to practice, practice, practice — which is exactly what the coin doctorers do.

Coin doctorers rarely fiddle with counterfeiting because the profits are small, the likelihood of getting caught is good, and the penalties for getting caught and convicted are so high. ("Tis death to counterfeit" is a popular phrase from colonial times.) On the other hand, it's easy to make a coin look better or more valuable with just a touch of chemicals here, a rub or two here and there, and a little repair work. Plus, I've never heard of a coin doctorer going to jail, even though the losses from their handiwork are just as damaging and insidious as the work of the counterfeiters.

Becoming Your Own Expert

Years ago, in a simpler and more innocent time, all you needed to detect fake coins was a good magnifying glass and a familiarity with the various coin design types. Back then, you could spot a fake fairly easily if you knew what a real coin was supposed to look like. Today, you need to know how to perform specific gravity tests and have access to electron microscopes, x-ray spectrophotometers, and other sophisticated equipment and techniques. As an alternative, you can send your coins to a certification service, where their experts are well versed in counterfeit detection and he equipment performs the proper analyses. Or, even better, you can take the time to find out how to detect counterfeit and altered coins on your own.

How do you go about becoming your own expert?

- ✔ **Read the basic grading guides (see Chapter 10).** These guides give you good insight into the history of coin grading, different approaches used by different authors and companies, how grading has changed over the years, and what it may be like in the future. Learning to grade is important because you must know what a coin is supposed to look like before you can tell whether it is actually different in any way. The processes that I outline in the "Finding Out about Repaired, Restored, and Recolored Coins" section, later in this chapter, changes how a coin looks, so you need to know how to tell the difference.

- ✔ **Look at lots of coins.** When you visit a coin shop or go to a coin show, take the time to look at as many coins as possible, even those you're not interested in, just to discover the characteristics of each type and date. For example, by looking at lots of Silver Dollars, you figure out soon enough that the 1890-O is almost always weakly struck, while the 1881-S is usually crisply struck and well detailed. After a while, you become so good that you can tell whether an 1893-S Silver Dollar is good just by looking at the front of the coin.

- ✔ **Ask questions.** Don't be shy — after all, it's your money that you're protecting. Why is the toning on this coin artificial? How do you know this coin had a hole filled? Were the hairline scratches on this coin caused when the dies were polished or because the coin was cleaned later? Is the red color on this copper coin original or false? Would you demonstrate the proper method for dipping a coin?

Dies are the cylinders of steel with a design on one end that are used to make coins. Before the dies are put in the coining press, they are usually polished to make the flat surfaces as smooth as possible. Sometimes the action of the polishing leaves fine scratches in the steel that become raised lines on the coin itself. Alternatively, hairline scratches occur when a coin is lightly wiped or rubbed. In many cases, the difference is subtle but can translate into a huge price difference because die polishing lines are acceptable but hairline scratches are not.

Teaching an old dog new tricks

ANA president Bob Campbell taught the difference between genuine and artificial toning on coins at the 2001 American Numismatic Association's Mid-Winter Convention in Salt Lake City, Utah. Bob has specialized in toned coins for many years, and he really knows his stuff. During his talk, Bob provided a slide show of enlarged, full-color images to illustrate real and artificial toning. At the end of his presentation, Bob put up slides of toned coins and polled the audience to see whether they thought the color was natural or unnatural. I admit to getting only three out of four right, but I came away from Bob's presentation better able to protect myself from artificially toned coins — and with a new-found realization that an old dog *can* learn new tricks!

Die polishing appears as raised lines on the surface of a coin while scratches go below the surface and into the metal. Ninety-nine percent of the time, die polishing lines affect only the fields, while hairline scratches will run up and over the raised design elements on the coin.

✔ **Read some more.** Keep up with the latest numismatic publications to find out about new techniques being used to improve coins, new fakes that are being discovered, and new methods being used to uncover frauds.

✔ **Go back to school.** Take a grading and/or counterfeit detection course at the American Numismatic Association's Summer Seminars. Listen in on the Numismatic Theater presentations at the American Numismatic Association conventions. Discover as much as you can from as many different sources as possible. Many presentations at coin shows are free. Others, like the ANA seminars, cost money — but believe me, it's money well spent. I look at this part of my education as insurance against getting stuck with a fake or fraudulent coin. Saving yourself from one expensive mistake may pay for the costs of these courses many times over.

Finding Out about Repaired, Restored, and Recolored Coins

Coin doctorers use a variety of means to improve the appearance of coins. Some results are obvious to the naked eye, but some are so deceptive that they are almost invisible. You can avoid many repaired, restored, and recolored coins by being aware of the traps discussed in this section.

Cleaned coins

How a coin is cleaned and what you use to clean it with are critical factors in determining whether the cleaning is a success or a failure. (In Chapter 3, I discuss cleaning coins and how easy it is to damage a coin and its value through improper or overenthusiastic cleaning.) What about the coins in your collection? Most likely, you can point out the coins in your collection that you've cleaned personally. But can you tell whether other coins in your collection have been cleaned by someone else? What about the coin you're about to buy?

Do you have the knowledge to determine whether a coin has been cleaned? If not, watch out for unnaturally bright surfaces. This is a good indication that the surfaces have been scrubbed. All coins possess a natural brightness (or *luster*) when they are brand new. As a coin wears, the luster begins to disappear. And by the time a coin reaches the grade of Very Fine, the luster is completely gone. (See Chapter 9 for explanations of the terms used to describe the condition of coins.)

Be suspicious of any coin below the grade of About Uncirculated that appears to have full luster — most likely, the coin has been polished. In Uncirculated condition, cleaning is harder to detect because coins are expected to be bright in those grades. Nevertheless, if you find out what real, original luster looks like, you're less likely to be fooled by a cleaned coin.

Walking the planchet

When the employees at the U.S. Mint get ready to make coins, they usually polish the die before placing it into the coining press. The result is known as a *Prooflike* coin — a reflective coin with a hard, metallic luster. A Prooflike silver coin resembles highly polished chrome — you can actually see your reflection in the surfaces of the coin. Each time the die is used to strike a coin, it begins to wear down microscopically as the metal of the *planchet* (blank piece of metal that becomes a coin when it is stamped with a design from the dies) spreads out underneath it.

Over time, the spreading metal of the planchets creates tiny grooves in the metal of the die, destroying the Prooflike luster and replacing it with what is termed *frosty luster.* The tiny grooves are known as *flow lines,* and you can actually see them under magnification — they radiate out from the center of the coin toward the edges. The conversion from a Prooflike to a frosty surface takes place in small degrees, so on many coins you see a wide variety of different surfaces, ranging from deeply mirrored Prooflike to heavily frosted (and everything in between).

It is easiest to detect cleaning on a Prooflike coin, perhaps because the reflective surfaces exaggerate any imperfections. Think of how easy it is to see scratches on the surfaces of your eyeglasses — the same is true of Prooflike coins. On coins with frosty luster, you must look for any disruption of the flow lines; this is why using a magnifying glass is so important. Sure, you can catch gross cleaning jobs with your naked eye, but the good frauds will fool you unless you take a closer look.

Until you feel comfortable in your ability to tell whether a coin has been cleaned or not, stick with *certified coins* — coins that have been authenticated, graded, and certified by an independent, third-party grading service (see Chapter 10). Reputable grading services will not certify a coin that has been cleaned (or else they will make such a notation on the holder label). This eliminates much of the uncertainty and lets you focus your buying on coins that look nice for the grade.

Dipped coins

Dipped coins have been immersed in a chemical cleaner to enhance their appearance. Dipping is usually done to remove toning from silver coins (read about cleaning your own coins in Chapter 3). When done properly, dipping improves the appearance of a coin and can't be detected. When done improperly, dipping can etch the surface of a coin and give it a cloudy appearance. Heavy dipping destroys the natural luster of a coin, be it Prooflike or frosty, and the result is a drab, lifeless coin. Copper coins develop an unnatural orange color, and silver coins turn pure white. Gold coins are less susceptible to dipping because of the inert nature of gold. But heavily dipped gold coins will develop a subtle grainy surface, as the natural luster is destroyed by the chemical action of the dip.

Light dipping has little or no effect on the value of a coin. But heavy, noticeable dipping should force a discount of about 30 percent of the value. Expect the impact to be even greater on Uncirculated coins.

Detecting dipped coins is difficult; it depends on the degree of chemical wear. Nevertheless, a good rule to follow is that any coin struck more than seventy-five years ago should show some natural toning. For example, if you see an 1800 Silver Dollar that has no tarnish whatsoever, it's a safe bet that the coin has been dipped. Whether that's good or bad depends on your personal taste, your preference for *toned* (tarnished) or *untoned* (untarnished) coins, and how the appearance of the coin was affected by the cleaning.

Sadly, the current demand for untoned coins has resulted in rampant dipping and the destruction of the natural beauty of many coins that should have been left alone in the first place. I suspect that many years from now we'll look back and wish we had been more selective and careful with our numismatic treasures.

Scrubbed coins

Cleaning coins with a harsh abrasive results in a coin with a scrubbed appearance. Scrubbed coins lack any luster whatsoever and have heavy *hairlines* (fine scratches) or brightly polished surfaces. Scrubbing lowers the value of a coin dramatically. In fact, unless the coin is a rarity, stay away from anything that's been scrubbed.

Erasered coins

As hard as it is to believe, some people use the eraser of a pencil to remove spots or toning from coins. Because of the abrasives embedded in pencil erasers, the result is a localized area of fine scratches. On most coins, they show up as a bright patch on an otherwise frosty surface. To see the scratches, you must turn the coin at just the right angle under a light source.

Whizzed coins

Ever heard of onomatopoeia? That's when a word sounds exactly like what it describes. When you hear the word "whiz," think of the nightmarish sound of a brush rotating at high speed and coming in contact with the surface of a coin. (A dentist's drill comes to mind.) Then, imagine what happens to the surface of the coin as the flow lines are disrupted and the metal is moved around. Sounds sickening, doesn't it? Whizzing is a cruel way to treat a coin, and the result is a bright but unnatural luster that has fooled many a novice collector. Thankfully, whizzing has declined in popularity; but there are a lot of coins floating around from the days of yore when whizzing was commonplace. After you see a whizzed coin, you'll never forget it. So ask your numismatic adviser to point one out to you. Just have your barf bag ready!

Repaired coins

A good coin doctorer can repair just about anything. I once saw a very valuable coin that had broken into two pieces, rendering it almost worthless. The two pieces were soldered together and the surface details reengraved with incredible skill. Had I not known what was done, I doubt whether I ever would have detected the repair work. I've seen holes filled, surfaces smoothed, scratches removed, rim dents hammered out, and details reworked.

 Coin repairs require the addition, removal, or movement of metal from one area to another. In many cases, a coin must be softened by heat to make the repair work easier. As you know by now, it is very easy to destroy the natural luster and appearance of the surfaces of a coin. Because most coin repairs are localized, coin doctorers try to cover up their work by cleaning and recoloring the entire coin. I've even seen repaired coins that were distressed to create natural looking marks and nicks. Be smart. Stay away from cleaned and recolored coins — they may be hiding a host of problems.

Recolored coins

Recolored coins come in two categories:

- Coins that have been stripped of color and retoned
- Coins that were original but have had color added to make them more attractive

The difference between the two categories is subtle but important. Stripping destroys the natural quality of a coin's surface, whereas the color on an artificially toned coin can usually be taken off and the coin underneath will still have original-looking surfaces.

Recoloring is most obvious on copper coins, where the original color has been dipped or stripped away, leaving a bright, unnatural orange-red color. Copper coins are usually stripped because their color is ugly to begin with or because of corrosion spots on the surfaces. About Uncirculated coins are often stripped to make them look like full red Uncirculated examples. Given time, this bright, unnatural color will tone down to a more pleasant brown color; such a process takes many, many years, and if you follow my recommendations in Chapter 3 for properly storing your coins, it may take forever. As a result, coin doctorers speed up the process by applying a salve of pure sulfur powder mixed in petroleum jelly to the surfaces of the coin until the desired brown color is achieved. As you may suspect, a lot of chemical activity takes place on the surfaces of a recolored coin. And as you already know from Chapter 3, chemical activity on a coin is always bad.

Under the right circumstances, a silver coin acquires the most incredible rainbow of iridescent colors. You'll see mouthwatering descriptions of these coins in auction catalogs and sales brochures (I've used 'em myself) — crystalline, sea-green hues, pearlescent luster, pale shades of lilac and gold, killer toning, and so on. A coin with the right color can fetch a huge premium over an untoned version of the same coin; so there is considerable profit awaiting the coin doctorer who can duplicate such a color. However, as hard as they try, no one has ever been able to duplicate killer toning on a coin. Usually, the results will fool new collectors but not anyone who has been around coins for any length of time.

Differentiating between real and artificial toning is difficult and requires the examination of lots and lots of coins. However, in the meantime, protect yourself either by staying away from toned coins entirely or by purchasing only coins that have been encapsulated by reputable grading services (which are very good at discovering and rejecting fake toning).

Curated coins

Curating is a term that entered the numismatic world only recently — it refers to a method of cleaning that improves the appearance of a coin without harming the surfaces. In other words, curating is good, cleaning is bad (even though curating itself is a form of cleaning). Proponents of curating liken it to the restoration of Michelangelo's frescoes in the Sistine Chapel or the removal of surface grime from an Old Master painting. Opponents call curating a deceptive term that allows some coins to get around the restrictions against cleaned coins at some of the grading services.

Coins are a lot like dogs. Ninety percent of them are perfectly safe, 9 percent of them will bite you, and 1 percent will maul you. Find out how to tell the difference, stay away from the bad 10 percent, and become best friends with the rest!

Curated or cleaned?

The gold coins and bars of the shipwrecked *S.S. Central America* rested on the bottom of the Atlantic Ocean for over 125 years before being discovered in 1986. When they were finally salvaged, many of the coins were covered with a red encrustation and/or attachments of sea life, all of which were removed before the coins were sold. The processes used to remove the encrustations left the coins in their pristine, original condition, with no outward indications that they had been cleaned (apart from the salvors saying so). Many of the coins were graded by the Professional Coin Grading Service (PCGS), which knew the whole story of the salvage operations and the fact that the coins had been cleaned (or curated or

whatever). When PCGS placed the coins in their special protective holders, they added a special notation to the paper insert sourcing the coins to the *S.S. Central America* shipwreck.

Purists decried this action, stating that by grading and certifying the coins, PCGS violated one of their own rules against certifying coins known to have been cleaned. However, having seen many of the coins, I can't tell from looking at them which have been curated and which have not. The collecting market has embraced the coins wholeheartedly, saying with their wallets, that curating is an acceptable form of cleaning. What do you think?

Chapter 5

Weaving Your Way through Price Guides

"*W*hat's my coin worth?" If I earned a nickel every time someone asked me that question, I'd be a rich man. People love old coins, but they're even more interested in finding out what the coins are worth. For some reason, people think that any coin over twenty years old is worth a million dollars — or they're interested in finding out how close to a million dollars their coin is worth. So far, I haven't been able to tell anyone that their coin is worth a million dollars (or even ten-thousand dollars, come to think of it). Nevertheless, as long as collectors keep asking, I'll keep answering — because I know, *I just know*, that sooner or later a million-dollar coin is going to show up. Perhaps it's hiding in your collection!?

Knowing that Raison d'Être Isn't a Cereal

One thing I've noticed in dealing with collectors is that they are very suspicious people, especially where pricing is concerned. That's why I like having price guides around. I open one up, point to a page, move over a row, drop down a column or two, and stab my finger repeatedly, saying "See, there it is in black-and-white."

Price guides serve several useful purposes:

▶ **They record prices.** Numismatic price guides are numerical history books, recording prices for coins sold in the recent past. The prices represent what a coin was or is worth, not what it should be worth. A good price guide includes pricing from a variety of sources, including dealer trades at the wholesale and retail levels, auction prices realized, private sales, and fixed price lists.

✔ **They set prices.** After coin prices are recorded, they tend to set prices for the near future. Collectors, wanting to know what to pay for a coin, look to the price guides for guidance. If the guide says $50, collectors expect to pay that price. If Dealer A prices his coin at $25, collectors consider that a good deal, and the coin sells quickly. If Dealer B tries for $75, his coin languishes in inventory. Thus, price guides create a self-fulfilling prophecy. After a price appears in print, it may as well be set in stone.

✔ **They add stability to the market.** Because price guides tend to set prices, they have a calming effect on any wild swings that occur in the market. For example, because of their reluctance to budge from published prices, customers may not support big price increases. On the other hand, if prices begin to drop, customers help keep prices up by buying what they think are bargains. In a sense, the market is most comfortable when it is close to the published prices. Price guides are like invisible fences that keep everything contained and under control.

✔ **They give the consumer confidence.** If Dealer X, whom you've never seen before in your life, offered you a coin for $100 and claimed that it was a good deal, would you buy the coin on his say-so? I would say not. The first thing you'd do is run for a price guide to see if $100 is a good deal or not. Now, why would you trust a price guide over nice Dealer X? Because the price guide doesn't lie. Price guides instill confidence because of their independent nature — they are blind to any transaction that takes place after the publication date, including the one you're about to enter into with Dealer X.

Different price guides serve different areas of the market. Collectors can choose between wholesale price guides, retail price guides, buy price guides, sell price guides, market price guides, certified coin price guides, and raw coin price guides, all from a variety of different sources.

Haggling with the Best of 'Em

The coin business has no secrets. I know of no other retail business that "tells all" like the coin business does. As coin dealers, we pretend that we have wholesale and retail price levels, but we have no protection for either side. Imagine going into Saks Fifth Avenue, picking out a $500 item, and then saying to the sales clerk, "I know that your company paid only $250 for this item, therefore I am willing to offer you $300, giving you a profit that should be plenty fair." They'd throw you out of the store. Yet this sort of thing happens at coin shows and in coin shops all the time. When is wholesale, retail and retail, wholesale? Try the coin market.

About five minutes after becoming a coin collector, you'll discover that no one pays retail prices and that prices are always negotiable.

Going whole (sale) hog

In *most* of the business world, *wholesale* refers to the prices at which dealers trade among each other. Professional dealers buy from wholesalers and sell the item at a retail price to their customers. Generally, the public is not allowed into this inner circle of wholesale pricing so that the retail dealer's business can remain protected. Rarely do the wholesaler and retailer compete with each other for the same customer. Also, it is rare to hear of a retail dealer offering a customer the same discount he would give to another dealer — except, that is, in the coin business.

In the coin business, *wholesale* is supposed to refer to the prices at which dealers trade among each other. However, wholesale prices are also available to the general public because of a lack of control in the market. Here's an example: At most coin shows, the period at the very beginning of the show is known as *dealer set-up* — a time when dealers bring in their coins, set up their booths, and trade among themselves. As you may expect, some of the best deals are found during set-up. Some coins may actually trade hands several times in the course of a dealer set-up, increasing in price at each transaction.

In theory, dealer set-up is for wholesale dealers only — those who have traveled from afar at considerable expense. In reality, anyone can gain access to this wholesale market quite easily. In many cases, you can buy your way into a dealer set-up by paying a fee (usually a fraction of the cost of a regular table or booth). If you're friends with a dealer who has a table at the show, you can arrange beforehand to be listed as an assistant in the booth. Your identification badge appears exactly like all the others (no one will know you're not a wholesaler), and you can compete with the dealers for the best deals. (To gain access to wholesale pricing, simply subscribe to the *Coin Dealer Newsletter* — the "Greysheet" — and its associated publications.)

The price guides that you carry identify you as either a retail mark or a savvy buyer. Whip out a Redbook to check the price of a coin and you may see a gleam in the seller's eye or a faraway look as he calculates how much to add to the asking price. Whip out a Greysheet and you'll be recognized as a serious buyer with whom to be reckoned!

Retailing the story like it really is

In most of the business world, *retail* refers to the prices charged to the general public. Retailers buy from wholesalers at a discount, add on some profit (their markup), and then offer the merchandise through retail locations in shops, malls, and mail-order businesses. Retailers in the United States frequently offer discounts through sales events, but even then prices are firm. The wholesale prices paid by the retailer are never divulged.

In the coin business, *retail* is a dream. Retail is the customer who pays the full asking price without haggling. Retail is the customer who hasn't yet discovered wholesale price guides. Retail is the customer who hasn't discovered eBay. Retail is the customer who hasn't discovered coin shows or the competitor down the street. Retail is the customer who will become wholesale soon enough.

Bidding a do

In the stock market, *bid* is the price someone is willing to pay for a particular stock. *Ask* is the price at which someone is willing to sell the stock. The difference between the bid and the ask prices is called the *spread*. Stocks that trade in large volume tend to have close spreads, while stocks that are rarely traded have larger spreads.

Similar concepts apply in the coin market. In theory, the *bid price* is the highest price a dealer is willing to pay for a particular coin, and the *ask price* represents the lowest price a dealer may ask for a coin.

My experience with the bid and ask prices in the *Coin Dealer Newsletter (CDN)* publications is that

- ✔ You can sometimes find coins priced below bid.
- ✔ You can almost always find coins priced right at bid.
- ✔ Only rarely must you pay the ask price.

For the past 38 years, the *CDN* has compiled and published Bid and Ask prices for U.S. coins. After the grading and certification services became established, *CDN* began publishing the *Certified Coin Dealer Newsletter*, containing bid and ask prices for certified coins. The dealer in the CDN publication titles refers to the user of the pricing information in each issue — you don't have to be a dealer to subscribe. Anyone willing to pay the price may order a subscription, and many collectors and non-dealers do!

Aiming your sights (unseen)

The term *sight unseen* came out of the electronic networks that were set up to facilitate trading in certified coins. To reinforce the notion that certified coins were universally acceptable, bidders began making sight unseen bids for certain coins — especially generic coins like MS-65 Morgan Silver Dollars or MS-63 $20 Gold pieces. In effect, the bidders were saying, "No matter how good or bad your coin looks, I will accept it and honor my bid."

Unfortunately, certified coins are not like stocks. Even though they may bear identical grades, no two coins are identical in appearance. Take a look at a handful of certified MS-63 Morgan Dollars and you can see differences in eye appeal, the number and location of marks on the coin, the luster, the strike, toning, and so on. Just from a standpoint of personal taste, you can probably sort them out into coins you like and coins you don't like. If you decided to sell only a few of them, which ones do you think you would ship to a sight unseen bidder? Naturally, you'd send out the ones you don't like and you'd keep the best ones for yourself.

Sight unseen bidders learned quickly enough that they were receiving only the worst coins, so they lowered their bids to the point where they would be comfortable accepting even the ugliest coin of any grade. To keep from having to buy ugly coins, dealers began making sight seen bids that represented higher offers for the same coins, but with a right to reject any unsatisfactory ones.

Simply put, we now have a two-tiered market that offers two options:

- ✔ High liquidity at a lower price
- ✔ Low liquidity at a higher price

In other words, you can sell your coins today at a cheap price, or you may be able to sell your coins for more money *if* you have the time and if your coin has the right look.

When selling, always try for the sight seen bid. You bought your coin because you liked it, didn't you? Chances are the next person will like it, too. You may find the difference in the sight seen and the sight unseen bids to be well worth your time and effort.

Rooting Out the Right Guide

What's the best price guide for you? How often do you need a new price guide?

Be aware that by the time price guides are published, the market will have already moved on and prices may be substantially different. The timelier the information, the better. So ask the publishers of your favorite price guide how much time elapses between the end of their compilation process and the beginning of the printing process.

✔ **Weekly price guides:** Subscribe to weekly price guides if you're buying and selling coins on a frequent basis. Weekly price guides reflect rapid changes in the market and are available for both the wholesale and retail markets.

- At the wholesale level, I recommend *Coin Dealer Newsletter* and *Certified Coin Dealer Newsletter.*

- For the retail market, try *Coin World's* "Trends of U.S. Coins." (It appears on a three-week cycle, so buy three consecutive issues of *Coin World* to get a complete set of their "Trends.")

Keep in mind that knowledge equals profits. Use your awareness of price swings to your advantage. If you know prices have moved up in a certain area, go buy coins from the less informed dealers. If you know prices have weakened in a certain area, sell your coins at yesterday's prices before everyone finds out.

✔ **Monthly price guides:** Monthly price guides are perfectly fine for collectors with a long-term approach to collecting and who don't need up-to-the-minute pricing. Because they include information over a longer period of time, monthly price guides tend to smooth out the volatility of weekly price guides. *Numismatic News* publishes "Coin Market," a handy guide that's easy to carry and use. The parent company of *Numismatic News,* Krause Publications, also produces the bi-monthly "Coin Prices."

✔ **Annual price guides:** Use annual price guides only if your collecting activity remains at a very low level. Annual price guides are like bread and flowers — they're best when fresh. Remember, the farther you get from the publication date, the less relevant the information will be.

- The premier annual price guide is *A Guide Book Of United States Coins,* by R.S. Yeoman (St. Martin's Press, Inc.), commonly known as the "Redbook" because of its distinctive red cover.

- For the last thirteen years, *Coin World* has produced an annual price guide for U.S. Coins.

- A third option is the *Blackbook Price Guide to United States Coins,* published by House of Collectibles (a division of Random House), now in it's 39th edition.

Pricing World Coins

Determining the value of world coins is a trifle more difficult than pricing U.S. coins simply because, in general, not as much information is available about world coins. Krause Publications produces some wonderful world coin catalogs that are great for general world coins, but they may be overkill if you're simply trying to find prices for a few coins from a specific country. Specialized publications exist for most countries, but they are hard to locate and are often written in the language of the home country.

The following are some options for working with world coin pricing:

- **Bite the bullet.** Make the investment and purchase all of the Krause "Standard Catalog of World Coins" catalogs. These catalogs are broken up by century, so you need to purchase one for each of the 17th, 18th, 19th, and 20th centuries. They're the size of telephone books and are fairly expensive, but if you have a sizable collection of world coins or if you're seriously interested in collecting them, buy these books before you buy a single coin.

- **Check with numismatic book dealers.** You never know what world coin books a numismatic book supplier may have in stock. If nothing else, you may be able to get a discount on the major titles (like the Krause catalogs). Check the Cheat Sheet at the front of this book or go on the Internet and search for **numismatic book dealers**.

- **Ask around.** Many U.S. dealers also have sidelines in world coins. In many cases, they'll have some of the specialized books you'll need. For example, I specialize in German coins, so I like to have some of the more important books on German coins on hand for collectors who are developing interests in this area.

- **Go to the source.** Get on the Internet and locate dealers in the country in which you have an interest. Ask them which publications are best suited for the coins you wish to collect. Ask whether they can obtain the publications for you. You must have patience in this endeavor, however — you'll run up against language barriers, currency exchange issues, and shipping challenges. However, if you want to know what your coins are really worth in their home country, finding these books is well worth the effort.

I still haven't found any decent world coin pricing information on the Internet, something I hope will be corrected in the near future.

Realizing Auction Prices

Coin auctions are a wonderful source of pricing information, especially for those rare and hard-to-find coins that only show up once in a blue moon. Each year, tens of millions of dollars worth of rare coins are sold by some of the biggest names in the business. Take a look at the list of the ten most valuable U.S. coins in Chapter 24 and see where the prices came from. You got it — auctions!

For some coins, auction records are the only source of pricing information. After each sale, auction houses publish a list of the prices realized for that sale. A good library of recent auction catalogues and their prices realized makes a wonderful resource for tracking coins, determining prices, and finding comparable sales.

Use auction prices realized with caution. As you will soon see, they may not be real.

Avoiding over-enthusiasm

When great collections are sold, the crowd can sometimes get, dare I say, carried away. You may have heard of *auction fever* or even been infected by it. As you're sitting in an auction, especially an exciting one, it's easy to get caught up in the action. It's like playing poker with chips — no actual money changes hands, so you lose all concept of value. All you're doing is raising a bidder paddle in response to the auctioneer's call, right? Nevertheless, you may have written your top bid right beside the catalog description for the lot you're bidding on, just to remind yourself not to get caught up in any bidding wars.

"But this auction is different," you think to yourself. "The market's hot, activity at the auction is greater than expected . . . hey, something's going on here and I'm gonna get a piece of it." You bid beyond your limit as you glare down your competitors, set your jaw, and keep that paddle in the air way too long. The next day, you pick up your lot and get an immediate case of *buyer's remorse,* that sickening realization that you've paid too much.

Over-enthusiasm at auctions leads to inflated prices that may not translate into real life. I've seen so many cases where a bidder paid twice what a coin is worth at auction, even though the same coin was available from any number of dealers at the coin convention 500 feet away. Yet, for some reason, you never see that bidder buying coins outside of an auction (even though he may save himself a lot of money).

Steering clear of manipulation

Auctions are sometimes used to establish a price record, even if the coin never sells. Here's an example: Dealer A buys a coin for $50,000. He places the coin in Auction B. During the auction, Dealer A bids on his own coin and buys it back for $75,000. Dealer A now has a price record to show to a potential customer to justify an asking price of $80,000. To the customer, Dealer A is a grand fellow who is making less than a 10 percent commission on an $80,000 sale. What a great guy!

In recent years, changes in the reporting of prices realized have minimized this problem. Most of the major auction houses will not report a sale if it fails to meet the seller's reserve or if the consignor buys back his own coin. Heritage Numismatic Auctions, Inc., of Dallas, Texas uses an innovative computer system that dings anytime a coin is bought back. The *ding-meter* also serves as an erstwhile market indicator — in a good market, hardly a ding is heard.

If you think you're the victim of a price record ploy, call the auction house that sold the coin and ask whether the dealer offering you the coin was the consignor, and then proceed based on the answer you receive.

Going Online for Price Guides

If you can't afford to subscribe to numismatic publications or price guides, you can still find valuable pricing information on the Internet. Most of this information is free.

However, be aware that some of the companies providing pricing information on the Internet are also trying to sell the information — the Internet version may be scaled-down and contain less information than the printed version. You may have to register to get to some pricing information, which raises privacy concerns. For example, how will your demographic information be used and/or will it be sold? Keep an eye on how often prices are updated — I found one site that claimed to update their prices weekly, but a notice at the bottom of the page was nearly five months old!

To locate online price guides, enter **Coin Prices** in your favorite search engine. (I like www.google.com.) The following two Web sites rise to the top like cream on freshly drawn milk.

Numismedia

Numismedia (www.numismedia.com) offers two tiers of pricing information — Fair Market Value prices and Market Prices (which you find links to on the right side of the page, under Price Guides).

- **Fair market value prices:** Defined at the site as "a reasonable charge over a dealer's wholesale price for a specific coin." In effect, Numismedia attempts to predict the actual price a dealer may charge you for a particular coin, taking the dealer's profit margin into account.

  It appears, at least to me, that the Fair Market Value is somewhere between wholesale and full retail price levels. This is a fair and realistic approach to coin pricing because, after all, you shouldn't expect to be offered coins at a wholesale price if you're not a coin dealer (even though I've pointed out that it happens all the time).

- **Market prices:** Reflect wholesale, dealer-to-dealer pricing. Fair Market Value prices are available on the Numismedia Web site for free, without any registration requirement. You can also subscribe (for a fee) to receive a hard copy of the information each month. To obtain

Numismedia's Market Prices, you must first complete their online registration process (an easy procedure that asks for your contact information). By registering on the Numismedia site, you will also be permitted to bid in the various auctions hosted there.

Numismedia has done a good job of filling in a lot of the holes for generic coin prices, but some of the rarities and obscure coins are still unpriced. Numismedia does not offer pricing information for World Coins.

The Professional Coin Grading Service's Daily Price Guide

The Professional Coin Grading Service's (PCGS) Daily Price Guide (www.pcgs.com) offers free pricing information for all United States coins, in just about every grade. PCGS calls their prices "the average dealer asking prices for properly graded United States coins," which sounds similar to Numismedia's Fair Market Value pricing with the added twist of proper grading. Certainly coins graded by PCGS would fit the bill, as may coins graded by some of the other certification services.

PCGS's pricing is gathered from a number of different sources. Some prices are updated daily, and all prices are updated at least once a month. PCGS does a good job of pricing coins across the board, but they sometimes leave out 'tweener grades like Very Good (VG) and Very Fine (VF) — probably because of space considerations.

To their credit, one thing that they don't do is price coins that simply don't exist. For example, you won't see a price for an Uncirculated 1802 Half Dime or an Extremely Fine 1797 Gripped Edge Half Cent — two coins that exist only in my sweetest dreams! I'll take that Uncirculated 1796 Half Cent, an order of fries, and a shake!

Chapter 6

Verifying . . . and Verifying Again

1 hate writing a chapter like this because I know it scares people away from coin collecting. Sadly, whenever money is involved, some bad apples will try to spoil the whole bunch for the rest of us.

Yes, this is an ugly chapter, but keep in mind that 99.9 percent of the time, coin collecting is a fun, exciting, interesting, and enjoyable hobby. You may never encounter any of the problems that I outline in this chapter, but it's good to be aware of them and know how to handle them. In Chapter 7, I offer tips for finding a good coin dealer. Follow the tips carefully and you may never have to return to this chapter.

Spouting the Cliché

If it sounds too good to be true, it probably is. If someone offered to sell you a $1,000 coin for only $100, would you buy it? What if someone asked $200 for a coin worth only $50 — would you buy it? Would you buy an overgraded coin for twice what it's worth?

Amazingly, people buy overgraded, overpriced, and fake coins every day — usually because they think they're getting the bargain of a lifetime. In just about every case, the bargain turns out to be a very bad deal and the customer ends up losing money. Worse, the customer gets fed up with coin collecting and leaves the hobby altogether.

Separating a fool from his money

Every month, Ken Bressett writes a Consumer Alert column for the American Numismatic Association's *The Numismatist* magazine. Ken does a great job of scanning various publications for coin offerings and alerting consumers to potential scams. You may think that after twelve years of writing the column, and over 600 files, Ken would be running out of scams to write about. Sadly, there's a new "bargain" every week — usually some variation on an old theme designed to separate you from your money.

Ken wrote about some 1943 "copper" Cents being offered at $2.47 each. These coins were actually regular 1943 zinc-coated steel cents that had been copper-plated. An authentic 1943 Cent on a bronze planchet is easily worth tens of thousands of dollars because only a few were made by accident. Recent reports in the news media incorrectly listed their value at

$500,000, a figure that captured the attention of the general public and prompted a rash of calls to coin dealers from people who were absolutely, positively sure that they had the real thing.

What's so bad about selling a 1943 copper Cent for $2.47? After all, how much money can a person lose on a $2.47 purchase? The shock value alone of showing the coin to a fellow collector and hearing them say, "Do you know what this is? Do you know how valuable this is?" is worth every penny of the purchase price. The problem comes down the road. Somewhere, someday, someone is going to try to pass this novelty coin off as the real thing, and I guarantee you that someone is going to pay a lot more than $2.47 for it. Not to mention the fact that coin dealers will be inundated with calls from customers claiming to have the rare 1943 Penny made out of "copper."

Don't think that you won't find bargains in numismatics. Dealers often give nice discounts on older material or overstocked items. Using your knowledge, you may find a rare variety worth several times the asking price. You may find a dealer or collector who is a bit too conservative in their grading. But, in general, you're not going to find $1,000 coins for $100 (especially when it comes to rare, key date coins). If you do, something's wrong.

Scams

Scam artists sell you something, take your money, and then never deliver the goods. You're most likely to encounter this problem when ordering coins through the mail, but I've also heard horror stories of people ordering thousands of dollars in bullion gold from local operators, only to have their money disappear.

Protect yourself before ordering by checking out the seller's reputation within the industry. Ask around — most dealers know who the bad eggs are. Be careful when giving your credit card number out to strangers — your card may be used to make bogus charges. On the other hand, if you do use a credit card to place your order, you may have recourse through your credit card company.

Misrepresentation

Sometimes the coin you receive is different from the one you ordered. At times, the difference may be obvious — at other times, the difference may be so subtle that you don't detect it until it's too late. In such cases, the seller hopes you won't notice, won't complain, or won't care.

If you order a 1900 Silver Dollar and receive a 1945 Half Dollar, the seller's shipping department probably made a simple mistake that can be cleared up with a quick phone call. If you order an Extremely Fine 1921 Half Dollar, and the coin you receive has nice details but big nicks on the rim that weren't mentioned in the description, you've probably been cheated.

Additional scams in this area include coins that have been repaired, artificially colored, altered, faked, or otherwise "improved" upon to make them appear more valuable.

Overgrading

Prior to the advent of the independent grading services, unscrupulous dealers made a nice living off new collectors by deliberately over-grading coins. Instead of making a 10 percent profit on a properly graded coin, they jumped the grade to the next level to take advantage of the higher price. In some cases, price differences between grades are significant, so the temptation to overgrade is strong. Fortunately, grading services eliminate much of this problem by providing an independent grade that is recognized and accepted by virtually every dealer and collector in numismatics. But be careful when buying *raw coins* (coins that haven't yet been independently certified or graded) — there may be a very good reason that the coin is not in a holder!

Undergrading

We would all like to buy a coin for a fraction of its true value. But would you do it by deliberately knocking the grade of someone else's coin to undermine its value? A lot of people would, it seems, because this is a common practice in numismatics.

Riiing . . .

During the past decade, telemarketers have received a bad rap for using high-pressure sales techniques and selling overpriced coins to people who had no clue what they were buying. Because of the many complaints received, the Federal Trade Commission (FTC) entered the fray and placed restrictions on how coins could be marketed over the telephone and established fines and punishments for violations.

Say you bought a coin for $500 in Extremely Fine condition. You've owned the coin for five years and you decide to sell it and use the money to buy other coins. The market value has gone up slightly since you purchased the coin, so you expect to get offers in the $475–$525 range. Dealer A looks at your coin, comments on what a lovely piece it is, and offers $250. "What!" you exclaim, "How can you offer $250 for an Extremely Fine coin worth more than $500?" Dealer A replies calmly, "But your coin is only Very Fine. The catalog price is $200, so I am being more than fair in offering you $50 over catalog." Welcome to the world of undergrading (which, by the way, never happens when Dealer A sells his coins)!

The problem of undergrading is one of the best reasons I can think of to certify your valuable coins. After you've settled the grading question, you can argue over the price, which is a whole other issue. For an explanation of how grading services work and tips for submitting your coins, see Chapter 10.

When you sell a coin, you can ask whatever you want for it. Even though a price guide values your coin at $100, nothing prevents you from asking $200 for it. Of course, you may have a hard time getting that price from a knowledgeable collector; but if you're dealing with someone who doesn't know any better or who trusts what you say, you may find a buyer. You may also have trouble sleeping that night!

When is a profit too much? If a 5 percent markup is fair, what about 10 percent? Is a 25 percent markup unfair? Would a 100 percent profit be unconscionable? Should the profit margin be tied to the cost of a coin, or should it be related to the market price? These are questions every dealer struggles with as they attempt to strike a balance between fairness and profitability. I'm a firm believer that any profit earned in a fair and equitable manner is well-deserved, no matter how large or small. On the other hand, I consider any profit earned by deliberate manipulation of any part of a transaction to be unconscionable, again no matter how large or small.

Cheap offer

Most dealers work on *close spreads* — they pay fair prices when buying, and ask fair prices when selling. However, there are some dealers who want to make a killing on every coin they buy or sell, and they do it any way they can. The dealers who make cheap offers are usually the same ones who under-grade your coins (their methods are the same).

This time, you take your Extremely Fine coin to Dealer B, again expecting to get an offer in the $475–$525 range. Dealer B looks at your coin and agrees that it is a lovely Extremely Fine, and offers $250. "What!" you exclaim, "How can you offer $250 for a properly graded coin worth more than $500?" Dealer B replies calmly, "But I have a lot of expenses running this operation, I don't need the coin for inventory right now, I don't have any customers for it, and I'm trying to conserve cash." Welcome to the world of cheap offers. Dealer B is hoping that you're desperate to sell, that you're stupid, or that you don't have anywhere else to sell the coin.

To combat the problem of cheap offers, get bids from at least three different dealers. If you're still not satisfied, try selling the coin yourself or offering it in an online auction (see Chapter 21). The extra effort on your part may pay off handsomely.

Caveating Your Emptor

Caveat emptor is Latin for "let the buyer beware." This concept means that the buyer alone is responsible for determining the quality of a coin before he buys it. Under this concept, the seller has no responsibility whatsoever to inform the buyer of any defects or flaws. If the buyer finds any defects or flaws after the transaction is completed, the buyer has no recourse against the seller. Sounds pretty one-sided, doesn't it?

CA from the FTC and ANA

In 1996, the FTC and the American Numismatic Association (ANA) teamed up to produce a Consumer Alert titled "Investing In Rare Coins." To obtain a copy, write to the FTC at 6th and Pennsylvania NW, Washington DC 20580, or visit the ANA's Web site at `www.money.org/ftcbro.html`.

Recent consumer protection legislation lessens the impact of *caveat emptor.* In many cases, the buyer does have some recourse against the seller. However, as a general rule, you should treat all of your coin purchases as if *caveat emptor* applies. Expect the worst, investigate each transaction as thoroughly as possible, and hand over your money only when you're completely satisfied that all is well.

Saving the Day: Return Privileges

Most coin dealers want their customers to be happy. Dealers realize that happy customers return to purchase more coins. Happy customers are more likely to tell their friends about the positive experience they've had with a particular dealer.

Businesses spend large amounts of money to attract new customers. The cost of retaining customers is much lower, but only if the customer is treated right. With this in mind, the typical coin dealer will usually offer a return privilege of some length. During this time, you may inspect the coins you purchased, choose to have the coins evaluated by an expert or certification service of your choice, and, if you're not happy with them, return the coins for a refund.

Return privileges are your chance to decide whether you really like the coins you purchased. My advice: If you don't like a coin, return it immediately. I guarantee that if you don't like a coin today, you'll hate it even more tomorrow. To this day, I own several coins that I simply can't stand. Every time I see them, I ask myself, "Why the heck did I ever buy this piece of (expletive deleted)." Instead, I should be asking myself, "Why didn't I return this coin when I had the chance?"

Return privileges appear in a variety of forms and lengths, ranging from no return privilege (the worst) to an extended, flexible period that is fair to both you and the dealer (the best). Most return privileges fall somewhere in between.

Before buying a coin, find out what kind of return privilege your dealer offers. Instead of a cash refund, you may be offered a credit against future purchases. Think twice before accepting a credit — you may never be happy with anything you receive from the seller. Never assume that you have a return privilege — ask.

No return privilege

If no return privilege is mentioned, there probably isn't one. No return privilege means that you are buying the coin *as is,* and you must accept it no matter how bad or how nice it is.

Never buy any coin as is unless you've inspected it personally and are completely satisfied that it is authentic and described properly. You have no recourse if you discover later that the coin is fake, repaired, or something other than you expected. Be sure to read the Terms and Conditions of Sale before bidding in auctions, especially as a floor bidder. (Swing on over to Chapter 8 for more auction advice.)

Ten-day return privilege

This is one of the most common return privileges in the coin industry. Ten days allows just enough time to examine the coin for yourself, but not quite enough time to show it to many experts, and certainly not enough time to submit the coin to any of the grading services. Make your own decision, and make it quickly.

Thirty-day return privilege

You won't find many return privileges longer than 30 days — only strong, confident companies offer such generous terms. Thirty days gives you ample time to make a decision for yourself. If you're willing to pay for expedited fees, you should have ample time to submit the coin to a certification service for their opinion.

Be sure to find out when the time period for the return privilege begins and ends. Does the 10 day period begin with the postmark date, the date the coin was shipped to you, the date you received it, or some other date? When must you return the coin? Is a postmark date sufficient for meeting the return date? What happens if you don't return the coin on time?

Negotiated return privilege

After you establish yourself as a legitimate customer, sellers are more likely to allow for negotiated return privileges. For example, you can arrange for the seller to submit your purchase directly to a grading service and then notify you when the coin comes back. If the grade comes back as expected, you take delivery of the coin; if not, the seller keeps it. The seller may grant an extended return privilege if you need extra time for authentication or grading. For example, some grading services utilize outside experts for specialized coins such as U.S. colonials or Native American peace medals. Processing times for such items are usually longer because of the extra time needed to get the coins to the experts and back.

The key to return privileges is fairness. The idea is to establish trust and a good working relationship between the buyer and the seller. State your requirements and negotiate your terms up front.

Before you become too entangled with a seller, try a test return and see how you are treated. If you encounter any problems, be wary and consider dealing with someone else. Some dealers hate returns, and they perceive anyone who returns coins as an undesirable customer — if you return a single coin, they'll never do business with you again. Other dealers take a more reasoned approach, understanding that legitimate differences of opinion exist among buyers and sellers. However, if you return eight out of ten coins from every order, something's wrong. Are you being too picky or are the coins really that bad? In either case, move on and try your luck with another seller.

Covering Your Behind with Guarantees

Many businesses use guarantees as a means of instilling confidence in potential customers. Guarantees are also used to induce customers to spend their hard-earned money. All else being equal, you're more likely to buy from someone who offers a guarantee than from someone who doesn't, aren't you? I know I am.

You should be aware that there are different kinds of guarantees and that a guarantee, like a return privilege, is only as good as the person offering it.

Lifetime guarantee

Lifetime guarantees usually apply only to *authenticity* (whether a coin is real). In theory, the *lifetime* in a lifetime guarantee refers to the life of the seller. In reality, lifetime refers to the life of the company. If a corporation shuts down operations, they are no longer required to honor any of their guarantees. Don't wait until ten years from now, after the seller may have already gone out of business, to find out that your coin is fake. Check it out today and enjoy peace of mind for the rest of your life.

Unconditional guarantee

An *unconditional guarantee* means that you can return the coin for any reason, no questions asked, within the time allowed for the return privilege. Unconditional guarantees are the best possible types of guarantees you can ever hope to get. They are offered only by sellers who are truly interested in satisfying their customers.

Guarantee of authenticity

Be sure that the seller is willing to stand behind the authenticity of any coin he or she sells. Steer clear of any seller who lacks the expertise, the willingness, or the financial ability to ensure the authenticity of their coins. A simple test return will reveal much about the dealer you've chosen.

Guarantee of grade

A *guarantee of grade* is great when you can get it. It assures you that the raw coin you purchase will meet a minimum grade if sent to a certification service. However, certification services are not all equal — nor are their grades equally valued by the market — so it's important to find out which service will be used. If your dealer guarantees the grade of a coin, ask him or her to submit the coin before you pay for it. Be prepared to pay for the grading fees — they are generally your responsibility, especially if the coin comes back under-graded or not graded. Look at such an expense as insurance. It's a lot cheaper to pay a grading fee than to find out much later that your coin is overgraded and worth substantially less than you paid for it.

Buy-back guarantee

Some firms offer to buy back the coins they sell. These firms will buy the coins back at a percentage of the future market or at a fixed price, usually above what you paid for the coin. This is a powerful enticement to some people because it seems as if there is no way for them to lose money.

Unfortunately, no firm, no matter how financially strong, can support such a guarantee. Even worse, when prices are dropping in a bad market, your seller may disappear along with your guarantee.

Most grading, authenticity, and pricing issues can be resolved if you stick with certified coins. The small premium you pay for certification may be some of the best money you ever spend, and you won't need no stinkin' guarantee.

Sorting Out Online Security

The Internet and e-mail have made it easier and more convenient for us to communicate with each other. Unfortunately, the Internet is perhaps the least secure way of communicating because your messages and transactions are subject to the prying eyes of hackers, crackers, and pirates who try to capture your information and use it for their personal gain.

For information on using the Internet, pick up a copy of *Internet For Dummies,* by John R. Levine, Carol Baroudi, Jordan M. Young, and Margaret Levine Young (Hungry Minds, Inc.). You can get the book in either Windows 98 or Windows Me version.

Sending e-mail

A large number of buyers and sellers communicate today via electronic mail. Many of the millions of messages that are sent every day contain sensitive or proprietary information. Before you click that Send button, be aware that sending a message via e-mail is like mailing a letter without an envelope — anyone can capture your letter and read what you've written.

When sending e-mail, be careful about what you say and what kind of information you give out. Beware of sending the following information via e-mail. Instead, call the appropriate person and pass it along over the phone.

- Social Security number
- Credit card number
- Home address and phone number

Using credit cards on the Internet

Years ago, you took a big risk when using your credit card over the Internet. The way data was transmitted from one place to another made your credit card information easy prey to hackers and online pirates. When businesses saw the growth potential of Internet commerce and the need for greater security, safeguards were put in place to offer better protection for online consumers.

Today, secure technology reduces the risk of data theft to nearly nothing; the chances of anyone stealing your credit card information are extremely remote. Sure, you may have read about hackers breaking into sites and stealing millions of customers' files, but I've never met anyone who has been a victim of a credit card crime. I've used my credit cards over the Internet for years with no problem. Nevertheless, don't hand over your credit card information to strangers or anyone you haven't checked out. Follow your gut instinct — if it doesn't feel right, forget it.

You can usually tell when it's safe to use a credit card online. Your browser will tell you that you're on a secure site. Sometimes there's a padlock-type icon on the bottom of the screen. It will show itself as locked (or closed) for secure pages. You can also look at the URL address to determine whether a site is secure. Secure pages will have an "s" after the http. The "s" stands for "secure."

Slamming the Scammers

If you feel you've been scammed, cheated, or otherwise defrauded, do something about it! Scammers hope you'll be too embarrassed or too busy to do anything, or that the cost of bringing a legal case against them will be so expensive and time-consuming that you won't pursue it. Fight for your rights and money! Sometimes all it takes is a little pressure to help resolve your case. By going after scammers, you protect yourself and anyone else who may be a potential victim in the future.

You may be mad as heck, but don't make exaggerated or outrageous claims. And be careful what you say about the seller. Don't make things worse by inviting a lawsuit for slander, libel, or defamation of character. Stick to the facts.

- ✔ **Try to resolve the problem with the seller.** Give the seller a chance to resolve the problem by communicating your wishes clearly and reasonably. Let the seller know that you are prepared to take additional steps if you do not receive satisfaction. You may be offered a discounted settlement that you must weigh against the costs of proceeding further.

- ✔ **Talk with an attorney.** Find out what your rights are under the law by contacting an attorney. A letter from your attorney lets the scammer know that you're serious and may result in a quick settlement.

- ✔ **Document your case.** Keep a diary of your case, including documentation of the original transaction, any correspondence, phone calls, and so on. Be as detailed as possible. Include dates, times, places, and anything that can bolster your case.

- ✔ **Contact the Better Business Bureau.** File a complaint with the Better Business Bureau, even if the seller is not a member. You can find the BBB's contact information in your local Yellow Pages.

- ✔ **Contact the postal authorities.** Mail fraud is a serious crime. If your case involves a transaction through the mail, file a complaint with the Postal Authorities.

- ✔ **Contact your credit card company.** If you used a credit card to make the purchase, file a complaint with the credit card company. You may be able get your money back through the credit card company.

✔ **Contact professional organizations.** File complaints with any numismatic or professional organizations of which the seller is a member. Some organizations have standard procedures for dealing with complaints, including hearings before ethics committees, arbitration proceedings, and expulsion of offenders.

✔ **Contact the Federal Trade Commission.** File a complaint with the Federal Trade Commission, which is already well aware of consumer fraud in numismatics. You can find their contact information in the Consumer Alert bulletin I mentioned earlier in this chapter, or you can visit their Web site at www.ftc.gov.

✔ **Notify law enforcement authorities.** Contact the Attorney General and local law enforcement authorities in the seller's state to see whether any laws have been violated. If laws have been violated, press charges. To find the appropriate phone numbers, check the listings in your telephone phone book; you can find sections in the front of the book devoted to important city, state, and federal government offices.

Communicate regularly with all parties involved in your case, including the scammer, to let them know that you're serious about getting results. Remember, the squeaky wheel gets the grease.

Chapter 7

Wheeling and Dealers

A coin dealer can be your best friend or your worst enemy. A good coin dealer can be a source of valuable information, wonderful guidance, and great coins. A bad dealer lies, cheats, and does anything else to get your money. Your goal is to find a coin dealer that you can trust and who will deal with you fairly. In this chapter, I offer advice on evaluating dealers and tips on moving up the numismatic ladder to maximize your collecting opportunities and pleasure.

Finding a Good Coin Dealer

Question: What does it take to become a coin dealer?

Answer: One coin and one customer.

Unlike most professions, the field of numismatics has no education requirements, no competency testing, no continuing education, no bonding, and no background check (except in rare instances). Therefore, just about anyone can obtain a business license, rent some retail space, and hold themselves out as a coin dealer. Governmental regulation of the coin business is virtually nonexistent, and self-regulation by the industry doesn't seem to be much better. Because money is the very essence of numismatics, the coin industry attracts people with a wide range of ethical values — to put it politely. To put it more bluntly, people lose money every year because of the unethical practices of some people in the coin business. As a result, you have Chapters 2 and 6 in this book.

Lest I appear to paint with too wide a brush, let me state at the outset that most coin dealers are legitimate businessmen and businesswomen who are ready and willing to serve your needs. They follow the rules and try to treat everyone fairly and with respect. But how do you, as a potential customer and a newcomer to the hobby, separate the good from the bad? How can you protect yourself from the unscrupulous dealer?

In Chapter 2 I cite Aaron Feldman's favorite saying, "Buy the book before you buy the coin." In this chapter, I create a new saying (and you can quote me), "Check out the coin dealer before you buy the coin."

With that in mind, don't be afraid to investigate dealers. Be sure to ask the following questions and stay away from anyone who does not give you satisfactory answers. Remember, it's your money on the line.

✔ **How long have you been in business?** Experience is a wonderful teacher. Seasoned coin dealers are familiar with market swings, market fads, and market trends. Staying in business for a long time requires perseverance, a good work ethic, desire, and a willingness to treat customers fairly and honestly. Con artists, on the other hand, have a hit-and-run mentality — they work an area until it is no longer profitable or until they are forced out of town, and then they head for greener pastures.

✔ **What are your professional affiliations?** Find out whether your prospective coin dealer is a member of any numismatic organizations and, more specifically, whether he or she subscribes to any code of ethics. A code of ethics may give you some recourse down the road, but remember that they are guidelines, not guarantees. Ask dealers about their affiliations with the following organizations: your local coin club(s), regional or state organizations, the American Numismatic Association, and the Professional Numismatists Guild. Ask about membership in service organizations, such as Kiwanis or Rotary International. Remember, mere membership in an organization may not be sufficient, particularly when the organization's code of ethics has no teeth. A code of ethics is only as good as the organization's willingness to enforce it.

✔ **Are you a member of the local Better Business Bureau?** Although membership in the Better Business Bureau is no guarantee of legitimacy, you can find out a lot about a business by inquiring whether there are any complaints against them. You may find that the reason your potential coin dealer is not a member is because they were kicked out!

Call the Better Business Bureau when you're out hunting for a dealer. Sometimes the Bureau receives complaints about people or businesses that aren't even members — those are the kinds of complaints you want to know about before you spend your first nickel with someone.

✔ **How large is your inventory?** The larger the inventory, the more likely you are to find items for your collection. A recent poster on the rec.collecting.coins newsgroup observed that one of the reasons many coin collectors buy their coins online (over the computer) is because of the poor inventory selection at their local coin dealer. Well-stocked dealers offer not only a wide variety of material, but depth as well. For example, some dealers won't have even a single example of the rare 1916-D Dime. But others may have several pieces in different grades, giving you a wider variety of choices.

✔ **Do you attend coin shows outside of your area?** If coin dealers can cut it on the show circuit, they can cut it anywhere. Competition on the show circuit is fierce, requiring finely honed grading skills, self-confidence, and a good horse-trading sense. Plus, coin shows are a great place for getting rid of old, dead inventory and acquiring new material to bring back home to customers like you.

✔ **Do you provide a want-list service?** Good coin dealers know what their customers want and will call them immediately if a coin becomes available. Better coin dealers make an effort to locate coins for their customers. The best coin dealers perform this service on a no-obligation basis, giving you an opportunity to buy or pass on a coin at your option.

✔ **Are you a member of any electronic exchanges?** When dealers have access to external markets and up-to-date pricing information, they are able to pay more for your coins and sell their own coins for less. Here's how having access to better markets works: Say a customer brings a coin into a coin shop. The dealer looks up the value in a price guide and finds that the coin is listed at $100. The dealer may not have a customer for your coin, but he may be willing to inventory it for $50, taking a chance that the coin will eventually sell to someone else. Is that good for the customer? Maybe not. What if the coin dealer is a member of a trading network, where someone is offering $90 for the same coin? Knowing that he or she can turn a quick profit, your dealer may offer even more money for your coin — say $80. You're thirty dollars richer, all because of the trading network. The same principle works on the other side, too. If your dealer can locate a coin for you and turn a quick profit, he or she is more likely to sell it to you for less than if the coin had been in inventory for months.

✔ **Are you a submission center for any of the certification services?** Some certification services require you to submit your coins through a *submission center* (dealers approved by the certification service). Submission centers provide a valuable service by screening your coins before sending them in to be certified. Prescreening helps eliminate any coins that have been cleaned, repaired, or recolored; it also helps eliminate any coins that are out-and-out fakes. (See Chapter 4 for more information about fakes.)

Generally, submission centers provide the prescreening service for free. Of course, you must still pay for the grading fees and postage, but all the required forms and supplies are provided for proper submission. As an added bonus, dealers who are submission centers may make a nice offer for your coins after they come back from the certification services, or they may make recommendations about resubmitting coins for a higher grade. Sometimes this information can be very, very valuable.

Localizing Your Efforts

You'll find a coin dealer in just about any city in the United States and in most of the big cities around the world. The larger the city, the more coin dealers you are likely to find. Big cities host some of the biggest names in numismatics, along with many dealers of lesser fame. But rest assured that they are all eager to do business with you.

✔ **Check out the telephone listings for coin dealers in your area.** Contact the dealers and check out their operations, inventory, and willingness to deal with you. Then decide which dealer(s) you'll visit again in the future.

- A quick phone call can give you a good first impression.

- Pay a personal visit to each of the dealers in your area.

- By meeting dealers face-to-face and seeing their operation, you can tell whether they handle the types of coins in which you are interested and whether your personalities are compatible. You may be surprised at the wide variety of presentations you encounter — ranging from dark, dingy shops to well-lit, beautifully maintained mall operations, and from expensive offices to scary joints in a seedy part of town. The proprietors you meet will be just as different, ranging from gruff, no-nonsense types to humorous, genial types.

- Attend the next coin show in your area. This is a good idea if you don't have time to visit each dealer individually. At the show, be sure to meet with and introduce yourself to the dealers in your area. Look over their inventory and discuss your particular situation with them. You can cover a lot of ground at a coin show. You can find out a lot about which dealers are active in your area. Plus, coin shows give you a good basis for comparing prices from one dealer to the next (an option not available in a single shop).

- If potential dealers are active on any of the online auction services, like eBay or Yahoo!, check out their feedback ratings. Steer clear of anyone with more than a few negative feedbacks. The way dealers handle their online transactions gives you a good idea of how they'll handle face-to-face transactions.

> ✔ **Join your local coin club and ask members about their experiences with local dealers.** This is a great source of feedback. You may find out some interesting information about who pays the most, who has the best deals, who deals fairly and honestly, and, most importantly, who doesn't deal fairly and honestly. Pay careful attention to this information — weigh it all together and keep it in the back of your mind as you meet with the individual dealers.

Going to the Nationals

Most of the time, your local coin dealer can take care of your collecting needs. But at some point you may need to go to the next level, which means going national. Think of the coin market as a feeder system — each level of the coin market is stronger financially, more knowledgeable, and has a broader customer base.

To show how this works, consider an 1808 Half Cent. The coin first shows up at a local flea market, where a dealer buys it for $20 as a common date. The flea market dealer takes it to the local expert who determines that the coin is the scarce 1808/7 overdate and buys it for $50. The local expert takes it to a regional coin show where a Half Cent specialist examines the coin, determines that it is the rarest overdate variety, and buys it for $5,000. The specialist takes the coin to a national firm, which places the coin in its next auction and highlights it as an extreme rarity and one of only ten known. A customer then buys the coin at auction for $15,000. At each step along the way, the coin becomes more valuable until it reaches the ultimate collector.

What's interesting about this story is the fact that you could have been the buyer at any step along the way. You could have purchased the coin from the flea market dealer, the local expert, the Half Cent specialist, or the rare coin auction company. Obviously, the earlier you jump in, the cheaper you will be able to buy the coin — the main advantage to going national. By attending national coin shows and dealing with national dealers, you are more likely to run into buying and selling opportunities that simply don't exist at the local level. At a national coin show, you can meet the flea market dealers, the local experts, the specialists, and the national dealers.

Your success in buying at national coin shows depends, in large part, on getting there early. In theory, everyone has an equal opportunity to compete for bargains at the opening bell. As the coins work their way up the feeder system, the coins you seek become more and more expensive. Therefore, get to the show as early as possible. Even better, find some way to get into the pre-show setup, when dealers conduct business before the show opens to the general public. (Ask a dealer friend to add you to their table as an assistant or buy your way into the show with an early bird badge.) Time is of the essence at coin shows.

One-way traffic

Several years ago, the German Deutschmark rose in value to over 70¢, and the German coin market was very active. Because of their economic advantage, German coin dealers made frequent visits to the United States to buy German coins and bring them back to Germany — effectively repatriating their own coins. Some German coin dealers offered long lists of buy prices, resulting in a constant stream of coins that headed from the United States, across the Atlantic Ocean, back to Germany. When the German market was strong, American collectors of German coins were at a distinct disadvantage. All the best German coins were being sucked out of the United States, and it was difficult to purchase German coins out of Europe because the prices were so high.

Now, in the year 2001, all that has changed. The coin market in Germany has finally cooled down, the Deutschmark has dropped in value to below 50¢, and the flow of traffic has reversed. Far fewer German dealers make the trip to U.S. coin shows. Instead, you see a lot more American dealers at German coin shows taking advantage of the low prices.

In a perfect world, traffic across the Atlantic would be equal in both directions. But because of various factors (such as the strength of currencies relative to each other, taxes, import and export restrictions, travel and shipping costs, and so on), one direction will always be stronger than the other.

Relationships with dealers are just as critical as timing. In the previous paragraph, I mention that everyone has an equal chance to compete for bargains at the opening bell. In reality, the opposite is true. When I enter a coin show for the first time, I know from experience exactly who to visit right away and who to visit later. I know who has given me good deals in the past and who is likely to have the coins I seek. I know who I haven't been able to buy from in the past and I either avoid them completely or save them for last. Before the show even opens, I try to work out arrangements with certain dealers to make sure that I have first shot at their inventories. For their part, these dealers are happy to do so because they know I'm always a strong buyer.

You, too, can develop similar insights and relationships for yourself. The first time you attend a national show, no one will know you or what you collect. As you introduce yourself and develop relationships of your own, dealers will be more likely to pull you aside and say, "Hey, I know you like Half Cents and I just ran across a nice 1808 that you can have for $50. . . ."

Going Global

You may find it necessary to go global and meet dealers throughout the world — especially if you collect world coins. What better place to buy German coins than in Germany itself? Or what better place to buy English coins than in London? Most developed countries have strong, organized internal markets. With a little research, you can find out whether it is to your advantage to buy from, or sell into, various countries. For example, you may find that you can buy world coins in your own country, sell them back to dealers in their country of origin, and then use the profits to buy coins for your own collection. You may also find dealers in other countries to be excellent sources of coins from your home country — it's amazing how coins travel around the world even more than we do!

A little-known secret is that many of the best U.S. coins have been found in Europe; they range from hundreds of thousands of gold coins in Swiss banks, to individual, classic rarities, to ordinary, run-of-the-mill coins that show up in the oddest places. By developing as many contacts as possible throughout the world, you are more likely to be offered first crack at some of these discoveries.

Looking at the pros

Consider the following reasons to go global:

- ✔ **Ready sources of the coins you seek:** When I first started dealing in German coins, American dealers were my only source. I found plenty of German coins in the United States, but certain ones showed up quite infrequently — I always got excited when one came my way. Then I made a trip to a coin show in Germany. Were my eyes opened! The coins that seemed so rare in the United States were in every dealer's case in Germany. The coins weren't necessarily cheaper in Germany, but at least I was finally able to fill some want lists that I've had for quite some time. I learned an important lesson on that first trip — go to the source for the coins you seek. If you want French coins, go to France! If you want Spanish coins, go to Spain!

- ✔ **Developing contacts with knowledgeable dealers:** I claim to know a lot about German coins, but I can't hold a candle to some of the German dealers. For information on rare varieties, errors, and pattern coins, I know to contact Guy Franquinet. For information on Bavarian coins, I don't know anyone more knowledgeable than Ernst Neumann. You can develop relationships of your own to gain the information you need and the coins you want. After you develop these contacts and relationships, you no longer need to make the actual trip — you can simply use the telephone, fax, or e-mail to stay in touch. Unless, that is, you need an excuse to get away!

Weighing the cons

Keep in mind the following reasons not to travel overseas to buy coins:

- **Overcoming language barriers:** You may find language barriers to be a real deterrent in conducting business with overseas dealers. However, larger firms usually have at least one person on staff who can speak and/or understand English — or understand your attempts at speaking their language. In addition, some translation programs in the computer world can make it easy for you to translate text files back and forth, from one language to another. Don't let your inability to speak a foreign language keep you from expanding your horizons. On the other hand, don't be an "ugly American" — make an effort to learn the language.

- **The costs of converting your currency:** When you deal overseas, you must factor in not only the transaction costs that I discuss in Chapter 2, but also the costs associated with converting your currency. When you enter a foreign country, one of the first things you usually do is change your money into the local currency. You always have to pay a fee to do so. The fee varies depending on where you make the conversion. A good rule: The closer you are to your point of arrival or destination, the higher the fees for conversion. For example, if you convert your money at the airport, you will pay a higher fee than if you convert your money in a bank near your hotel.

  Whenever possible, use a credit card to pay for overseas purchases. The currency conversion is done automatically, and the conversion fee is often as good, if not better than any rate you can find yourself.

- **The difficulties and risks of overseas mails:** Sending or receiving coins overseas is often a risky proposition. Theft is a big problem with overseas shipments. You run the risk of loss even when you ship to "safe" countries using insured or registered mail. You may find that the U.S. Postal Service does a great job in delivering packages to foreign countries, but at some point, they must give the packages to a foreign postal service over which they have no control. My experience in sending packages to Germany is that I lose about one out of every twenty shipments. Germany is supposed to be a "safe" country, and I can only guess at how many packages I'd be losing if I were sending them to an "unsafe" country. Insurance and registration covers some of the loss, but check to see if these options are even available. The U.S. Postal Service Web site at www.usps.com provides information (including rates) on the various options for shipping overseas.

- **Clearing coins through customs:** I keep hearing horror stories about what happens if you don't use a customs broker to handle your commercial shipments into and out of the United States. But in all my years of shipping overseas, I've never used one, nor have I had the need for one. When you ship coins through the U.S. Postal Service, you must declare the contents of your package and/or fill out a customs form. Generally, when your package arrives at its destination, the foreign customs will either forward the package or ask your customer to come in and pick up the coins in person. When your customer receives the package, he or she will have to pay any required customs fees. You should not have to pay any customs fees for coins shipped from overseas countries to your address in the United States.

Physically carrying coins into or out of another country is a whole other story. If you declare the coins, be prepared for a bureaucratic nightmare. If you don't declare the coins, be prepared for confiscation of the coins, hefty fines, and/or prison time. Having tried it both ways, I would never recommend carrying coins yourself. Pay the extra money and have the coins shipped. Believe me, you'll be glad you did!

Surfing for a Dealer

Millions of collectors have discovered the Internet, and thousands of dealers understand the advantages of having an online presence. Many dealers report that they now conduct the majority of their business over the Internet. Each day, more and more collectors find the coins they want by searching through online auctions or dealer inventories. Collectors are no longer limited by geography and time. You can order coins from Australia at 3:00 in the morning, pay with a credit card, and have them at your doorstep within a week, all without having spoken to a single person.

The Internet offers plenty of advantages:

✔ New technologies make ordering online easier and more secure.

✔ Shopping cart technologies allow you to complete a virtual order form, check out, and pay for your order with a credit card, all from the convenience of your home.

Making a mint

The level of interest in coins on the Internet is huge. The U.S. Mint began online sales in April 1999 and recorded its first $1 million month in May 1999; its first $1 million week during July; and its first $1 million day on October 18, 1999. Total online sales amounted to $26.5 million for the period of October 1 through December 31, 1999. The Mint projected online sales of more than $125 million for the year 2000, placing it among the nation's top e-tailers. The U.S. Mint has also reported a single hour sale of $2.7 million and a sale of 12.8 million coins in two hours!

✔ The coin in which you are interested will often be illustrated with enlarged, full-color photos. Some numismatic sites offer new zoom technologies that give you close-up views of coins so you can see every bit of detail and surface quality.

✔ Search tools allow you to pick through millions of Web sites to hunt down just the right coin for your collection. Online auctions offer thousands of coins every day, many of which are simply unavailable from your local coin dealers.

✔ You can access a staggering number of coin dealers, not only in the United States, but throughout the world. More importantly, you'll meet people that you would not otherwise meet in a million years. I refer to the hundreds of thousands of collectors and part-time dealers who do not have a store presence in real life, who have never been to a coin show, and who are making a part-time living buying and selling coins on the Internet.

The Internet gives the collector access to more coin dealers and more coins than ever before in history. Unfortunately, the downside is that you may not know the dealer on the other end of your Internet connection or whether the coins are properly graded — giving you even more reasons to follow the advice in this chapter. And if you need help with the World Wide Web itself, check out *The Internet For Dummies,* by John R. Levine, Carol Baroudi, and Margaret Levine Young (Hungry Minds, Inc.).

Chapter 8

Going Once, Going Twice: Buying at Auction

Auctions offer an interesting and exciting way to buy and sell coins. You get to pay what you want and you have just as good a chance of buying a particular coin as the next person — assuming you have enough money. Auctions generally contain better coins than you're used to seeing in your local coin shops; plus you can bid in auctions from the comfort of your own home by submitting your bids by mail or over the Internet. If you really want to experience some excitement, plan to attend any of the major coin auctions scheduled for the upcoming year — it's an experience you will remember for a long, long time.

In this chapter, I explain how coin auctions work and I give you complete instructions on how to participate. Along with the benefits of buying at auction, I also provide sage advice about some of the pitfalls to watch out for.

Most price records for coins have been set at auction, so get ready to go where the action is.

Flying Like Bees to Honey

If you want the best quality coins and the rarest numismatic items, you're more likely to find them in a coin auction than anywhere else. Sure, you can find nice coins at numismatic conventions and at your favorite dealer, but the crème de la crème seem to gravitate toward auctions. Why is that?

You can't buy publicity like this

In many cases, the publicity gained from buying a particular coin is more valuable than the coin itself. Here's an example:

In May 2000, a fellow named Frank Wallis discovered a very unusual coin that mistakenly combined the front of a Sacagawea One Dollar with the front of a Washington 50 States Quarter Dollar. This was the first documented appearance of a U.S. coin with two different denominations. The discovery created quite a stir in numismatic circles. The national press picked up the story and millions of Americans began searching through their change in hopes of finding a similar treasure. The discovery coin was consigned to a major rare coin auction house with the sale scheduled for August 9, 2000. The auction house featured the coin in all of its publicity for the sale. In the meantime, two additional examples of the coin were found. One sold right away on eBay for $41,935, while the other was sold preemptively in an auction on August 6, 2000 for $31,050. When Wallis' discovery coin finally came up for sale on August 9, members of the media were there to witness the event and record the sale. The coin sold for $29,900, which was less than either of the two that had been discovered later but sold earlier. However, because of all the hype attending the sale, the high bidder became the beneficiary of millions of dollars worth of national publicity — the kind of publicity that money can't buy!

Seeking a rare flower

Getting the best price for a coin means finding the best buyer. Actually, coin sellers should find the two best buyers and get them to bid against each other. Auctions attract the biggest and best buyers because the sales usually contain a concentration of coins that may not be found anywhere else. For example, if a sale contains a complete collection of Large Cents by *die variety* (minute differences in the coins), you can bet that every major collector will either be at the auction or be represented because there is simply nowhere else to find those rare varieties. When you have several well-heeled collectors frothing at the mouth to buy the same coin because they haven't had a chance to buy it for decades, you can bet the action will be fast and furious, and the final price will be high.

Rare coin auctions draw crowds because they give buyers the chance to engage in a little conspicuous consumerism, to be seen paying top prices for coins, and perhaps to get a little publicity in the meantime. Watch what happens anytime a really rare coin is sold at auction. As soon as the bidding starts, the members of the audience crane their necks and scan the room to see who the bidders are. When the auctioneer finally hammers down the lot, the audience applauds and the auction stops for a moment to allow the winning bidder to bask in the limelight and perhaps grant an interview or two to the press.

Getting stung

Another reason auctions attract the best coins is a thing called auction fever. *Auction fever* occurs when bidders lose control and bid well beyond their normal limits. Several things contribute to auction fever:

- ✔ The coin market is particularly strong. Prices are advancing and buyers have difficulty obtaining the coins they want.

- ✔ The auction is held at a fast pace. Bidders must make decisions quickly, often with very little time to think about what they're doing or how much they are spending. It's very easy to make a bad decision if you haven't prepared properly for the sale.

- ✔ A buyer is frustrated at not being able to buy any coins in an auction. This results in a twisted determination to buy anything just to get something.

- ✔ A buyer wants a *pedigreed* coin. Sometimes people overpay for otherwise common coins just to buy something from a famous collection.

Whatever the motivation, auction fever almost always results in *buyer's remorse,* a sickening knowledge that you've overpaid for a coin.

Auction companies love auction fever because that's how records are set. An auction company exists to get the highest price for the coins it sells, so they encourage auction fever all along the way. Presale publicity is meant to excite the collecting community, the sale catalog is designed to entice buyers with its wish-book styling, the auction venue itself is designed to create an air of anticipation, and, because they are using bidder numbers instead of actual cash, buyers tend to forget that they are spending real money.

The best defense strategies against auction fever are good preparation and sticking to your limits.

Preparing to Buy

The auction itself signals the end of a long process of preparation that begins the moment you receive your catalog. Holding your bidder card up in the air at the auction is the easy part — in fact, many bidders allow their spouses and/or children to do the bidding for them. The hard part is deciding on what to bid and how much to pay. Here are some tips you can use to prepare for the big day at the auction.

Obtaining the catalog

When you see your first rare coin auction catalog, you understand why the auction companies don't give them away. Auction catalogs have come a long way from the days of small, thin booklets with minimal descriptions. Today, they are thick, glossy publications chock full of images (many in color) and lengthy, well-researched descriptions. In fact, the best catalogs are saved by collectors and used as excellent sources of information for future research.

Because of all the work and expense that goes into the catalogs, expect to pay to obtain a copy. Most firms offer a yearly subscription to their publications, which gets you all the auction catalogs they produce, plus any additional promotional literature or newsletters. See the Cheat Sheet at the front of this book for a list of major rare coin auction houses.

In most cases, auction houses use subscription fees to cover the costs of producing the catalogs and also to keep out the riff-raff. Before calling a company to order a catalog subscription, save yourself some money by checking to see whether the firm offers an Internet version. Then, if you like what you see, or if you still need a hard copy, ask for a sample copy instead of ordering a full subscription. Here's a secret — some auction companies offer free subscriptions to buyers who can prove that they purchased a certain amount of rare coins in the past. For example, you may get a free subscription if you can provide invoices showing that you've purchased over $1,000 worth of coins over the past year. Don't be afraid to ask — auction companies love serious buyers.

Reading the Terms of Sale

To avoid any unpleasant surprises, read the Terms and Conditions of Sale in the auction catalog before you even think about bidding. Be sure that you understand how the sale will be conducted *before* you place any bids. You may call it the fine print or legalese, but the Terms and Conditions of Sale explains your rights and obligations as a bidder.

When you place a bid in an auction, you actually enter into a legally binding contract with the auction house. In cases of dispute, courts look to the Terms and Conditions of Sale to determine what rules to apply when resolving the case.

Although most auction houses conduct their business in similar fashion, all of them have their own Terms and Conditions of Sale which can be dramatically different from one company to the next. Even if you deal with only one company, their terms may change from one sale to the next. For example, buyer's fees have jumped from 10 to 15 percent in recent years. Although most companies have been very good about announcing this significant change, they are not required to do so; the announcement may be a single line buried in the Terms and Conditions of Sale. It's up to you to notice any changes in the fine print!

As you read through the Terms and Conditions of Sale, pay particular attention to the following terms:

- ✓ **Buyer's fee:** Most auction houses charge a *buyer's fee* — an additional charge added to the final selling price. For example, if the buyer's fee is 10 percent and a coin sells for $100, you pay $110 ($100 plus 10 percent of $100). For many years, the buyer's fee in most coin auctions stayed at 10 percent. But in recent years, the fee has crept up to 15 percent. Because the buyer's fee impacts what you pay for every coin, make sure that you know what the percentage is, and be aware that the buyer's fee can change from company to company and sale to sale.

- ✓ **Warranties/guarantees:** What guarantees does the auction company offer? What if the coin turns out to be fake, repaired, or overgraded? How long are the guarantees good for? Will you have time to get a coin checked out by a competent expert before the warranty period expires? What options are available to you after the expiration date?

- ✓ **Credit:** Some auction houses extend credit to their bidders, often allowing 15 to 30 days after the sale to make final payment. The availability and cost of credit may or may not be listed in the Terms of Sale and may have to be negotiated on an individual, case-by-case basis — so be sure to discuss the possibilities with the auction house principals.

- ✓ **Return privileges:** What are your return privileges in an auction, if any? On what basis can you return a coin? Generally, if you're a floor bidder, you can't return a coin for any reason (because floor bidders are deemed to have examined the coins beforehand). As a mail bidder, you may return coins under certain circumstances, but the reason had better be good or you may be dropped from the company's mailing list. Again, how long is the period in which you may return a coin?

- ✓ **Resolution of disputes:** How do you settle disputes with the auction company? Do you go into arbitration, or can you go directly to the courts? If you go to court, where do you file? By nature, most Terms of Sale favor the auction house. So, if you live in Maine, you may find it inconvenient and expensive to file a lawsuit in California.

Be sure to ask your important questions before you bid, not after!

Registering to bid

In order to bid in an auction, you must identify yourself to the auction company. This involves providing personal contact information and references so that the auction company can verify that you are a real person and that your reputation within the industry is good. You may be asked to provide credit references, particularly if you plan to spend a lot of money in the sale. You should register well in advance of the sale date in order to give the auction company time to check out your references.

Studying the catalog

After you're satisfied with the answers to your questions about the Terms of Sale, give the auction catalog a good once-over to see what coins are being offered and how the material is arranged. Mark the pages that contain items of obvious interest, and go back through the catalog and take a look at every *lot* (each of the numbered items in the sale) to see whether you missed anything. For example, some auction houses offer certified coins in one section and *raw* (uncertified) coins in another. Therefore, you may find a coin you're looking for in one section and miss the same coin in another section.

Don't expect the listings in auction catalogs to follow the same sequence found in reference books. Many auction houses prefer to offer the most expensive coins in the evening sessions, when most people have finished their workday and are able to attend. Listing sequences vary from company to company and even from catalog to catalog, so looking at every lot becomes essential. To find out what's being sold when, take a peek at the schedule in the front of the sale catalog — here you can find the times for each session of the sale and which coins are included in each session.

You may find treasures hidden in the *bulk lot section,* where cheaper coins are lumped together into big, single lots. For example, you may find a rare half dollar variety mixed in with a partial collection; or you may find a valuable, high-grade coin mixed in with a bunch of low-grade junk.

The ultimate in hidden treasures

Normally, an auction company presents coins in their best light. Rare coins receive lavish descriptions and are scheduled to sell when the greatest number of bidders will be in attendance. Sometimes, however, unusual circumstances prevent an auction house from doing their best job, resulting in a presentation that defies description.

A classic example is the 1954 sale of the collection of King Farouk, the former king of Egypt. Farouk was a voracious collector of coins from around the world (especially coins of the United States) and he had just about every significant rarity you can imagine. After Farouk abdicated in 1952, the Egyptian government arranged for his collections to be sold in an attempt to recoup some of the money he had spent as King. The coins in the sale were arranged together with seemingly little regard for rarity and value. For example, one lot contained a set of Liberty Head Nickels — normally not a big deal, but in this case, the set contained an example of the extremely rare 1913 Liberty Head Nickel! Another treasure was the unique 1907 Indian Head $20 Gold coin that was given hardly any description at all (today, this coin would receive a full-page spread)! When King Farouk purchased the coin from Abe Kosoff and Abner Kreisberg, he paid nearly $10,000. Guess who the buyer was at the Farouk sale in 1954? Abe Kosoff. He bought the coin back for the bargain price of $3,400!

Choosing your battles

If you're like most people, you can't afford to purchase entire sales — especially at today's prices — so you must winnow your wish list down to an affordable level. Prioritize your list between the following:

 ✔ Coins you absolutely have to own no matter what the cost
 ✔ Coins you're willing to fight for to a reasonable level
 ✔ Coins you'd like to own but wouldn't get too upset if you were outbid on
 ✔ Coins in which you have no interest

Try to feel out your competition. Although *collusion* (secretly agreeing with another bidder not to bid against each other) is illegal, there's nothing wrong with discussing with other bidders their interest in various lots, or in trying to find out how high bidders are willing to go for certain coins. Careful investigation before the sale may give you a good idea of your potential for success with a particular lot, allowing you to adjust your bidding strategies accordingly. As you speak with other potential bidders, be careful what you say. After all, your competitors may be trying to get information from you as well. Never, ever tell someone how much you are willing to pay for a particular coin or lot — you may end up bidding against yourself!

Collusion is an agreement between bidders, whereby one bidder agrees to refrain from bidding in return for a fee or commission. In effect, collusion cheats a consignor out of money to which he or she may otherwise be entitled. The penalties for collusion are hefty, so if someone asks you to *lay off* (not bid), whether for free or for a fee, say no.

Setting your limits

Before the sale takes place, decide what you want to pay for each and every coin on your wish list.

1. **Consult your favorite price guides to determine the top price you are willing to pay for each lot.**

2. **Calculate backward to take into account the buyer's fee.**

   Add 1 to the buyer's fee (as a percentage) and divide your top price by that number. For example, if your top price is $200 and the buyer's fee is fifteen percent (.15), divide $200 by 1.15 for an adjusted limit of $174 (rounded from $173.91). This is the most you should pay for the lot.

Setting your limits in advance of the sale accomplishes two things: You avoid the mistakes made by trying to calculate bids during the heat of an auction, and you immunize yourself against the dreaded auction fever.

If you have a spending limit for the entire sale, be sure to keep a running total of the lots you've won during the auction. When you've reached your limit, pack up your stuff and leave the room, or put your bidder card away and enjoy the rest of the auction as a spectator. Otherwise, you may spend more than you can afford.

Bidding

You know which coins you want. You know what you are willing to pay. You know your spending limits. Now it's time to separate the wheat from the chaff.

In person

An auction goes something like this:

1. **You register in advance so that you can bid in person in a rare coin auction.**

   By registering in advance, the auction company can verify that you are a legitimate bidder.

2. **You receive a *bidder number* (usually printed in bold numbers on a card or paddle) that you use to signify your bid to the auctioneer.**

3. **As the auction begins, the auctioneer calls out the lot number, and a representative of the auction company shouts out an opening bid.**

   Known as *book bids*, opening bids may represent a minimum amount required by the consignor, or they may be offers received from an absentee bidder through the mail.

4. **The auctioneer opens the bidding up to the *floor* (the bidders in the room), allowing them to compete against the book.**

   In order to be the winner on a particular lot, a floor bidder must beat not only the book but also every other bidder in the room.

5. **After the bidding ceases, the auctioneer raps his/her hammer, indicating that the lot has sold, and announces the final price and the number of the successful bidder.**

The whole process happens very quickly. In an auction where the book is weak or there is a lot of bidding by the floor, expect a rate of about 100 to 150 lots per hour. In an auction where the book is strong and the floor offers little competition, the rate can increase to 300 to 400 lots per hour.

Great moments in auction bidding

When the late John Jay Pittman really wanted a coin, he marched to the front of the room, faced the audience, and held his bidder card aloft. Whether this bold move intimidated his competitors into not bidding, or whether he may have had his bid nudged up a little bit by his competitors is debatable, but this bidding method helped Mr. Pittman acquire some of his most important and valuable coins.

Similarly, when J.R. Frankenfield bid on the extremely rare 1795 Sheldon-79 Large Cent, he taped his bidder card to the wall and left it there until he finally won the lot for over $100,000, setting a record price for the variety.

On the other hand, I've seen plenty of bidders try these same tactics, only to wilt as the price goes higher and higher. It's amazing how heavy a bidder card can get as the bidding approaches your spending limit. It takes a strong person to keep that card in the air.

How you bid is almost as important as how much you bid. You can take the sly approach and hide your bids from your competitors by bidding with a wink, a slight nod, or a flick of your pen (just be sure that the auctioneer notices your bids). Or, you can take the intimidating approach, where you extend your arm fully and raise your bidder card high in the air, sending a message that you will not and cannot be beaten on this lot. Just be prepared to pull your card down as fast as possible in case your bluff is called!

By mail

As an alternative to bidding in person, you may find bidding by mail (also known as *absentee bidding*) to be easier and more convenient. To submit a bid, simply fill out the bid form included with the auction catalog and mail or fax it to the auction house.

Absentee bidding saves the cost of traveling to the auction itself, but it also means that you can't examine the coins beforehand. Plus, you give up a certain measure of control over your bidding. In fact, the biggest complaint I hear from absentee bidders is that they were beaten by a floor bidder with the next increment over their bid. On the other hand, absentee bidding prevents you from catching auction fever, which can be a very expensive disease!

If you bid by mail, you can increase your chances of success by placing many more bids than you have money to spend and instructing the auction company to limit your successful bids to a specific dollar amount. As the sale progresses, the auction company will keep a running total; when your limit is reached, the remainder of your bids are discarded. Use an *either-or* bid when there are two or more identical coins in a sale — that way you buy one or the other, but not both.

As a mail bidder, stay away from those little check-off boxes on the bid sheet where you authorize an automatic increase of 10 to 30 percent "if necessary." What you're really saying when you check off one of these boxes is that your top bid is not really $100, its $130. Although most reputable auction houses reduce your bids where possible, you expose yourself to *jamming,* where your bid is entered for the full amount with no reduction whatsoever.

Reserving Yourself

In theory, auctions represent the classic coming together of willing buyers and willing sellers to achieve a perfect market price. The price realized at auction is thought to represent the true value of an item because the process is open, public, fair, and unbiased.

In reality, auctions are not always what they seem to be.

Here's an example of how an auction can be used to dupe a customer. Say, for example, I have a coin that I purchased for $20,000. I consign the coin to an auction company that agrees to charge no commission on the sale and will allow me to bid on my own coin. I enlist the aid of a friend to bid against me at the auction and we run the bid up to $30,000. Of course, I end up being the winner on my own coin, but I can then offer the coin to a customer for $32,500, justifying my asking price by pointing out that the very same coin just sold at auction for $30,000!

I can use the same tactics to set a world record price for a coin, just to get some of that publicity I mentioned earlier in this chapter. If I had an 1804 Silver Dollar to sell at auction (and, oh, how I wish I did), and I could get an auction company to go along with me, I could bid my own coin up to $5 million, setting a new price record for a U.S. coin, and no one would be the wiser.

To their credit, no reputable auction house would knowingly participate in such shenanigans. Because of pressure from government watchdog agencies and consumer groups, most auction houses do not include *buybacks* and unsold lots in their list of prices realized printed after the sale. That is why you often see jumps in the numbering sequence on the list of prices realized. The missing numbers represent coins that failed to meet the seller's minimum price.

Hauling Yourself to Online Auctions

The Internet has changed the face of numismatics forever. At any given moment, hundreds of thousands of rare coins are available for sale on the Internet — many of them through online auctions. The variety of material being offered on the Internet is incredible and greater than you will ever find at any coin show. In fact, I know of many collectors and dealers who have literally quit going to coin shows — instead, they are able to buy and sell every coin they need over the Internet.

Getting Internet versions of auction catalogs

Most major auction houses now publish their auction catalogs on the Internet. In many instances, the online version of the catalog is more useful than the hard copy. For example, an online version may contain images of every coin, while the printed version illustrates only the most important pieces. Online images are usually larger and more detailed than those found in the printed versions, and they may be in color instead of in black-and-white. At least one company, Heritage Numismatic Auctions, Inc., publishes its catalogs in three different formats — online, as a CD-ROM, and as a printed version. Their CD-ROM version gives you all the benefits of online viewing without the lengthy download times often associated with the Internet.

Depending on the level of sophistication of a rare coin auction house's Web site, you may even be able to bid online, right up to the sale deadline.

Using eBay

No discussion of modern numismatic auctions is complete without a mention of eBay, the online person-to-person auction that took the entire world by storm in 1995 and has been growing ever since. Peter Omidyar started eBay as a way to help his wife sell her Pez Candy dispensers. What started out as a simple model grew into the most popular means of buying and selling items of all types on the Internet.

Today, millions of items are posted each day, a nice chunk of which are rare coins. To find out what's for sale, go to www.ebay.com and enter a search term for the coin you seek. For example, I typed in **Silver Dollar** and came up with over 3,500 listings, including everything from U.S. Silver Certificate bills, to modern U.S. Silver Eagle bullion coins, to all types of Silver Dollars. In my search, bid prices ranged from a starting bid of 1¢ all the way up to $2,350; I've seen some coins sell for much more in the past. The quality is just as varied, ranging from low-grade circulated coins all the way to Gem Uncirculated and Proof coins.

Here's how it works:

1. **Register by providing personal contact information and a credit card with which to pay any auction fees.**

   You receive a user ID and a password.

2. **Find an item of interest by searching through the vast offerings.**

3. **Place a bid and enter your user ID and password.**

   eBay tells you whether your bid is too low, at which time you can bid again. You can bid as many times as you wish until you either give up or are the high bidder. In what is called *proxy bidding,* you can enter the top price you're willing to pay and have eBay bid for you until the auction reaches your price level.

   However, as long as the auction remains open, other bidders can come along at any time and outbid you. All eBay auctions expire after a certain period of time. The bidding is often fast and furious in the last moments of an auction as bidders try to sneak in a final bid.

4. **If you win, you receive an e-mail with the seller's contact information.**

eBay uses a feedback rating system that includes comments about buyers and sellers. A high positive feedback rating indicates a reliable member. Negative feedback ratings indicate potential problems with a member; use your judgment in dealing with anyone with negative feedback.

Although other companies have tried to emulate eBay's success, eBay maintains its dominant position by providing the largest audience of active buyers and sellers, and the largest number of items for sale. For complete information on using eBay, locate a copy of the popular *eBay For Dummies,* 2nd Edition, by Marsha Collier, Roland Woerner, and Stephanie Becker (Hungry Minds, Inc.) or *Internet Auctions For Dummies* by Greg Holden (Hungry Minds, Inc.).

Chapter 9

Affecting Value through the Condition of Your Coins

In This Chapter

▶ Understanding how condition relates to value
▶ Recognizing how coins are graded

*T*he condition (or *grade*) of a coin is the key to its value, no matter the coin's age, rarity, or metal. Being able to determine condition accurately is critical because a slight difference in grade can mean a huge difference in price. For example, if you telephone a coin dealer and ask the value of your 1900 Silver Dollar, the first question you'll be asked is, "What grade is it?" By knowing the grade, you can use current price guides (discussed in Chapter 5) to determine the value of your coin.

In this chapter, I introduce you to coin grading, how condition is determined, and important terms you need to know to talk to coin dealers. Chapter 10 gives specific information on how to grade your own coins.

Knowing Your Grade: Art or Science?

Is coin grading an art or a science? For years, numismatists have debated this question, with no successful resolution of the issues:

✔ **Art:** On one side, you have those who say that no two people can agree on a grade, that many of the factors that determine the grade of a coin are arbitrary and subjective, that beauty is in the eye of the beholder or that grading standards change depending on whether you are the buyer or the seller.

✔ **Science:** On the other side are those who believe that the grade of a coin can be determined with a high degree of scientific accuracy using a set of established standards and that anyone using these standards will arrive at the exact same grade.

Some people believe that ownership of a coin improves the grade. Certainly, I've purchased coins at shows and been suddenly surprised at how much nicer they looked after I purchased them. Or when someone has offered to sell me a coin, I've become overly critical or unfairly strict in my grading, only to relax those standards after the coin became mine. You may find yourself doing the same thing.

In order to be a good grader, you must appreciate the subjective side of numismatics (the colors, the luster, the eye appeal, and other imprecise traits), but you must also be able to look at a coin objectively and remove yourself from any of the emotional aspects of buying and selling. Being unemotional when grading is difficult to do, but coin grading requires your head, not your heart.

Committing to Memory the Big Four: Strike, Eye Appeal, Luster, and Wear

The four biggest factors that make up the grade of a coin are as follows:

- ✔ Strike
- ✔ Eye appeal
- ✔ Luster
- ✔ Wear

Each factor must be evaluated carefully and weighed against the other factors in order to come up with a comprehensive grade. This section covers what each term means; as you're adding to your collection, think about each one as you consider the condition of potential purchases.

Many new collectors make the mistake of favoring one factor over another, resulting in an incorrect grade and an overpriced coin. For example, many collectors of Large Cents (see Chapter 16) go for details, such as strike, over surface qualities like luster and eye appeal; in fact, the most desirable copper coins are those with choice, glossy surfaces.

Strike

To make (or *strike*) a coin, steel dies crash together with a thin *blank* (piece of metal) between them. The pressure of the impact forces the soft metal of the blank into the recessed areas of the hard steel die, thus creating raised areas on the coin that represent the design elements. The harder the dies come together, the better the impression made on the metal blank, and the resulting coin shows full, complete details.

Falling out of fashion

Not too many years back, toned coins were the rage and if your coin had the right color, you could demand (and get) huge premiums. Today, most collectors prefer white, essentially colorless coins. Why the change of heart?

Two things changed the market's mind about toned coins. One changed involved *coin doctorers* (see Chapter 4). As soon as the first toned coin sold for a premium, the coin doctors started applying color to everything in sight. By baking, spraying, smoking, painting, and gassing coins, coin doctors came up with some pretty convincing artificial toning that fooled a great many collectors. Because artificial toning was so good, virtually all toned coins came under suspicion.

The straw that broke the camel's back was the debate over what toning really represents. On one side stood the toning enthusiasts, proclaiming the beauty and desirability of natural toning. On the other side stood those who framed the debate in chemical terms. Upon hearing that toning was oxidation and/or a degradation of a coin's surfaces, and that toning often hid underlying defects, the tide began to turn against toned coins. Soon, collectors began demanding coins with no color whatsoever, so guess what happened to all the toned coins? Many were stripped of their color in order to reveal their underlying whiteness.

Tastes have changed in the past and they will change again in the future. When the pendulum swings back to toned coins, people may regret having cleaned all those former beauties. Nevertheless, your goal is to learn what works today and to focus your attention on the types of coins that get the best grades. In other words, give the market what it wants.

However, coiners at the mints learned long ago that by slightly reducing the pressure used to strike coins, they could prolong the life of the dies. So, we end up with a trade-off between quality versus quantity, with the mints going for quantity and collectors seeking quality. Unfortunately, collectors have no say in the minting process — collectors take what the mints provide and hope for the best. Many coins come well struck and others look as flat as pancakes the moment they're made. Ask coin dealers to describe the most common characteristic of Silver Dollars from the mint at New Orleans, Louisiana, and they'll tell you the coins have *flat strikes*. On the other hand, Silver Dollars from the San Francisco, California, mint generally have *bold strikes*.

If the quality of strike is a product of the minting process, how does it affect the grade of a coin? Think about your own preferences. If you had a choice of two examples of the same coin — one well struck and the other weakly struck — which would you choose? Poorly struck coins rarely have the highest grades assigned to them, even if they are strong in the other three factors.

Eye appeal

Eye appeal refers to the visual appearance of a coin and can be classified as below average, average, and above average. Take a look at your own coins. You probably have some that look ugly, some that look so-so, and others that are simply beautiful.

Eye appeal is the most subjective of the big-four factors and depends on your personal tastes. If you prefer coins with no toning (see Chapter 3), you may discount a coin that has color even if the toning is beautiful. Some people prefer a luster that is soft and satiny, while others want coins with highly mirrored surfaces. The final judgment rests with you, but you also want to know how others view the same coins. Check your preferences against coins that have been graded by experts or third-party grading services (see Chapter 10). Do they add points for nice toning or do they favor untoned coins? What characteristics do the nicest coins possess?

Rest assured that your collecting tastes and preferences will change over the years. As you become more experienced in numismatics, you'll discover what "nice for the grade" and "nice for the coin" really mean and you can appreciate the true rarity of coins with great eye appeal.

Luster

Luster is the natural surface gloss imparted to each coin as it is struck. The first uncirculated coins (see the "Valuing Your Coin Based on its Circulation" section, later in this chapter) made from a fresh pair of dies may have brilliant luster, or they may have a satiny, frosty luster. Luster can be dulled by cleaning, wear, contact marks (discussed in the following section), or the natural wear of the dies as they are used over and over.

Each year, the U.S. Mint makes special Proof coins for sale to collectors. *Proof* coins are specially prepared so that the finished coin will have deeply mirrored surfaces and a crisp, strong strike. (See the "Being Blinded by Proofs" section, later in this chapter.)

As you examine various coins, keep an eye out for those with dazzling luster. You'll know them when you see them — their luster jumps out at you and almost blinds you. The next time you visit a coin shop or a coin show, take a look at some uncirculated 1881-S and 1884-O Silver Dollars — you'll notice the difference. The 1881-S almost always comes with bright, flashy luster while the 1884-O is usually satiny and creamy-looking.

Luster is a key component of eye appeal. For example, a coin with *subdued* (dull) luster usually has poor eye appeal while a coin with blazing luster is visually dazzling. All factors being equal, buy the brighter, more lustrous example of any coin for your collection.

Wear

At first blush, wear appears to be a measurement of how much deterioration has occurred on the surface of a coin, because wear is usually caused by friction (as when coins rub against each other in your pocket). However, *wear* is a broad term that includes such defects as marks or dings caused by mishandling coins, chemical reactions from natural causes or deliberate cleaning, and any alteration of a coin's surfaces. In short, anything that causes the coin to deteriorate after it is struck can be considered in determining wear.

Contact marks occur when coins knock against a hard object, leaving a *hit* or *ding* on the surface of the coin. Contact marks caused when two coins knock against each other are called *bagmarks*, because these sort of marks tend to occur when coins are transported loose in canvas bags, as they often are.

Rubbing occurs first on the highest points of a coin, sort of like the peaks of a mountain range, because those areas are the most exposed. Therefore, if you see any change in the color or luster on the highest points of a coin, you're probably seeing wear. For example, a coin with uniform toning should not have any breaks in the color on the high points. If a coin is bright white and untoned, expect the luster and color to be exactly the same on the high points as it is in the *fields* (lower points), unless the coin is worn.

How you determine wear is not so easily defined because other big-four factors can confuse the issue. For example, a heavy layer of tarnish (resulting in ugly eye appeal) on a silver coin may obscure friction or problems on the underlying surfaces. As another example, a poorly struck coin will show soft details and may appear to be worn when it is actually in perfect, original condition. You can see how the problem may be compounded when you come across a coin that is both heavily toned and poorly struck.

Determining the amount of wear on a coin is no easy task. Unfortunately, no machines exist that can scientifically examine a coin and spit out a report that says the surfaces have deteriorated by, say, 10 percent. Nevertheless, an evaluation must be made, so it helps to have lots of experience. This is why I suggest in Chapter 4 that you examine as many coins as you can when opportunities arise. After all, the coin you don't collect today may be the coin you love tomorrow, so it pays to find out how to grade it now (see Chapter 10). To fine-tune your grading skills, purchase one or all of the grading guides listed in the Cheat Sheet at the front of this book and match your coin to the written descriptions and/or the photographs found there.

Valuing Your Coin Based on Its Circulation

Technically speaking, an *uncirculated* (brand new) coin never entered circulation and remains as nice, or almost as nice, as the day it was made. A *circulated* coin entered into everyday money exchange and has become worn, even if only to a small degree. As collectors accumulate coins, the natural tendency is to acquire as nice an example as possible or to buy a circulated example and replace it with a nicer coin later.

U.S. coin collectors use a 70-point grading scale, ranging from the worst grade of 1 to the best grade of 70. The scale is not linear, because 20 points are allocated to the grade of Very Fine (discussed in the following section), while the Uncirculated level gets only ten points, even though the biggest differences in price occur at the Uncirculated level, where the distinctions between grades are sometimes so fine that many people can't tell them apart.

Dividing the circulated grades

Collectors began to make distinctions among circulated grades as a sort of shorthand to help them describe their coins to other collectors and dealers. After all, collectors in the 1800s couldn't just slap their coin on a scanner and send an image via electronic mail to any number of recipients around the world. Instead, they developed a set of labels to create word pictures in the minds of interested parties. Grading words have changed somewhat over the years, depending on how collectors and dealers apply them: Yesterday's grade of Fine is probably today's Very Fine because the underlying definition of Fine may have changed.

The following list summarizes grading words and their rough meanings — rough because these grades must be applied to a number of different denominations, series, and even individual coins, all of which have their own little grading quirks.

Try to memorize this list — you'll hear and use these terms all the time.

- **Poor (or *basal state*):** A coin that has been worn almost completely smooth. The only thing that keeps this from being a washer is that just enough detail allows you to positively identify the coin.

- **Fair:** Extremely worn, but you may be able to make out some details and the date.

- **About Good:** Very worn, but this one has more of the design left. The main design features may be outlined, but most of the wording on the outer edges is worn smooth.

Technical and marketing grading — a real-life example

The difference between technical and market grading exists not in the minds of numismatic theorists, but in everyday life. Perhaps the most glaring difference exists in the world of copper coins. Take a look at any of the recent auction catalogs produced by Superior Galleries, a firm that has made a nice niche for itself in the copper coin market, and you find dual grades on many of the Half Cents and Large Cents (see Chapter 16). For example, you may see a coin with a PCGS (Professional Coin Grading Service) grade of AU-55 and an EAC (Early American Coppers) grade of EF-45. Worse yet, you may even see coins with both uncirculated and circulated grades! I applaud Superior Galleries for being open and honest about the real differences between technical and market grading.

For years, collectors of copper coins have maintained a Condition Census, a ranking of the highest condition coins that exist of each die variety (see Chapter 14). While market grading has changed over the years, copper collectors are forced to stick with the more conservative technical grades in order to maintain the integrity of their condition rankings. Market grading messes up the Condition Census by appearing to raise the technical grade. For example, a coin that was once the third Finest Known may suddenly appear to be the Finest Known after a market grade is applied. Therefore, beware of confusing the two approaches to grading — it may be a costly or embarrassing mistake.

✔ **Good:** A well-worn coin that shows most of the design elements in outline, some of the *legends* (wording), and a partial date. Parts of the rims are worn down into the tops of the legends.

✔ **Very Good:** Full, complete rims on both sides. Some of the details within the design outlines begin to show, but don't expect much detail on a Very Good coin.

✔ **Fine:** Still well worn, but all of the design elements and legends should be clear and bold. Expect about half of the design details to show.

✔ **Very Fine:** Lightly circulated, with about two-thirds of the design details visible.

✔ **Extremely Fine:** At this level, you start to see some luster, although only in the protected areas around the raised lettering and design elements. Wear is slight and should affect only the high points of the coin.

✔ **About Uncirculated:** A coin that is so close to being uncirculated that the novice collector easily confuses the two. About Uncirculated coins should have full, original luster and only slight traces of wear on the very highest points of the design.

Carving up the uncirculated grades

Collectors extended their labeling system to uncirculated grades because they noticed that certain uncirculated coins were nicer than others. For example, uncirculated copper coins begin life with a bright red color that can soften down to a rich, brown color over time. To some collectors, the full red example is worth substantially more than a brown coin, so collectors need a way to identify special coins that are at the top rung of the condition ladder.

Memorize these labels, and you'll be able to talk like a pro:

- **Uncirculated:** An average uncirculated coin. Some of the luster may be subdued, the surfaces may be covered with a drab or dark toning (tarnish), or you may see a few too many contact marks or hairline scratches on either side.

- **Choice Uncirculated:** This coin has full luster, attractive toning, a few light bagmarks, but not too many. If your coin is uncirculated but poorly struck (flat design details), it belongs in this category.

- **Select Uncirculated:** The visual quality is very attractive. A Select coin has few marks, the luster is above average, and the eye appeal is impressive. The depth of the strike is important but not critical.

- **Gem Uncirculated:** A fully struck coin with exceptional luster, great eye appeal, and only small contact marks (which are few and far between).

- **Superb Uncirculated:** The difference between a Gem Uncirculated coin and a Superb Uncirculated coin centers mostly around eye appeal. Superb Uncirculated coins are often referred to as "killer" or "monster" coins because of their amazing quality and eye appeal. Many coins simply don't come this nice, which is why superb coins often set records when they appear on the market.

- **Perfect Uncirculated:** This term refers to coins that are as perfect as the day they are made. Only a few very special coins ever fall into this elite category.

Playing the numbers game

When rising prices made grading issues critical in the late 1970s and early 1980s, collectors and dealers began using the Sheldon Grading Scale to rank a coin's condition. The morph was easy, as Sheldon's scale already applied numerical ranges to some of the grading terms mentioned in the two previous sections, and the system had already gained wide acceptance among collectors of copper coins. At last, the market had the perfect shorthand method for describing coins, establishing standards, instilling confidence, and attracting investors. Even more importantly, the market finally had a way to fine-tune those pesky uncirculated grades.

Here's how the numbers from the Sheldon Grading Scale translate into the word labels listed in the two previous sections:

- ✔ **1:** Poor, usually seen as BS-1
- ✔ **2:** Fair, shown as Fair-2
- ✔ **3:** About Good, notated as AG-3
- ✔ **4 to 6:** Good, most often seen as Good-4, Good-5, or Good-6
- ✔ **7 to 10:** Very Good, usually seen as VG-7, VG-8, VG-10, but for some reason, never as VG-9
- ✔ **11 to 19:** Fine, usually seen only as F-12 or F-15
- ✔ **20 to 39:** Very Fine, most often seen as VF-20, VF-25, VF-30, and VF-35
- ✔ **40 to 49:** Extremely Fine, commonly seen as EF-40 and EF-45
- ✔ **50 to 59:** About Uncirculated, seen as AU-50, AU-53, AU-55, and AU-58
- ✔ **60 to 70:** Uncirculated, with every level commonly used as follows (the MS stands for *mint state*):
  - • **MS-60 to MS-62:** Average Uncirculated
  - • **MS-63:** Choice Uncirculated
  - • **MS-64:** Select Uncirculated
  - • **MS-65 and MS-66:** Gem Uncirculated
  - • **MS-67 to MS-69:** Superb Uncirculated
  - • **MS-70:** Perfect Uncirculated

Were Doctor Sheldon alive today, he would marvel at how coin prices have skyrocketed since the days when he developed his valuation scale. Who knows what his scale would look like today had he made adjustments for the huge differences in price at the high end of the scale. Most likely, his highest number would no longer be 70, but something like 700 or even 7,000.

Beware of descriptive grading terms that are meant to conceal and confuse. When in doubt, always turn to the numeric grade, especially one assigned by a reputable certification and grading service. The importance of understanding how grading terminology is used increases along with the price of a coin.

Being Blinded by Proofs

Proof coins are special coins made just for sale to collectors. The process starts with specially processed and polished blanks, and then the coins are struck using polished dies in a press using higher-than-normal pressure. The result is a coin with razor-sharp details, brilliant surfaces, and blinding, chrome-like luster. *Proofs* (as Proof coins are known) are meant to represent perfection in coining. The difference is obvious when you place them side-by-side with the same coins made for circulation.

Some purists will say that Proof is a method of manufacturing and not a grade, but some Proofs end up in circulation. Even though Proof coins are sold for more than their face value, many of them were spent or mishandled and will actually show wear from circulation. In such cases, the coins are still graded on the Sheldon scale, but the designation is always Proof (for example, instead of calling a mishandled Proof coin Extremely Fine-45, it's simply called Proof-45 to indicate to collectors that it was a Proof coin that has been impaired in some fashion. I believe that the reason for this difference is that some collectors prefer coins made just for circulation — they do not want Proof coins in their collection, even if the Proofs did spend time in circulation.

The first Proof coins made from a pair of dies will often have design elements that appear frosty instead of brilliant. Such coins actually look like little cameos (the kind you see in jewelry stores) and they are known as *Cameo Proofs*. As more and more coins are struck, friction between the dies and the coin blanks slowly polishes the designs until they also become brilliant. While brilliant Proofs are still desirable, they are not as attractive — or as rare and valuable — as Cameo Proofs.

Beware of coins that have been polished to look like a Proof. Fake Proofs have an unnatural shininess and uniform gloss or brilliance, and they lack the crisp detailing of a true Proof. Fake Proofs have little or reduced value. Also, be aware that some coins made for circulation may have been struck from leftover Proof dies or the dies may have been polished before coins were struck. These are known as *Prooflike* coins. Prooflike coins will look like Proofs but, again, they fall short of the perfect qualities of a true Proof. Prooflike coins sometimes sell for huge premiums because of eye appeal. (See the "Eye appeal" section, earlier in this chapter.)

Grading Damaged Coins

Every coin deserves a grade, even those that have been damaged, repaired, cleaned, or otherwise altered. But, how does one adjust for the negative aspects of a coin?

Several of the main grading services don't make such adjustments. If a coin has serious problems, they refuse to grade and encapsulate the coin (see Chapter 10). For example, the Professional Coin Grading Service lists several reasons for rejecting a coin: cleaning, PVC contaminations, environmental damage, altered surfaces, and so on.

What happens to coins with problems? They go to other grading services that utilize what is known as *net grading*. Basically, net grading determines a coin's grade as if the coin had no defects, then discounts the grade based on the severity of the problems to arrive at a net grade. For example, you may see a grade such as, "Very Fine details, cleaned, net Fine-12" or, "About Uncirculated, planchet flaw, net Extremely Fine-40." (A *planchet flaw* is a natural defect in the blank used to strike the coin.)

Net grading gives every coin a chance. Not everyone wants (or can afford) to collect perfect coins. In many cases, a collector can find some great bargains in net-graded coins, yet still have a coin with many redeeming qualities.

Understanding That Condition Equals Value

Which came first, condition or value? Does the grade determine the price of a coin or does the price determine the grade? These are important questions because you'll come across two approaches to determining a coin's grade:

- **Technical grading:** Using the technical approach, the criteria outlined throughout this chapter are used to come up with a numerical grade, and then the price of the coin is determined.

  In theory, a technical grade should never change. A coin graded MS-63 10 years ago should still be an MS-63 coin today and even 100 years from now. Certainly, the value of a coin goes up or down as demand waxes and wanes and market conditions change, but a technical grade should never change. The only way for a technical grade to change is if the underlying standards change. However, if a standard changes, it isn't really a standard, is it?

- **Market grading (also known as *commercial grading*):** With market grading, the grade of a coin is determined by the price. In other words, if an 1875 Twenty-Cent piece has a proper market value today of $7,000, the market considers the coin to be an MS-65. If the same coin is valued by the market at $2,200, it must be an MS-64. The problem with the market grading approach is that the market is fickle and subject to change. When money gets tight, grading standards tighten; when money flows, grading standards loosen, which means they aren't really standards.

  In my opinion, market grading is just another attempt to loosen standards. Market grading may fool some of the people some of the time, but it can't fool the market itself. Anytime grading standards are dumbed down, the real market adjusts by lowering real values. The market knows that you can't make a silk purse out of a sow's ear.

Buy the best looking coin you can find for a particular grade. The market always favors attractive coins.

Grading Standards as Malleable as Copper

Considering how grading has changed in the past, one can say with a high degree of confidence that grading will change in the future. But how? Will slabs (see Chapter 3) survive, or will new products arrive to replace them? What about computer grading? Will the grading scale be expanded to encompass 100 different grades instead of only 70? Will the current lineup of grading services remain the same, or will some be out of business five years from now? Will new grading services pop up? Will new technologies make coin grading more efficient and accurate? Will technical and market grading methods ever reconcile?

Clearly, change will occur. As a numismatist and a coin grader, you must be prepared to adapt to whatever changes take place.

Chapter 10

Grading Coins: Your Best Defense

● ●

In This Chapter

▶ Knowing how to grade coins

▶ Improving your grading skills

▶ Practicing your grading techniques

▶ Putting your money where your mouth is

● ●

Knowing how to grade coins (defined and discussed in Chapter 9) instills confidence and creates the self-reliance necessary to make you a better coin buyer. Coin grading skills can be used over and over again as you evaluate potential purchases and determine the value of your own collection. As a buyer, you can use your grading skills to protect yourself against over-graded coins. When you become confident and proficient enough, you can save yourself hundreds, if not thousands, of dollars by grading your own coins and bypassing grading services (listed in this chapter). Ultimately, you can use your skills to ferret out under-graded coins and resell them for handsome profits.

Gathering the Tools of the Trade

To get any job done right, you need the proper tools. Coin grading is no exception. Therefore, to start on the path to coin-grading nirvana, make sure you have the following equipment.

Good eyesight

When was the last time you had your eyes checked? Grading coins requires lots of close-up work that puts extra strain on your eyes. Before you begin grading coins, your eyes should be in tip-top shape and your corrective lenses or contacts should be up to date. Grading coins can become a miserable and unpleasant task if you end up with migraine headaches and eyestrain. If you haven't had your eyes checked and/or your glasses adjusted in the past year, make the investment and go see your eye doctor right away. If you wear glasses, make sure the lenses are clean and free of scratches.

Grading guides

Good grading guides are a must. Just remember that each guide brings a different bias to the table and that one guide's interpretation of standards may be different from the interpretations offered by another guide. Buy as many of them as you can afford (see the Cheat Sheet at the front of this book for a listing of suppliers of all sort of coin-related publications), because they may be the most important investment you make in your numismatic career.

Chapter 9 reminds you that "standards" aren't standards at all. Proper coin grading requires the ability to reconcile standards that are sometimes close and sometimes far apart.

Magnifying glass

I know a lot of graders who never use a magnifying glass to examine coins — instead, they prefer to examine coins with their naked eyes. I've tried that myself and I always end up missing a hairline here, a bit of repair work there, or some other defect that seems to escape my inspection. Come to think of it, if you evaluate a coin for the big-four factors (see Chapter 9), you're probably safe at the eyeball level when looking for luster, strike, and eye appeal, but when you get to the technical factor of wear, you must look closer to see whether the coin has any friction, scratches, bagmarks, or flaws — hidden or otherwise.

How strong should your glass be? A lot of dealers use a 10× magnifying glass. In my opinion, 10× works great for detecting counterfeit or altered coins, but the view is too close for grading. A simple 2× or 3× glass should suffice.

Lighting

The type of lighting used to illuminate coins affects their appearance, hence their grade. Therefore, choose the best possible type of lighting and use it consistently. You simply can't expect the same results using Tensor lamps, incandescent lighting, halogen, fluorescent, and daylight to grade coins.

To achieve results similar to those of the grading services, mimic their setups as closely as possible. For example, when I worked in the grading room at one of the certification services in 1999 (as a cataloguer, not a grader), the room was darkened, and each station had a desk lamp with a 75-watt incandescent bulb. Now, whenever I grade coins at my office, I turn off the overhead fluorescent lighting, switch on the desk lamp, and grade like a maniac.

Even though I recommend sticking with one light source, keep tabs on how appearances can change under various lighting conditions. Learning this technique may come in handy some day, because you never know under what sort of lighting you may have to grade a coin. Lighting at coin shows differs from venue to venue. The rooms at some coin shows (see Chapter 2) are dark and poorly lit, while others are so bright that every coin appears to have a grade of Gem Uncirculated (see Chapter 9).

Here's my opinion of various light sources:

 - ✔ **Halogen:** Too bright, because it brings out too many defects on the coin's surfaces, resulting in an ultra-conservative grade.

   These bulbs are extremely hot and can give you a nasty burn if you touch them.

 - ✔ **Tensor:** A bit on the bright side, but the small size and portability of the lamps makes them perfect for travel to coin shows.

 - ✔ **Incandescent:** A 75-watt incandescent bulb is optimum. However, incandescent bulbs are large and so are the lamps that use them, so they are not the most convenient lights for traveling. They also give off a lot of heat.

 - ✔ **Fluorescent:** Fluorescent lighting tends to flatten out the luster on coins, but some newer fluorescent lights provide good lighting in a portable form.

 - ✔ **Daylight:** Too inconsistent due to changes in the amount and direction of the light, depending on the time of day, weather, time of year, and other factors. However, this may be the only lighting available at the flea market, so practice grading coins in daylight.

Beware of the lighting at some coin shows. For example, *Long Beach lighting* refers to the bright overhead lights of the convention center in Long Beach, California where the Long Beach Coins & Collectibles Exposition convenes three times a year. Long Beach lighting makes many coins look better than they actually are, so most dealers learned long ago to check the coins carefully under another light source before making a purchase. It's not the promoter's fault — it's just the way the convention center has been for many years.

Attending Grading Seminars

Wouldn't it be great if you could sit down with experts from the grading services and ask them all the questions you have about coin grading? Wouldn't it be great to actually handle rare coins in a wide variety of grades and values and learn the special characteristics of each one? Wouldn't it be great to compare your grades with those of the experts and then find out what you're doing wrong or right?

Actually, you can do all that and more by attending one of the grading seminars offered by the American Numismatic Association (ANA), the largest and one of the oldest organizations of U.S. coin collectors.

The ANA conducts seminars in conjunction with its annual convention, its smaller mid-winter convention, and at seminars held during the summer at the ANA headquarters. The summer seminars are weeklong sessions held in Colorado Springs. A reasonable fee ($510 for the 2001 Summer Seminars) includes full tuition for the grading seminar, lodging in a dorm room at nearby Colorado College for six nights, and all meals. The seminars at the convention sites last only three days and cost $325 for ANA members and $425 for non-members (convention seminars include only the cost of the course itself, not lodging or meals).

The ANA offers an advanced grading course to those who successfully complete the initial grading course. To find out more about the ANA coin grading seminars, dates, and fees, visit their Web site at www.money.org or use the contact information in the Cheat Sheet at the front of this book.

Polishing Your Skills on Your Own

While seminars give an immediate boost to your grading skills, you may not be able to afford to take a week off from work and the fees for a grading seminar. In that case, you can still learn to grade from the comfort of your own home. Assuming you've gathered up all the tools listed in the "Gathering the Tools of the Trade" section, start by reading through your grading guide(s), paying careful attention to the terms and suggestions listed therein. Learning to grade is like learning a new language: Before you can speak the language, you must know the vocabulary.

One of the easiest grading guides to use is *Photograde,* which teaches you grading as you match your coins up with actual photographs of coins in the book. Other grading guides may use line drawings to illustrate different grades, along with word descriptions.

To begin the grading process, do the following:

1. **Turn off the lights in your room and turn on your grading lamp.**

   Your eyes should be level with the light source and looking down (see Figure 10-1). The goal is to have the light bounce off the coin and into your eyes.

2. **Remove your coin from any holder it's in so you have an unobstructed view of the surfaces.**

3. **Hold the coin by the edges (that's the proper technique, thank you) under the light source and give both sides a quick once-over.**

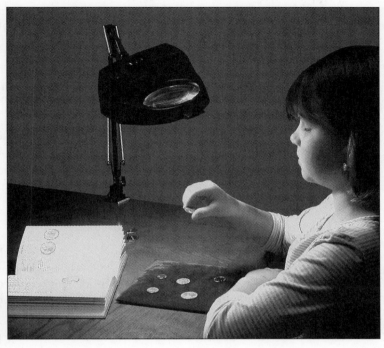

Figure 10-1:
Proper
positioning
of a grading
lamp.

4. **Look for any obvious flaws and then judge the coin's quality based on the criteria set forth in your grading guide.**

    Generally, grading guides lay out specific criteria for each grade level. Remember to discount for any unusual flaws using the instructions from the grading guide.

Grading circulated coins presents less of a challenge to the beginning numismatist because most of the evaluation centers on the amount of wear that the coin has received.

For uncirculated or Proof coins (see Chapter 9), keep in mind the big-four factors: luster, wear, eye appeal, and strike. As you consider each of these factors, ask yourself the basic question: "Is my coin average, below average, or above average?"

Evaluating the eye appeal

First, consider your coin's eye appeal. Move your coin in the light and use your unaided eyes to look for any gross defects such as heavy scratches, corrosion spots, rim nicks, polishing, or any other unusual flaws. Is your coin toned (tarnished) or untoned? If toned, is the toning dull, dark, attractive, colorful, iridescent, light, or heavy? Rate your coin based on the following criteria:

- ✔ **Below-average eye appeal:** Heavy, drab, dark, ugly, splotchy, or artificial toning. A dull, lifeless appearance. Heavy distracting marks, spots or corrosion. Obvious repair work. Any other distractions that make the coin unattractive.

- ✔ **Average eye appeal:** Light, original toning. Normal luster. Clean, problem-free appearance.

- ✔ **Above-average eye appeal:** Blazing luster. Exceptionally clean surfaces. Intense, bright colors. Rainbow toning. Superb quality.

Assessing the luster

Evaluate your coin's luster. Luster can be judged by how much light the surfaces reflect. Sometimes, toning affects the amount of light reflected by a coin. Is your coin flat and lifeless? Has the luster been stripped off by a cleaning agent? Is the luster nice and pleasing, or is it blazing and blinding? Rate your coin based on the following criteria:

- ✔ **Below-average luster:** Dull, drab, lifeless, cleaned, polished, or overpowered by toning.

- ✔ **Average luster:** Normal brilliance and natural brightness. Creamy, frosty, or satiny surfaces.

- ✔ **Above-average luster:** Blinding brilliance, blazing brightness, and dazzling surfaces.

Establishing the strike characteristics

Evaluate the amount of detail remaining on your coin. Is your coin *well struck* (nicely detailed), are the details flat, or do they appear worn? A flat strike will be most evident on the highest points of the coin, which is also where you will notice any wear.

Worn areas show friction — flatly struck areas do not. Rate your coin on the following criteria:

- ✔ **Below-average strike:** The coin will have flat areas where the metal didn't flow into all the deep recesses of the die.

- ✔ **Average strike:** Eighty to ninety percent of all details visible, with the only weakness appearing on the high points.

- ✔ **Above-average strike:** One hundred percent of all details visible

Estimating the wear

Wear is a negative term as far as coins are concerned, so as you consider the surface quality of your coin, treat wear the opposite of how you treat eye appeal, luster or strike. In other words, there is no such thing as good wear, and above-average wear is a bad thing.

✔ **Below-average surface quality:** Friction or color changes on the high points. Heavy or numerous contact marks. Rim dings, marks, and bruises. Heavy scratches. Obvious cleaning. Corrosion, pitting, or other surface damage.

✔ **Average surface quality:** An acceptable number of light contact marks or perhaps a single, large mark. No wear or friction. A hairline scratch or two. No pitting or corrosion.

✔ **Above-average surface quality:** Near-perfect surfaces. Few contact marks, any of which will be small. No scratches. No surface imperfections. Glossy, smooth surfaces.

Making the final judgment

After you rate your coin in each of the big-four areas, make a final judgment based on a combination of all four factors. For example, if your Uncirculated coin rated average in all four areas, your coin would merit a grade of 63 on the 70-point grading scale (see Chapter 9). If all four factors are below average, your coin earns a grade of 60. Above-average ratings in all four factors equate to the grades at 65 and above.

What if your coin has average ratings in three categories and above-average in the fourth? Your coin may make the 64 level. The important thing is to be aware of the thought processes that go into grading a coin. Your first grading decision may seem painstakingly slow, but as you practice on more and more coins, your evaluations will become faster and almost automatic. Practice helps perfect your skill, so get plenty of it.

Most grading guides offer specific instructions for determining the grades of uncirculated and Proof coins, but this remains an area of difficulty for most collectors and even many dealers. To become a great grader you must practice — and practice often.

Taking Your Grading Skills on the Road

Grading coins in theory and in the classroom differs greatly from grading coins on the road. At coin shows, you encounter different lighting conditions, the emotions involved in a buying-and-selling situation, and the pressure of having to make a number of snap grading decisions on short notice. To be a good grader, you must practice your grading skills under all conditions. After you feel comfortable examining and evaluating coins at home and as your confidence increases, take your grading skills on the road. Begin by visiting your local coin shop and check out some of the coins to see whether you agree with the grading.

In addition, attend a coin show and make a point to visit as many tables as possible to get a flavor for how different dealers grade their coins. While many dealers get awfully defensive if you question their grading, don't be afraid to ask them to explain their grade if you don't understand or agree with it. Explain that you're a new collector interested in learning how to grade coins. While you're at the table, make a courtesy purchase of some inexpensive coin to show your appreciation for the help. Dealers love to think they have a potential customer in the works.

Understanding Third-Party Grading

Coin grading is definitely not a spectator sport — to achieve any degree of competency, you must spend a lot of time viewing and evaluating coins. For some people, the demands are too great or the opportunity to see lots of coins just isn't there. Perhaps you have no interest in learning to grade coins — you simply want to enjoy your hobby with a minimal amount of effort. That's okay, that's why we have grading services.

For a fee, a *grading service* evaluates your coin by confirming its authenticity, checking it for any unusual damage or defects, rendering an opinion as to its grade, and then sealing the coin in a tamperproof holder to protect and preserve it. By employing world-class graders, grading services eliminate much of the guesswork involved in determining a coin's condition. Reputable grading services enjoy the respect of a large number of coin dealers and collectors, some of whom accept the grades blindly (sight unseen) over trading networks and in transactions between complete strangers. Grading services have helped eliminate many of the abuses of the past, including counterfeiting and over-grading.

Introducing the grading services

Wouldn't it be great if you could hire the best coin graders in the world and have them tell you the grades of your coins? Unfortunately, top experts in the field make huge incomes, so they're not likely to even take your phone call, nor would they have the time to grade your coins even if they wanted to.

Fine-tuning your eyeballs

Here's a great way to practice your grading skills and to fine-tune your eyeballs against those of the world's best grading experts: When you examine a coin that has already been graded and encapsulated, put your thumb over the grade as you pick up the holder, being careful not to give in to the natural tendency to cheat and peek first at the printed grade. Run through your normal evaluation process and come up with your own grade for the coin. After you've set the grade in your mind, lift up your thumb and look at the grade assigned by the grading service. If you match the grade, good for you! If not, reexamine the coin and try to understand where you went wrong. You may find this exercise frustrating at first, especially if your batting average is low, but I can think of no better way to practice your grading skills. You will improve over time. And, if you can raise your batting average high enough, you may have a shot at the six-figure incomes that some graders reportedly earn!

But, what if a specialized company hired top graders and offered their services to anyone who wanted to have their coins examined? Then, if you had one coin or a thousand, you could obtain the opinions of world-class experts for a small per-coin fee, thus giving you full confidence in your coin's grade at a reasonable price. That's exactly what the grading services have done. And on top of that, the grading services tell you whether your coin is authentic, they sometimes photograph your coin, and they sometimes determine the die variety to see of you have a rare coin — all for a fee, of course.

To be fair and objective, I list the following grading service in alphabetical order, and I describe some of the features and highlights of each:

- **American Numismatic Association Authentication Bureau (ANAAB):** ANAAB is located in Colorado Springs, Colorado and is the authentication arm of the American Numismatic Association. ANAAB does not grade coins, but identifies and authenticates numismatic items, including coins, medals, tokens, and obsolete paper money. For a fee, ANAAB provides die variety numbers for members of most U.S. coin series, information about numismatic conservation, and custom photography. ANAAB does not encapsulate coins but does issue photo certificates.

  For complete details about services, fees, submission policies, and guarantees, contact ANAAB by visiting their Web site at www.money.org.

- **ANACS:** ANACS, which used to stand for the American Numismatic Association Certification Service, but now just means ANACS; is located in Columbus, Ohio and was the former grading arm of the American Numismatic Association. ANACS authenticates and grades regular issue, commemorative, and pattern U.S. coins, a wide variety of world coins,

Civil War tokens, Hard Times tokens, and So-Called Dollars. For a fee, ANACS researches die varieties of most U.S. coin series. (If you already know the variety attribution number, ANACS will verify the number for free.) The plastic holders used by ANACS (to encapsulate the coins they grade) are the smallest and most compact of all those offered by the grading services listed here.

ANACS encapsulates problem coins and issues dual grades, one for sharpness that identifies the problem and another net grade that's discounted for the problem (see Chapter 9). For complete details about services, fees, submission policies, and guarantees, contact ANACS by visiting their Web site at www.anacs.com.

✔ **Independent Coin Grading Company (ICG):** ICG is located in Englewood, Colorado and is the newest of the grading services listed in this chapter. ICG differentiates itself by using a third-party receiving company to ensure that no submitter receives preferential treatment. ICG claims that its Intercept Shield holders offer maximum protection from atmospheric corrosion. ICG authenticates and grades most ancient and world coins, any numismatic item listed in the current *Guidebook Of United States Coins,* and casino chips. For a fee, ICG researches die varieties of most U.S. coins.

ICG may not encapsulate coins with previous damage, questionable toning, altered surfaces, or negative eye appeal. For complete details about services, fees, submission policies, and guarantees, contact ICG by visiting their Web site at www.icgcoin.com.

✔ **Numismatic Guaranty Corporation (NGC):** NGC is located in Parsippany, New Jersey and claims to be the largest third-party grading service. NGC began grading U.S. coins in 1987 and later expanded into world coins and error coins. NGC identifies die varieties through its VarietyPlus Service and offers a neat PhotoProof product (essentially a slick report that combines enlarged, full-color images with a well-researched history of your coin).

NGC is the official grading service of the American Numismatic Association. NGC will not encapsulate coins that are counterfeit or that have problems, such as harsh cleaning, artificial toning, altered surfaces, damage, corrosion, rim filing, and so on. NGC claims that the seals on its holders were the tightest in a test of holders from various services.

Submissions may be made through authorized dealers or through the American Numismatic Association Submission Center. Authorized dealers prescreen your coins, pointing out problem coins that may not make it through the grading process. Because most grading fees are non-refundable, even if the coin never gets graded, this can be a valuable time- and money-saving service.

For complete details about services, fees, submission policies, and guarantees, contact NGC by visiting their Web site at www.ngccoin.com.

✔ **PCI Coin Grading Services (PCI):** PCI is located in Chattanooga, Tennessee and has been grading coins for over a decade. PCI claims to have the lowest fees of any grading company. PCI authenticates and grades most U.S. coins. Variety attributions are free and problem coins are encapsulated in holders with a distinctive red label so as not to confuse them with the normal PCI holders.

PCI accepts submissions directly from the public. For complete details about services, fees, submission policies, and guarantees, contact PCI by visiting their Web site at www.chattanooga.net/pci/index.html.

✔ **Professional Coin Grading Service (PCGS):** PCGS is located in Newport Beach, California and claims to have pioneered the sonically sealed, tamper-evident, hard plastic cases known as *slabs* (see Chapter 3). PCGS began certifying and grading U.S. coins in 1986 and has since graded more coins than any other service (over 6 million coins with a combined value of nearly 9 billion dollars). In addition to U.S. coins, PCGS certifies and grades world coins, U.S. colonial coins, error coins, and California Fractional Gold coins.

PCGS is the official grading service of the Professional Numismatists Guild and provides holders with bar coding for use with computerized inventory management systems. PCGS will not encapsulate coins that are counterfeit or that have problems such as artificial toning, excessive cleaning, environmental damage, PVC damage, major scratches, or obvious natural defects. Submissions may be made through authorized dealers or through the PCGS Collectors Club.

For complete details about services, fees, submission policies, and guarantees, contact PCGS by visiting their Web site at www.pcgs.com.

✔ **Sovereign Entities Grading Service, Inc. (SEGS):** SEGS is a relative newcomer to the field of coin grading, but has captured the attention of many collectors and dealers with its innovative holder and the fact that SEGS will grade many of the problem coins that other services reject. The top of the SEGS slab has a clear window through which you can read a thin label that identifies the coin and the grade, allowing you to quickly scan the tops of the holders to find the coin you seek.

SEGS will not encapsulate coins that are counterfeit or altered with the intent to deceive (added mintmarks and so on). Submission may be made directly to SEGS without having to go through an authorized dealer.

For complete details about services, fees, submission policies, and guarantees, contact SEGS by visiting their Web site at www.segsgrading.com.

Should you use a grading service?

If you have a *raw* (unencapsulated or uncertified) coin, when should you consider submitting it to a grading service? When does the value of a coin justify spending more money on having it graded?

Actually, collectors obtain certification for a coin for two reasons:

✔ When you suspect the coin may be counterfeit or altered

✔ When you would like an expert opinion of the grade

All of the companies listed in this chapter include authentication of coins as a part of their services. All of the companies, with the exception of ANAAB, render an opinion of the grade. Therefore, you're really getting two opinions for the price of one.

Grading fees range from $7.50 to $100 per coin, depending on the company and the level of service you request. Usually, the higher fees entitle you to a faster turnaround, which can be important if time is of the essence or if your return privilege is about to end. (See Chapter 6 to find out more about guarantees and return privileges.)

Base your decision to submit a coin to a third-party grading service on the time you have and the value of your coin. Generally, I recommend submitting any coin worth over $200, any coin that shows big jumps in value from one grade to the next highest, or any coin that is commonly counterfeited.

I consider the grading services to be equity builders. By eliminating one of the most important arguments in a buying-and-selling transaction, grading services enable the average collector to buy with confidence and sell for the highest possible price. Grading services, especially the early pioneers, deserve a lot of credit and respect for adding liquidity to the market and instilling the confidence that wary buyers need to entice them into the market.

Evaluating the grading services

Each grading service offers a unique service that separates it from all the other companies. However, regardless of how innovative a particular feature may be, the true test comes from market acceptance. Which company does the market consider to be the most accurate and, hence, the most valuable?

Perhaps the best measure of the market's confidence in a particular holder is how the assigned grade measures up against real market values. For example, is an 1882 Silver Dollar more valuable as a PCGS MS-64 or as an ANACS MS-64? This question is answered by the *Coin Dealer Newsletter* (CDN), a weekly publication that ranks different grading services based on how valuable their grades are compared with listed values. As an example, in the January 19, 2001 issue, PCGS coins were valued at an average of 89.26 percent of CDN prices, NGC coins at 81.65 percent, ANACS coins at 67.20 percent, and PCI coins at 69.41 percent. Based on these rankings, the market appears to place the highest level of confidence in the grades of PCGS, high confidence in the grades of NGC, and lower confidence in the grades of PCI and ANACS.

This difference in confidence confirms that grading "standards" are not really standards at all. Even relying on third-party grading services may not be enough to protect you. Pity the poor collector who pays full retail value for a slabbed coin with a confidence rating of only 60 percent. Ouch!

Putting Your Money Where Your Mouth Is

Okay, suppose you've learned how to grade, you've practiced your skills at home and on the road, and now you have the confidence to buy your first coin. It's time to put your money where your mouth is.

Theoretically, you should be able to search dealers' cases at a coin show for that one undergraded coin that can make you hundreds of dollars. So here's my challenge to you: Find the most undergraded coin you can, buy it, and submit it to one of the grading services in this chapter. After the coin comes back from the grading service, you will know one of several things:

✔ **You missed something:** If the coin comes back without having been graded, you may have missed something such as cleaning, PVC contamination, artificial toning, or some other defect that would cause the grading service to reject the coin.

✔ **You need more work:** If the coin comes back with a grade less than you expected, practice your grading skills before you buy another coin. Take a good second look at your coin and try to discover why the grading service assigned a lower grade than you thought it would.

✔ **You're a great grader:** If the coin comes back with the grade you expected, all your practice and preparation paid off. If you bought the right coin, you probably also made some good money because of the price differential between what you paid and what the coin is now worth. Consider a career in numismatics.

✔ **You're too conservative:** If the coin comes back with a grade higher than you expected (I'd be surprised if this happens), your standards are way too strict. All this means is that you won't buy too many coins in the future because few of them can ever meet your expectations. On the other hand, you probably made a huge amount of money on this purchase, which is a nice consolation prize.

Don't let the results of this simple exercise affect your confidence too much either way: Don't give up and don't let it go to your head. Instead, use this exercise as a chance to discover your strengths and weaknesses on your path to becoming a world-class coin grader.

Even the most talented coin dealers make mistakes, and a 60 percent success rate is considered good. My longtime friend and fellow coin dealer, Jeff Garrett, once told me, "Anyone can make a killing on a coin now and then, but few people can make a 10 percent profit on a consistent basis." Jeff is right — you need a good eye and real talent to work on a small profit margin while buying lots and lots of coins.

Part III
Choosing Coins for Your Collection

The 5th Wave   By Rich Tennant

©RICHTENNANT

"Along with my Franklin Nickels and Roosevelt Dimes, I've collected several McDonald's Quarter Pounders. Many of them are missing a pickle and show an off-center patty."

In this part . . .

Coin collecting is a journey that begins with a single coin. The first coin leads to another, the second leads to a third, and so on. Along the way, your tastes develop in such a way that your previous choices influence what the next coin will be. Every collector's path is unique and different, which is why collectors have such a great time getting together to talk coins and swap stories about the paths they have chosen.

Nevertheless, most collectors stay where they start, usually because they are unaware that there are other types of coins to collect or because they're intimidated by their lack of knowledge in other areas. I've heard enough collectors say "I wish I had started collecting such-and-such a coin years ago," or "I can't believe the bargains that you can find in such-and-such an area" that I point out several paths you may be interested in taking.

In this part, you get a sneak preview into several major collecting areas, not so much to convince you to collect them, but to open your eyes to them and give you more choices when adding coins to your collection. So, take a seat on your numismatic tour bus and enjoy the ride.

Chapter 11

Showing Their Age: Ancient Coins

Mention the word *ancient* and your mind probably pictures Roman gladiators, Spartan warriors, Greek gods, Emperors, Caesars, Cleopatra, Alexander the Great, and so much more. Similarly, ancient coins remind collectors of history because they are, in fact, historical records. Long after papyrus and sheepskin records have rotted away, coins remain to tell the story of people and events from long ago.

To the novice collector, ancient coins seem intimidating. Aren't ancient coins rare? Aren't they expensive? How can you tell what the coins say? Where does one go to buy them?

In reality, ancient coins are like members of any other coin series. They are no more mysterious than U.S. Half Dollars, Spanish Doubloons, or Austrian Schillings — they're just older and a little harder to read. Just as with any modern coin, you can find helpful books that tell you all about ancient coins. Give ancient coins a chance, and they may turn out to be your favorite coins of all.

With that in mind, this chapter introduces you to the world of ancient coins, giving you just enough information to whet your appetite. Get ready to enter the worlds of Julius Caesar and the goddess Athena, and come face-to-face with other famous names from the past.

Ancient Coins — of Gods and Men

Simply put, ancient coins are all about history. Without newspapers, mail, telephones, faxes, overnight delivery services, e-mail, and the Internet, the best way to spread information throughout a kingdom 2,000 years ago was with coins. For example, each Roman ruler issued his or her own coins upon assuming the role of emperor or Caesar. Thus, you find Roman coins with portraits of Julius Caesar, Brutus (the brute who killed Caesar), Nero (he fiddled while Rome burned), Marc Antony (Cleopatra's lover), and other Roman rulers. Greek coins, on the other hand, favored the images of gods and goddesses such as Apollo, Athena, Zeus, and Hercules, not to mention lesser figures like Pegasus the horse and various nymphs and mythological figures. Even the goddess Nike (named after the shoes you're wearing, or was it the other way around?) appears on Greek coins, often driving a chariot pulled by four horses.

Coins put people in direct touch with the people of ancient times — they're like time machines that bring the ancient world to us and transport us back in time to a world that was much different than the one we live in today. Although historians provide stories of the ancient world, coins provide additional insight. Coins provide permanent records of military victories, marriages, deaths, new rulers, births, places, and events. In some cases, coins are the only historical records we have. By looking at the evolution of coins over time, you can tell a lot about the strength or weakness of a nation. Strong nations issue coins of gold and silver; weak nations could barely afford to make coins of copper and bronze. Hence, the decline of a nation or empire is mirrored in its coins.

Deciding Which Ancient Coins to Collect

The field of ancient coins is so broad that it would be impossible and frustrating, if not mentally unhealthy, to try to collect them all. Therefore, collectors gravitate to certain areas that have become very popular. In this section, I highlight areas in which you may want to develop an interest, as well.

Ancient Greek coins

The Greeks learned about coinage from the Lydians (their neighbors and inventors of the first coins). Greece and its city-states produced some of the most beautiful coins the world has ever known. Early Greek coins are crude little bean-shaped pieces with punched designs of animals or other objects. However, over time, the designs became more sophisticated and the beans flattened out into the thin, round pieces that are the hallmark of coins today. Between 500 and 400 B.C., hundreds of Greek city-states issued coins, copying each other but at the same time coming up with new and innovative designs of their own.

During this time, the Greeks at Athens issued large silver coins called Tetradrachms with a bug-eyed owl on one side (see Figure 11-1). The owl was the symbol of the goddess Athena, who considered the bird sacred. In turn, Athena was revered by the people, who considered her sacred and named their city after her. The ultimate Greek coin was the impressive Decadrachm, a large silver coin from Syracuse (Greece, not New York).

A *drachm* or *drachma* is the basic unit of Greek money, even in modern times. *Tetra* means four, so a *Tetradrachm* equals four drachma. Also, because values of coins were based on their weight, a Tetradrachm weighs exactly four times as much as a drachma. A *Decadrachm* equaled 10 drachma.

Figure 11-1: Athena's sacred owl in coin form.

The Greeks employed interesting and unusual designs for their coins, including grapes, a rose, ears of wheat, eagles, crabs, dolphins, and rabbits, not to mention images of many of the Greek gods and goddesses. Yet while they made liberal use of images of gods and animals on their coins, they shunned portraits of real people. Even Alexander the Great's image never appeared on his own coins until after his death, and by then he had been converted to a god by many of his successors and fans. Some of the neatest Greek coins show Alexander wearing a lion's head as a helmet; another shows him with the tusked head of an elephant atop his own head!

As Greek civilization declined, so did its coins. At one point, the Greeks became so desperate for metal for their coins that they made them out of bronze and then silver-plated them to make them look like their more valuable counterparts. They even melted down the statues of the goddess Nike to make gold coins.

Ancient Roman coins

Rome started out as a *monarchy* (ruled by kings), then became a *republic* (ruled by representatives of the people), then veered toward a dictatorship as the Romans created a worldwide empire. Unlike the Greeks, the Romans loved to place images of their rulers on their coins, and they used their coins as propaganda pieces to tout their military victories and record important events. Like the Greeks, the Romans revered their gods and sprinkled their likenesses liberally throughout their coinage.

One of the most famous Roman coins is the *denarius,* or penny (see Figure 11-2). This silver coin was roughly the diameter of a modern U.S. Cent or Dime. Because the denarius was issued over hundreds of years, collectors have an opportunity to collect a wide range of rulers and design types. Rome also issued a number of unusual coins, such as the big bronze coin known as an *Aes Grave,* the *golden aureus,* and the *silver didrachm.*

Figure 11-2:
The denarius, the backbone of Roman numismatics.

Some of the most popular Roman coins include Brutus' "Ides of March" denarius, the coins of the twelve Caesars, and the series of "JVDEA CAPTA" coins that commemorated Emperor Vespasian's victory over the Jews in 70 A.D.

The nice thing about many ancient Roman coins is their low cost. Small copper coins can be purchased in quantity for under $5 each. A nice silver denarius costs $20 to $50. Even Roman gold coins are surprisingly inexpensive.

Biblical coins

The Bible mentions several coins by name, including the Roman denarius, the Jewish Shekel, and the Widow's Mite. Something about these coins evokes a special feeling in collectors.

If you think about it, what other relics do we have from Biblical times? The Dead Sea Scrolls exist, but who can own them? Ancient manuscripts are all locked up in museums. The Shroud of Turin, yes, but you can't touch it!

When you get down to it, coins are the only tangible reminders we have of the people, places, and events of Biblical times. When you hold a tiny Widow's Mite in your hand, you realize why such a worthless coin can mean so much. And you wonder if, perhaps, you may be holding the very coin that the old woman gave as an offering.

Byzantine coins

The Roman Empire fell gradually but surely, to be replaced by the Byzantine Empire centered in Constantinople, Turkey. Beginning in 498 A.D., Anastasius introduced a new copper coin called a *follis,* worth 40 *nummi.* The Byzantines also issued beautiful coins of gold and silver. Byzantine coins are known for their religious symbols, and common themes include crosses, images of Christ, and other reminders of the Christian religion (see Figure 11-3). Like the earlier Roman coins, many Byzantine coins bear the images of the rulers of the time.

Figure 11-3:
Byzantine
coins,
promoters
of
Christianity.

Byzantine coins, like so many ancient coins, are quite affordable. Many of the gold coins can be purchased for under $200, and Byzantine bronzes often sell for less than $20.

Understanding How Age Affects Value

The first mistake non-collectors make concerning ancient coins is the false assumption that because a coin is 2,000 years old, it must be worth hundreds, if not thousands, of dollars. Nothing could be further from the truth.

One of the reasons ancient coins are so common is because of the many coin hoards that have been discovered over the years. In ancient times, people carried their wealth with them. There were no banks, ATMs, checking accounts, or credit cards. The wealth of the ancients was measured in cash (coins) and jewelry (precious metals). Money was accumulated in small pots or jars (kind of like our modern change jars). At the first sign of trouble, people would bury their money, then return to claim it after the crisis passed. As you can imagine, many people forgot where they buried their coins, were killed by invaders (and the location of the coins "died" with them), or went off to war and never came back.

Modern construction projects have uncovered many hoards of coins that eventually get dispersed into the coin market. Hand-held metal detectors have uncovered untold quantities of ancient coins.

The ancient world, especially the Roman Empire, spread over a vast area and lasted for centuries. True, only so many hoards of coins can be buried, and many of them have already been found, but I suspect that many more are waiting to be discovered. Each discovery makes more coins available to collectors and helps keep prices affordable. How long will the prices of ancient coins remain low? I have no clue, but I suggest enjoying it while it lasts!

It's All Greek to Me!

Many collectors are intimidated by the unusual letters, words, and symbols on ancient coins. "How," they ask, "can you identify your coin if you can't read and understand the lettering and designs?" Actually, ancient coins are no more difficult to collect than some of the modern coins that contain non-English inscriptions and symbols. For example, people who can't read or understand either Japanese or Chinese have no problems collecting coins from those countries, yet the same collectors may fear venturing into ancient coins.

Most Roman coins bear Latin inscriptions that are fairly easy to translate. After you understand the abbreviations used on Roman coins, the rest is easy. The only stumbling block with Greek coins is the Greek alphabet and the unfamiliar shapes of some of the letters. Again, after you learn the abbreviations used on the coins, translations are readily available.

Knowing Where You Can Get 'Em

You may have never seen or heard of one before in your life, but ancient coins are everywhere. Your local coin dealer probably has some in stock and you can find a big variety of ancient coins at any coin show. At the biggest shows, especially international coin shows where dealers attend from Europe, you may even see a collection of coins from a hoard that was dug up. Imagine having a chance to buy inexpensive ancient coins fresh out of the ground. If you want a real conversation piece, pick up an ancient coin (or two) and share it with your friends.

Don't forget eBay (www.ebay.com). I just performed a search for **ancient coin** and came up with 1,212 possibilities!

Chapter 12

Making a Safe Bet with U.S. Coins

*I*f you want to be where the action is (and who doesn't?), start collecting U.S. coins. No other area in world numismatics is as active, involved, or exciting. In general, the U.S. coin market enjoys the most active collectors, the most valuable coins, and the best innovations in research and grading. Ample opportunities exist for collectors at all levels — from kids to adults, and from beginners to advanced collectors.

In this chapter, I examine U.S. coins and explain some of the special characteristics that make them so attractive to collectors. See Part IV of this book for the lowdown on specific types of U.S. coins.

Discovering a Finely Tuned Market

The market for U.S. coins is perhaps the largest and strongest in the world, and tremendous amounts of good information are available for the beginning collector. Most U.S. coin series have been extensively researched and published, allowing a new collector to enter the market without any knowledge, and in just a short time, become nearly as expert as any seasoned collector.

In terms of pricing, the U.S. market is a fine-tuned machine. Most U.S. coins have buy and sell prices that are so close to each other that collectors can get in and out of the market with relative ease and little expense. Several different guides track and set prices at both the wholesale and retail levels — price guides are even available on the Internet (see Chapter 5).

The grading of U.S. coins has been elevated to a degree of sophistication seen nowhere else in the world. The 70-point grading system (see Chapter 9) allows for fine differences in most grades, especially those at the top end of the scale where attention is the greatest. The rise of third-party certification and grading services (see Chapter 10) has added a certain amount of standardization to an area of the market formerly subject to abuse and manipulation.

Many markets exist for U.S. coins, making buying and selling an easy prospect, even for those with a do-it-yourself mentality (see Chapter 21). From local dealers to coin shows to major auctions, collectors and dealers have quick, easy, and frequent access to major markets. The Internet and online auctions bring the coin markets and millions of collectors to your home. Many dealers who once struggled to stay in business are now thriving with sales through the Internet. Today, collectors can sort through thousands of coins offered by hundreds of dealers. When they find a coin they like, they can view a digital image, make their selection, pay with a credit card, and wait for their coin to arrive. What could be more convenient?

Understanding Why U.S. Coins Are So Popular

Coins from the United States are so popular for a number of reasons:

- ✔ **Wonderful designs:** In over 200 years of making coins, the United States has produced a plethora of lovely and interesting designs to entice the collector. The recent success of the 50 States Quarters program (see Chapter 19) and the millions of new collectors it has brought into coin collecting are proof that designs matter.

- ✔ **Challenging series:** Whether you're looking to collect mundane, common coins or something more challenging, U.S. coins have it all, including many different denominations and types, inexpensive coins, super-rarities, big coins, small coins, and everything in between. The sky is the limit, but you can also keep your feet on solid ground.

- ✔ **Affordability:** Contrary to popular belief, you do not have to be rich to collect U.S. coins. Just ask any kid who collects the 50 States Quarters, Proof sets, and the new Sacagawea Dollar coins (see Chapter 17). Of course, being rich makes your coin collecting experience so much nicer, but that's true of any collecting pursuit that requires money!

- ✔ **Availability of commemorative coins:** You want commemorative coins? The United States has 'em. Since 1892, the United States has commemorated scores of national events, people, places, and organizations. If you choose, you can spend your entire collecting life just in this specialized area. See Chapter 19 for details.

✔ **Availability of gold coins:** If you like the yellow metal, the United States produced tons of coins made from gold (see Chapter 18). Many U.S. gold coins are priced just above their metal value, making them very affordable.

✔ **Active markets:** Coins can be bought and sold at local shops, at local coin shows, at regional and national coin shows, over electronic exchanges, over the Internet, over the phone, through the mail, and so on. In short, something is always happening in U.S. numismatics.

✔ **Social benefits:** You can meet and make new friends at coin club meetings, at coin shows, over the Internet, through newsgroups, and so on. Numismatists from the United States love to talk coins and compare notes.

U.S. coins have some of the most beautiful designs of any coins of the world (see Chapter 25). In addition, the history of the United States can be seen on its coins. Through coins, you can see how the American colonies struggled to gain their independence and why a stifled economy and a lack of coins were such common complaints. Over the years, a young Miss Liberty has aged gracefully. A religious motto ("In God We Trust") was added to U.S. coins in response to the Civil War. A number of statesmen have appeared on U.S. coins, from presidents to other great national icons like Benjamin Franklin. Peace was proclaimed on Silver Dollars after World War I, and later coins honored conflicts in World War II and the Korean War. The United States issued commemorative coins celebrating just about every event you can think of, from the founding of Delaware to the new 50 States Quarters to the Cleveland-Great Lakes Exposition.

In short, U.S. coins are steeped in a long tradition of history and remembrance. Collectors like you have contributed to the preservation of that heritage.

Recognizing Desirable Coin Characteristics: Liquidity, Liquidity, Liquidity

Realtors tell you that three most desirable characteristics of a piece of real estate are location, location, and location. If you're buying a coin with the hopes of making a profit, the three most desirable characteristics of a coin are, in my opinion, liquidity, liquidity, and *liquidity* (which means how fast they can be sold). Your coin can be the most beautiful thing in the world, the rarest coin ever known to humankind, and of the highest quality obtainable, but if you can't sell it quickly to take advantage of market opportunities, it's worthless.

Liquidity requires the following:

- Access to the markets
- Uniform pricing
- Public acceptance of the product
- Ease of transportation and storage

In general, U.S. coins meet all of the above requirements. In fact, one of the reasons for the success of third-party certification services (Chapter 10) was their perceived ability to make coins more liquid. In the early days of its existence, the Professional Coin Grading Service (PCGS) went so far as to establish a sight-unseen trading market for PCGS graded coins. Even today, some certified coins trade on a sight-unseen basis, but most require a visual examination and acceptance by the buyer.

How liquid are U.S. coins? The answer depends on the price level and how much time is available to complete the transaction. For example, many coin dealers use the *Coin Dealer Newsletter* (also known as the *Grey Sheet*) to set their buy and sell prices. If you need to sell today, most anyone will pay 30 percent below the *Grey Sheet* bid prices. If you can wait and do a little shopping around, you can find several dealers that will pay ten percent below bid. If you have enough time, you can eventually find just the right person to pay full bid or even more.

Thus, as far as coins are concerned, liquidity may not mean the best price. Nevertheless, if any coins are liquid, U.S. coins are the most likely to meet this definition.

Avoiding the "I" Word

Are coins an investment? For many years, especially during the 1980s, U.S. coin dealers became enamored with the idea of coins as an investment, particularly an investment that could attract Wall Street money. The idea of money pouring in from Wall Street investors was especially appealing because it represented an expansion of the U.S. coin market at a time when demand was particularly low. The hope was that an influx of money would reduce the supply of coins on the market and thereby increase demand and prices.

Dealers began using terms from the stock market to describe the coin market. Phrases such as "coins are liquid," "coins are fungible," "coins are tangible assets," "standardized grading has led to uniformity of product," "an active market exists where buyers and sellers can meet," and "coins have out-performed all other investments for the past ten years" were used to entice investors. Several rare coin investment funds were established, including one by Merrill Lynch. The funds met with mixed success, much of it depending on the state of the economy when the coins were sold.

Problems began when telemarketing firms began touting coins as an investment, often promising unusually high returns, guaranteed buyback programs, and even guaranteed profits. Unfortunately, many of the coins sold in this fashion turned out to be over-graded and over-priced, or the commissions charged by the so-called investment firms were so high that the buyer had little or no hope of ever recovering the purchase price, let alone making a profit.

Eventually, the Federal Trade Commission (FTC) got wind of the abuses in the coin market and began taking steps to protect the consumer. One result was that the word *investment* is rarely used in conjunction with coins anymore. The mere hint of a promise of future gains can land a coin dealer in a lot of trouble.

By definition, coins are not an investment. Unlike traditional investments, coins generate no income or interest. Rather, they cost money because of storage and insurance fees. However, coins are an excellent vehicle for the speculator. The coin market has taken some pretty wild swings in the past two decades, which means that big profits could have been made if you bought at the bottom of the market and sold at the top. In Chapter 24, I list a couple of very expensive coins that sold for a lot more money the second time they appeared on the market, even if it was only a few years after their first appearance. By the same token, if you bought coins at the top of the market in 1989, you would have faced some pretty heavy losses just a few years later — losses that have never been fully recovered, even in today's hot market.

If you're looking at coins as an investment, look elsewhere. If you're looking at coins as a speculative vehicle, understand that you are just as likely to win at a casino or a racetrack. If you're looking at coins with the intention of forming a meaningful collection and having fun, I encourage you wholeheartedly.

Chapter 13

Globetrotting with World Coins

W orld coins offer tremendous collecting opportunities for numismatists at all levels. If you're a beginning collector, you have literally hundreds of countries and thousands of different coin designs from which to choose. If you're a collector of average means, you can find lots of great values in world coins, including coins for as little as ten cents each and $100 rarities that would cost thousands of dollars if they were U.S. coins. Advanced collectors appreciate the many research opportunities that exist in the coinages of other countries, where collectors have not always taken the time to classify, evaluate, or publish information about their coins.

World coins can take you beyond your borders into foreign lands and different cultures that you may not otherwise experience. To collect world coins is to understand new languages, appreciate other cultures, and "visit" other countries that you now know only by name.

Giving a Few Hints to Beginners

You can build a meaningful collection of world coins in many ways. This section shares a few of the more popular methods of collecting them.

Collecting by country

There's a whole world out there! So where do you start? The world is full of countries from A (Albania) to Z (Zambia) and everything in between. The face of world numismatics changes constantly as old countries fade into obscurity or break up and new countries and governments take their place.

Many collectors attempt to obtain one coin from as many different countries as possible. This collection includes coins from countries that no longer exist, countries that have just formed, others that have been around for awhile but have undergone name changes, breakaway republics, and much more. Other collectors try to obtain as many different coins from the same country as possible, but this can be a tough challenge if you choose a country that has issued coins over several centuries.

Collecting by denomination

The United States uses Cents and Dollars, but as you travel around the world, you run into odd and interesting coins like Groschens, Lire, Dreilings, Centavos, Dongs, Ponds, Marks, Schillings (see Figure 13-1), Petermengers, Qirsh, Rupees, and so on. The number of different denominations used around the world is surprisingly large, and the resulting collection is a lot of fun to create and display.

Figure 13-1:
The 5
Shilling of
Austria.

Collecting Crowns

In the context of numismatics, Crowns are not the golden hats worn by kings or the diamond tiaras worn by queens, but the large, Silver Dollar-sized coins issued by many countries around the world. Most European Crowns are known as Thalers (pronounced *tall*-ers with a hard *t*), which are the forerunners of U.S. Dollars (notice how the two words sound almost the same?) Virtually all of the Crowns prior to 1965 are made of silver. However, in recent years, most countries discontinued the use of silver and began making Crowns out of a silver-colored mix of copper and nickel. A high percentage of Crowns were made to commemorate special events or people, so a collection of these large, impressive coins can be filled with interesting and unique designs.

Collecting by date

Pick a date and try to collect coins minted in that year from as many different countries as possible. You may choose the year of your birth or some other year with personal or historic significance. You may find that the year you choose has special significance in another country, as well, but probably for a different reason.

You can also focus on a particular century and try to obtain as many different coins minted in that century from as many different countries as possible. Not surprisingly, collectors focus a lot of attention on modern coins and tend to overlook older ones, where lots of good values hide. You can find some really good values in coins from the 17th and 18th centuries. For example, you can buy old Thalers from the 1600s for under $200, while many of the lower-denomination coins from the same period can be had for $20 or less.

Collecting topically

Topical collecting means forming a collection of coins with similar themes or topics. Popular topics include animals, presidents, plants, trains, Olympics, the FAO (Food and Agriculture Organization of the United Nations), kings, queens, airplanes, bees, and many others. Topical collections are limited only by your imagination.

Recognizing the Hot and Cold Countries

Collecting tastes for world coins run hot and cold depending on factors such as the strength of the home country's *collecting base* (the number of collectors within a country and how active they are), currency exchange rates, import/export restrictions, and the types of coins issued by the country. The following is my take on some of the most visible (although not necessarily the most popular) countries:

- ✔ **Africa:** Yes, Africa is a continent and not a country, but none of the African countries stands out as having a particularly strong collecting base. Nevertheless, the coins of Egypt, Ethiopia, and South Africa get honorable mentions.

- ✔ **Australia:** Because of the British affiliation, Australian coins started out with lots of fans back in England and have now developed a following of their own "down under." As Australia's economy and population grow, expect to see even greater collecting activity in this country's coins.

- ✔ **Canada:** Collectors love coins from this country. Canadian coins from the 19th century are rare and valuable in high grades (see Chapter 9). In recent years, Canada has minted a lot of interesting commemorative coins that have created thousands of new collectors.

- ✔ **China:** A huge population, a growing economy, and an emerging middle class all point to a powerhouse market as the Chinese become increasingly aware of and interested in their numismatic history.

- ✔ **France:** French coins are slow and steady. You won't see any big swings up or down in France's low-key coin market.

- ✔ **Germany:** Blistering hot for over a decade, German coins have cooled down in recent years. Nevertheless, this country is a perennial favorite in the U.S., and a strong market for German coins exists in Germany, too.

- ✔ **Great Britain:** England has been making coins for so many centuries that you have lots of great pieces from which to choose. Great Britain is famous for its well-made coins.

- ✔ **Japan:** Prices for Japanese coins have followed their economy from dizzying heights to anemic levels. The Japanese love their coins, so look for prices to rise sharply if Japan can get its economy back on track.

- ✔ **Mexico:** As a colonial Spanish power, Mexico was a prolific producer of silver coins, the most important of which were the *Eight Reales* or *Pieces of Eight,* the coins commonly found on shipwrecks. Any coins struck prior to 1900 are in great demand — after 1900, the use of silver drops and interest wanes.

- ✔ **Netherlands:** Catalog values remain high but coins from this country are usually hard to resell.

- ✔ **Russia:** Russian coins are hot, hot, hot — especially for older coins from the 18th and 19th centuries. If the Russian people ever get their hands on extra spending money, watch Russian coin prices explode!

- ✔ **Spain:** Demand for coins later than 1900 is weak, but the demand for older Spanish coins is huge, especially for coins from the Spanish colonies in the Americas (Mexico, Bolivia, Peru, and so on).

- ✔ **Switzerland:** Like Germany, the weakening of the Swiss Franc relative to the U.S. Dollar resulted in lower prices in recent years, which is good news if you've been waiting to pick up some bargains from this country.

Collecting tastes are fickle. Coins from your favorite country may be hot today and cold tomorrow. Be ready to adjust your collecting strategies: If prices for coins from your favorite country jump up, shift your attention to a country that's out of favor. If prices begin to drop, buy while the getting's good.

TIP

Teaching your kids history and geography

I've discovered more about history and geography from coins than I ever did in my high school and college courses. There's something about picking up a coin from a foreign country and reading the wording on both sides to figure out where the coin came from and when. Some coins are easy to decipher. For example, Australian coins bear the word "Australia," South African coins say "South Africa," and Argentinian coins say "Argentina." From there, you need only a basic knowledge of foreign languages to know that coins with the word *Espana* come from Spain, and coins with the word *Française* come from France. At a more advanced level, you soon discover that coins from Germany bear the words *Deutsches Reich* or *Bundesrepublik Deutschland*. However, the going gets a bit tougher when you encounter coins from *Norges* (Norway), *Oesterreich* (Austria), and *Sri Lanka* (Ceylon). And if you start collecting Islamic coins (shown in the following figure) and Oriental coins, the alphabets are unique and even the dating on the coins must be converted into something you understand.

The funny thing about working with world coins is that you don't even know that you're learning about history and geography while you identify the coins, which is why collecting world coins is such a great hobby for kids. Coins attract a natural curiosity that is hard to produce any other way. The limited information displayed on coins leads to new areas of inquiry such as, "Who is the person pictured on this coin?" or, "What does this symbol mean?" or, "Why was this coin struck?" The answer to one question leads to another, and soon you know a lot more about world history, people, events, and geography than you ever thought possible. Plus, you've enjoyed the educational process.

I love giving young collectors a handful of inexpensive world coins. It's amazing how excited they get as they discover coins from distant lands and times past. They always come back for more.

Knowing that Changing Economies Equals Great Values

The low cost of collecting world coins makes it the perfect hobby for parents and children to share. In particular, young collectors love digging through boxes of loose world coins in dealers' shops and at coin shows. For a few bucks, your child ends up with a fistful of coins and hours of priceless fun identifying and evaluating them.

Collectors familiar with the dizzying prices for U.S. coins are amazed at the wonderful values found in world coins: With world coins, you receive better quality, higher rarity, and greater variety.

World coin values are tied closely to currency exchange rates, impacting the two-way traffic that exists between the currencies of different nations. When the U.S. Dollar is strong, world coins flow into the United States; when the Dollar weakens, the flow of the traffic reverses. Although world markets adjust their prices to compensate for changes in the value of their currency, you always encounter short periods of time when a sharp collector can find some great bargains.

Some world coins are worth half of the values listed in price guides (see Chapter 5); others are worth the full amount; still others are worth much more than published price listings. World coin prices depend a lot on timing, availability, and demand. For example, if you have a coin that some collector has been searching for, expect to ask for (and receive) full catalog value. However, if no one wants to buy the coin, expect to discount it heavily or own it for a long time. Get a feel for current pricing by discussing with world coin dealers the relative strength of various countries, following the pricing on actual coins, and checking auction selling prices.

Understanding that Grading Standards Are Not All the Same

U.S. numismatists work with a highly developed grading system (described in Chapter 9) that classifies minute differences between grades. While attempts have been made to impose these standards on the rest of the world's coins, most countries are perfectly happy with their own, simpler grading standards.

Obsession with quality is okay — to a point

For the most part, collectors of world coins are not as obsessed with quality as are U.S. collectors. For example, collectors in Germany are more interested in obtaining as many different coins as possible, and whether the coin is circulated or Uncirculated isn't very important. This means that collectors aren't willing to pay much of a premium (if any) to obtain an Uncirculated coin when they're just as happy with a nice, high-grade circulated coin.

The reason I bring this up is because there is great danger in assuming that foreign markets support the huge premiums that Americans pay for the best quality coins. Here's an example: In 1989, the U.S. market hit a cyclical peak. Coin prices were extremely high, dealers were making lots of money, and the economy was good. *Slabbing* (coin grading and certification) of U.S. coins was only a few years old, while the slabbing of world coins was brand-new. Collectors and dealers from the United States began paying huge premiums for high-grade world coins, partly because money was loose and partly because of perceived rarity. Gem coins (MS-65 or Proof-65) began selling above the values published in catalogs; anything better (MS-66 or Proof-66 and up) brought multiples of the catalog value. Unfortunately, the only ones paying the premiums were U.S. dealers and collectors — buyers in foreign countries thought the Americans were nuts. And so, it seems, they were right, because as prices for U.S. coins fell, so did the premiums being paid for world coins. (See Chapter 9 for definitions of Gem Uncirculated coins and other grading terminology.)

Extremely Fine is not Extremely Fine is not Extremely Fine

Grading systems differ throughout the world. For example, an Extremely Fine coin under the U.S. coin-grading system shows only light wear on the high points and you can generally expect to see some luster on the coin (see Chapter 9). The equivalent under the European grading system is *Vorzuglich* (sometimes abbreviated as *vz*). However, to qualify as Vorzuglich, a coin must look more like the U.S. version of About Uncirculated, meaning that the luster should be full and strong, and the highest points of the coin should show only traces of wear — a much stricter standard. The problem comes when you try to translate the grades of one system into prices in another, and vice versa.

To illustrate, many of the German States coins listed in the *Standard Catalog of World Coins* (Krause-Mishler) show big jumps in price as you move from Very Fine to Extremely Fine, then a smaller jump in price between Extremely

Fine and Uncirculated. A coin may be listed at $30 in Very Fine, $600 in Extremely Fine, and $850 in Uncirculated condition. If you go to one of the German price guides, you may find the same coin listed at the equivalent price of $600 in Vorzuglich, so it would appear that the prices match for the Extremely Fine and Vorzuglich grades. Therefore, if you see the coin being offered at a U.S. coin show for $450 in Extremely Fine, it must be a good deal, right? Not necessarily so, and here's why: Given a choice between a $30 and a $600 example of the same coin, the average collector both in the United States and elsewhere will settle for the $30 example. At the $600 level, the U.S. collector says, "I'd rather spend $250 more and get a nice Uncirculated example" and the German collector says, "For $600, I want a much nicer coin than the one you're offering." Therefore, the $600 Extremely Fine coin becomes trapped in a numismatic limbo, shunned on one side because of price and shunned on the other because of quality.

Before buying world coins, learn how they are priced and graded in their country of origin. Beware of imposing U.S. grading standards and values on another country's coins because you may find yourself paying unnecessary premiums for coins that are actually quite common.

Chapter 14

Exploring the Wild Side with Rare, Expensive, and Esoteric Coins

- -

- -

*L*ike people, coin collecting can be plain and simple or wild and crazy. "Plain and simple" would mean working on completing your collection of Lincoln Head Pennies in Extremely Fine condition (see Chapter 9 for an explanation of coin grading). Such coins are readily available at most coin stores, they're affordable, and if you miss the chance to buy one, you can probably find it somewhere else. "Wild and crazy" would be trying to obtain the finest Lincoln Head Pennies known. These are the kinds of coins that require a considerable effort to find and a considerable income to afford. You have to know what you're doing and be ready to pounce when the right coin comes along — if you miss it, years may go by before you have the chance to buy another.

In this chapter, I describe some areas that require active participation and a high level of commitment in terms of time or money — or both. In return, you'll be rewarded with some of the most interesting, unusual, and valuable coins, not to mention the thrill you'll receive from hunting them down and capturing them.

So if you're looking for a little more excitement in your collecting career, check out some of these wild areas!

Looking for the Best of the Best

Quality is an important goal in numismatics. Coin dealers preach incessantly that you should buy the best quality you can afford. (Of course, higher quality equals higher price, so such advice may work to the coin dealers' advantage.) To some people, quality is important; to others, quality is everything.

Collecting Finest Known coins

Some people collect only the finest example known of particular coins (called *Finest Known* coins), paying some very impressive premiums for that privilege. For example, a coin worth $50 in Choice Uncirculated condition could be worth $5,000 (or even $50,000) in Superb Uncirculated condition.

Finest Known does not always mean fine quality, however. Many of the earliest U.S. coins are not available in Uncirculated condition, and the finest example known may rate a grade of only Extremely Fine or worse. Only a few coins, most of them modern, are known in the top grade of 70 on the Sheldon Grading Scale.

The Sheldon Grading Scale rates the condition of coins using a scale from 1 to 70, with 1 being the worst condition and 70 being the best. For the most part, 70 is a theoretical grade representing absolute perfection. See Chapter 9 for the lowdown on coin grades.

Even coins of the same denomination from the same year may have wildly different Finest Known examples. For example, the finest 1865 $10 Gold pieces graded by the Professional Coin Grading Service (PCGS) are two examples at the MS-63 (Choice Uncirculated) level. By the same token, the finest PCGS graded 1865-S $10 Gold piece is a single AU-53 (About Uncirculated). This is the opposite of what collectors expect to find, because more than four times as many $10s were minted at San Francisco as Philadelphia in 1865. What it really means is that fewer of the 1865-S $10 Gold pieces were saved because most of the major collectors at the time lived in the eastern United States, and only a few of them were concerned with collecting coins with different *mintmarks* (the tiny letters on coins that tell where a coin was made).

Therefore, a collection of Finest Knowns may contain coins ranging from Extremely Fine (circulated) all the way to Superb Uncirculated. While the appearance and quality of the coins in such a set won't be uniform, you can bet that any numismatist worth his or her salt would drool over it!

Collecting only Finest Known coins carries one huge risk — that a better coin may come along tomorrow. Imagine paying $69,000 for a 1953-S Half Dollar graded PCGS MS-66 with Full Bell Lines, as someone did in January 2001. (*Full Bell Lines* refers to the design lines in the Liberty Bell that appear only on the very sharpest Franklin Half Dollars minted from 1948 to 1963 — poorly made examples have no, or only partial, bell lines.) What will happen to that person's investment if an MS-67 Full Bell Lines, or even another MS-66 Full Bell Lines, shows up tomorrow? Think it can't happen? Keep in mind that there was a time when no MS-66 Full Bell Lines examples had yet been graded. And there are still a lot of ungraded 1953-S Half Dollars out there!

Collecting Finest Known world coins (discussed in Chapter 13) can be particularly treacherous because far fewer world coins have been submitted to grading services and, as far as I have seen, very little Condition Census research (discussed in the following section) exists for world coins.

Checking Condition Census

For many years, Large Cent collectors have maintained a listing of exceptional examples of different die varieties. (I explain these in the "Collecting by Die Variety — the Spice of Life" section, later in this chapter.) Known as the *Condition Census,* this listing gives collectors a good idea of what conditions are available for each variety and how their coins stack up against the best-known examples. If you come across a particular variety in Extremely Fine condition, you can check the Condition Census listing to see whether your coin is important. Generally, if you own a coin that's listed in the Condition Census, or if you discover a new example that warrants inclusion, you have a special and valuable coin.

Along those lines, PCGS developed the PCGS Set Registry on its Web site at www.pcgs.com. The *Set Registry* lists the finest condition coin sets in existence today and the finest condition sets of all time. Not surprisingly, the Set Registry contains only coins that have been graded by PCGS or evaluated by one of their experts. The information contained in the Set Registry lets you know how your collection stacks up against those around the world. Your collection need not be complete to merit inclusion in the Set Registry, but if you're working on a popular set, such as Mercury Head Dimes (see Chapter 17), you'll have to have as complete a set as possible in the finest grades, or your collection will be way at the bottom of the list.

Most of the major grading services publish reports showing all the coins they've graded and the condition of each coin. Use these reports just as you would a Condition Census to see whether your coin is no big deal, special, or even Finest Known.

When using the condition reports published by grading services, be aware that they do not include coins from other services that may be significantly better. Be aware that the very same coin can earn different grades at different services. Beware of common coins minted since 1964 — they will show only a few listings and may appear to be rare simply because they are so inexpensive that very few are sent in to be graded.

Recognizing Odd and Curious Money

Wait until you see the things people around the world have used for money! I mention a few of them in Chapter 1, including the dried carcasses of the Bird of Paradise and the heavy stone disks used by the Yap Islanders.

If you really want to get wild, try your hand at building a collection of odd and curious money from around the world. The following are a few items to look for:

- Bricks of tea used as money by the Chinese
- Billion Mark emergency coins used by the Germans following World War I (see Figure 14-1)
- Porcelain disks from Siam
- Clay tablets with cuneiform inscriptions used by the Babylonians
- Heavy copper plate money used by the Swedes
- Thin, oval plates of gold, called *oban,* from Japan

Figure 14-1:
1923 Billion
Mark Coin
from
Westphalia.

Investigating Tokens, Medals, and Miscellaneous Coins

Tokens and *medals* are privately-made, coin-shaped pieces of metal that may or may not have a stated value. This section offers you some areas to investigate.

Hard Times tokens

In the 1830s, President Andrew Jackson refused to recharter the Bank of the United States, helping to plunge the United States into a depression. Small change disappeared from circulation, and merchants had great difficulty conducting business without coins. A number of privately issued copper pieces, called *Hard Times tokens* (see Figure 14-2), appeared in response to the need for small change. Usually the size of a United States Large Cent (see Chapter 16), these tokens feature a variety of contemporary political slogans, a few of which lambasted President Jackson. Many of the tokens are quite rare, but enough of them are affordable that you can assemble a nice collection.

Figure 14-2:
1837 Hard Times token.

Good For tokens

Good For tokens (see Figure 14-3) are tokens that give the bearer some sort of premium, such as, "Good for One Ride" on a carousel or "Good For Ten Cents" against a purchase in a dry goods store. Merchants created Good For tokens to advertise their businesses and get buyers into their establishments.

Because so many different Good For tokens have been made over the years, collectors have come up with innovative ways to collect them:

- ✔ **By city:** Some collectors try to obtain Good For tokens from as many different cities as possible.

- ✔ **By state:** Some collectors try to obtain Good For tokens from as many different states as possible.

- ✔ **By product:** Some collectors specialize in tokens that offer a certain product, such as cigars or boots.

Figure 14-3:
Good For
token.

- ✔ **By merchant:** Some collectors try to obtain as Good For tokens from as many different merchants as possible.

- ✔ **By denomination:** Some collectors try to obtain as many different denominations as possible, such as "Good For One Dollar" and "Good For 10 Cents."

Civil War tokens

During the Civil War, people began hoarding coins just in case fighting forced them to flee their homes with all their worldly possessions. As a result, merchants had difficulty conducting business, just as they did during the Hard Times of the late 1830s. Private companies worked to satisfy the need, this time by issuing small coins the size of today's One Cent pieces (see Chapter 16). You see many political themes on Civil War tokens, mostly patriotic ones aimed at supporting the Union cause. But you also see a lot of tokens whose purpose was not only to supply loose change but also to advertise the merchant's business at the same time (see Figure 14-4).

Civil War tokens appear in two major categories:

- ✔ **Patriotics:** Tokens with purely patriotic or political themes and no references to a business or merchant

- ✔ **Store Cards:** Tokens with at least one side that refers to a business or merchant

As you may have guessed, a lot of designs from the Patriotics were also used on Store Cards.

Most Civil War tokens were made of copper, although a number of off-metal pieces were made for collectors out of silver, brass, nickel, copper-nickel, lead, and other metals and alloys.

Figure 14-4:
Civil War
token.

Check out this fascinating series — collecting Civil War tokens is affordable, educational, and fun.

Washington medals

George Washington was not only the father of the United States, but a popular subject for coins, medals, and tokens (see Figure 14-5). In Chapter 15, I discuss the U.S. colonial coins that bear his image; in this section, I introduce you to some of his medals and tokens.

Figure 14-5:
George
Washington,
a popular
subject on
tokens and
medals.

Special medals were made to honor Washington at his Presidential Inauguration, at his death, at the centennial (100th year) of his birthday in 1832, at the U.S. centennial celebration in 1876, at the bicentennial (200th year) of his birth in 1932, and for just about any other occasion you can think of. A collector can find literally hundreds of Washington medals, tokens, and coins. Most are affordable, some are very rare and valuable, and all are interesting. A collection of Washington medals makes a fascinating display, and you won't have to explain to your non-numismatist friends who that fellow is on the coin!

Collecting by Die Variety — the Spice of Life

Here's the simplified explanation of a die variety: A *die* is a cylindrical piece of steel with a design on one end. An *engraver* cuts a design into the steel. Stamping a blank piece of metal with the die creates a raised design on the blank. To make a coin, you need two dies — one for the front and one for the back of the coin. Any combination of front and back dies is known as a *die pair* or a *die combination*.

Sometimes, an engraver makes more than one front die (say, Die 1 and Die 2) and more than one back die (say, Die A and Die B). To make a coin, a press operator uses one of the front dies and one of the back dies, places them into a coining press, and begins stamping coins. During one day, the press operator may choose Die 1 with Die A, but the next day, it may be Die 1 with Die B, and so on. The more dies the engraver makes, the higher the number of possible combinations the press operator has.

In the early days of the U.S. Mint, engravers cut the designs into the dies by hand, meaning that each die had unique characteristics that separated it from all the others. Through careful study, collectors have identified most of the die pairs used to strike coins in the 1800s, especially in the early part of the century. Each unique die pair is known as a *die variety*. Collectors who seek to acquire a coin from each different die variety are known as *variety collectors*.

Why the big fuss over variety collecting? Some varieties are extremely rare and valuable. Just a small difference between two die varieties can translate into a huge difference in price.

The following are some areas in which variety collecting has become particularly strong. For information on the various clubs listed, flip to the Cheat Sheet at the front of this book.

- **Colonial coins:** Rabid variety collectors can be found searching just about every colonial series (see Chapter 15), but the ones who really froth at the mouth focus on the New Jersey Coppers, Connecticut Coppers, and Vermont Coppers. Less intense collectors work with Massachusetts Half Cents and Cents, Nova Constellation Coppers, Voce Populi Coppers, and other series. (If these names sound strange to you, flip to Chapter 15.) If you're interested in this area, check out the Colonial Coin Collectors Club.

- **Half Cents:** I used to collect Half Cents by die variety, and I look back on that part of my numismatic career as one of the most enjoyable of all. Half Cents were made from 1793 to 1857, and there are roughly 100 varieties (if you don't count the rare dates in the 1840s that were made only for collectors). Some of the best people in the world collect Half Cents and Large Cents. I encourage you to meet some of them! If you're interested in this area, check out the Early American Coppers Club.

- **Large Cents:** The community of collectors for Large Cents is even larger than that of Half Cent collectors. Large Cents present a greater challenge for you as a variety collector, as you can find literally hundreds of different varieties, some of them quite rare and valuable. If you're interested in this area, check out the Early American Coppers Club.

- **Half Dollars:** The name of their club says it all — these folks have gone nuts for Half Dollar varieties. If you're interested in this area, check out the Bust Half Nut Club.

- **Silver Dollars:** The high cost of early Silver Dollars requires deep pockets if you want to collect them by die variety, but if you have the money, go for it! Just watch out for that 1804 Silver Dollar, one of the world's most valuable coins (see Chapter 24)! If you're interested in this area, check out the John Reich Society.

- **Other series:** Collectors have scrutinized just about every U.S. series for die varieties, and each series has its proponents. The key to success and happiness is finding a series that you enjoy. You may want to settle into a series that has been fully explored or venture into uncharted waters, do the research, and discover the next new variety on your own.

Many more opportunities exist for the collector looking for a little excitement. If nothing else, I hope I've encouraged you in this chapter to explore new and different ways of collecting. Let your collection mirror who you are, whether you're mild or wild!

Part IV
Focusing on U.S. Coins

The 5th Wave   By Rich Tennant

"That's right! A 1943 bronze Cent in a pair of penny loafers. Denise is checking it out now."

In this part . . .

In this part, I take you on a trip through the fascinating series of U.S. coins, beginning with colonial coins, tokens, and medals, to the copper and nickel coins, to valuable silver and gold coins, through special commemorative coins, and finally to rare and unusual coins, like patterns, pioneer gold, Confederate coins, and much more.

The first official coins of the United States appeared over 200 years ago. The designs on the coins evolved from images of Liberty and a simple eagle to patriotic representations of some of America's most famous and revered people. On U.S. coins today, you see Abraham Lincoln, Thomas Jefferson, Franklin Roosevelt, George Washington, John Kennedy, and Sacagawea. (Hey, she wasn't a President.) Tomorrow's coins will surely be completely different, especially as the United States continues to grow and change.

Chapter 15

Colonial Coins:
America's Ancients

*I*n a sense, colonial coins are the U.S. version of ancient coins. Some colonial coins, like the Massachusetts Silver coins, predate the first official U.S. coins by more than a hundred years.

To the new collector, U.S. colonial coins are every bit as intriguing and mysterious as old Roman and Greek coins. Colonial coins, like wine, are an acquired taste: It takes a while to learn and appreciate them. Many collectors view the year 1792 (the year the first U.S. Mint was established) as a sort of boundary over which they will not cross. However, after you cross that line and get a taste of U.S. colonial coins, your collecting days may never be the same.

Colonial coins are rich in history and stories. Holding a colonial coin, you imagine the events and people of long ago. How many different people held this coin? Who were they? Anybody famous? What battles, if any, has this coin endured? Where has this coin been all these years?

In this chapter, I introduce you to U.S. colonial coins with the hope of arousing your curiosity just enough to induce you to take a longer look.

Recognizing a Colonial Coin

Prior to the adoption of the U.S. Constitution in 1789, America was a loosely knit conglomeration of territories and colonies owned by England and a number of other countries. Despite their cultural differences, the colonists had one thing in common — they needed money, especially coins, to conduct their daily business. To satisfy this need, they relied on a unique mix of coins of different origins, metals, values, and quality.

There is no hard and fast definition of what represents a colonial coin. Tradition can be just as important as fact in deciding which coins qualify. Nevertheless, over the years, colonial coins have been defined as those that fall into one or more of several categories:

✔ Foreign coins used in the U.S. colonies

✔ Coins officially sanctioned by a colony

✔ Privately issued and other miscellaneous coins and tokens

✔ Quasi-official national issues

✔ Washingtoniana

Locating Foreign Coins Used in the American Colonies

Many countries controlled land in the colonies. Because they viewed their possessions as investments and sources of needed goods, foreign countries had a vested interested in making the colonies work. In keeping with that philosophy, they often made coins specifically for use by the colonists.

French coins

The French owned a lot of land in the colonies, both within what became the United States, including the Louisiana Territory, and in what was to become Canada. Naturally, as French people emigrated to America, they brought coins with them. Other coins were made specifically for use in the French colonies. Being realists, the colonists welcomed any kind of money, including any of France's silver and copper coins, up to the mid-1700s.

Experts still don't agree on which French coins may or may not have been used in the colonies. My advice — tell the experts to hoist themselves on their own petard and collect what you want to!

Irish coins

A number of Irish coins made their way to America, either deliberately or because no one else wanted them.

The earliest Irish coins used in America were the copper St. Patrick Farthings and Halfpennies of the late 1600s (see Figure 15-1). The front of both coins shows King David playing a harp beneath a crown. The back of the Farthing shows St. Patrick driving the snakes out of Ireland. The back of the Halfpenny shows a crowd of people surrounding St. Patrick.

Figure 15-1:
St. Patrick
Farthing.

Here's a neat anecdote: To make the crown look golden, a small plug of brass was added to the coins before they were struck.

In 1722, a fellow named William Wood began making copper Farthings and Halfpennies for Ireland. Unfortunately, the Irish rejected the coins because they were too light, so guess who ended up with them? Yep, you guessed it — the colonies. Today, these coins are known as *Wood's Hibernia Farthings* and *Halfpennies.*

British coins

Considering how important the colonies were as a trading partner, the British supplied precious few coins, preferring instead to trade tea for rum, sugar, cotton, and tobacco. Nevertheless, many British coins and tokens made their way to America, but they were usually lightweight or fake coppers. In the 1790s, several types of tokens were made privately for use by colonial merchants or for sale to collectors. In the first category, the Talbot, Allum & Lee (TAL) tokens stand out (see Figure 15-2). Originally made for the New York merchants of the same name, many of the TAL tokens were later cut down in size and used as blanks to make U.S. Half Cents.

Figure 15-2:
The Talbot,
Allum & Lee
token.

Spanish coins

In the 1700s, Spain had one advantage over all the other countries that controlled territories in North America — it owned Mexico. The vast silver mines of Mexico provided Spain with plenty of the whitish metal, most of which was turned into coins before being shipped to the coffers in Europe. Many of the Spanish coins made their way to the colonies, where they were highly regarded and accepted by just about everyone. The most popular coin was the *Eight Reales* or *Piece of Eight* (see Figure 15-3), a large silver coin that served as the standard for U.S. Dollar coins.

Figure 15-3:
Spanish
Piece of
Eight.

London Elephant tokens

In the late 1600s, several interesting Elephant tokens were created (see Figure 15-4). Because some of them refer to Carolina, they have all become a popular part of the colonial series. These are the only colonial coins that display pachyderms. (Sounds like a disease, doesn't it?)

Figure 15-4:
The
Elephant
token.

Appreciating How Colonies and States Expressed Themselves

Generally, the colonies were under tight control by their mother countries. Except in rare instances, they could not issue their own coins. This section covers some exceptions.

Massachusetts

Specially authorized individuals made copper Half Cents and Large Cents for the state of Massachusetts in 1787 and 1788 (see Figure 15-5). The front of the coins feature a Native American holding a long bow and a spear. The backs of the coins feature an eagle with outstretched wings and a shield on its chest.

Figure 15-5:
The Mass-
achusetts
Half Cent.

New Jersey

New Jersey authorized private contractors to produce copper coins (known as *New Jersey Coppers*) for use in the state. Dated 1786, 1787, and 1788, these interesting coins feature a horse and plow on the front and a shield on the back. A number of varieties exist, most with the horse's head facing right, but a few with the head facing left. Some have a small running fox on the back, while others show the horse's head shaped like that of a camel!

Practice trying to distinguish the different New Jersey die varieties (see Chapter 14). Rare ones can easily be worth from $5,000–$50,000!

Figure 15-6:
New Jersey
Copper.

Connecticut

Connecticut farmed out its coining contract in 1785, beating New Jersey by a year. The contract lasted through 1788, during which time thousands of coins, known as *Connecticut Coppers* (see Figure 15-7), were produced representing many different varieties. In this series, you can find varieties with such quaint names as *African Head, Muttonhead, Laughing Head, Horned Bust,* and others. In recent years, prices have risen dramatically for rare varieties and even for common varieties in Very Fine or better condition. (See Chapter 9 for an explanation of coin grading.)

Figure 15-7:
Connecticut
Copper.

Vermont

Beginning in 1785, Vermont produced some of the most eagerly sought-after collector coins. Known as *Vermont Coppers,* the first issues show the sun peeking over the Green Mountains, with a plow in the field beneath. The back of the coin bears the legend "Quarta Decima Stella" (meaning "fourteenth star" and referring to Vermont being the fourteenth colony and state). Later coins in this series have busts that face either left or right. Although 40 varieties were produced, many of them are quite rare and valuable.

New York

Unlike New Jersey, Connecticut, and Vermont, the state of New York never awarded a coinage contract. Nevertheless, several coins were made by private mints, and individual coins bear images that are near and dear to New York. Chief among these are the *Nova Eborac Coppers* and the several varieties that feature the Arms of New York on one side (see Figure 15-9). Most New York coins are rare — only the Nova Eborac copper coins were made in quantity.

Virginia

In 1773, King George III of Britain authorized the coinage of copper coins for Virginia. Known as *Virginia Coppers*, these royal coins featured a bust of George on one side and his coat of arms on the other (see Figure 15-10). The coins were struck in England and then sent to Virginia for use by the colonists. How did the people of Virginia repay their good king? By joining with the other colonies and declaring their independence just three short years later.

Figure 15-10:
Virginia
Copper.

Collecting Privately Issued Coins, Tokens, and Medals

A pocketful of coins in early times may have included some interesting tokens and medals made by enterprising individuals who sought (among other things) to promote their businesses, tinker with coin-making, or get rid of copper from their mines.

Mott Token

The Mott Company of New York produced a token dated 1789 that features a tall, pendulum-driven clock on one side and an eagle on the other (see Figure 15-11). The Mott Token had no stated value and was used to promote the watch-making business in the same way that we use business cards today.

Figure 15-11:
The Mott
Token.

Brasher Doubloon

In 1787, Ephraim Brasher, a New York jeweler and goldsmith, created one of the rarest and most enduring of all colonial coins — the *Brasher Doubloon*. Brasher's coin is significant because it is one of the few early colonial coins made out of gold. The weight of Brasher's coin came very close to that of the Spanish Gold Doubloon, hence the name. Brasher not only signed one of the dies used to strike his Doubloons, but he also punched each one with his hallmark "EB" stamp. Check out the list of the ten most valuable coins in Chapter 24 — the Brasher Doubloon used to be at the top but now merits only an honorable mention. However, no Brasher Doubloon has sold at auction since 1979 and I suspect that if one shows up today, it will rank right up there near the top of the list.

Higley Coppers

Dr. Sam Higley once owned a copper mine in Connecticut. Like any enterprising businessman, he sought out ways to convert his raw materials into a valuable product, so in 1737 he started making coins with the value of Three Pence. The front of the coins bore an image of a deer; the back of the coin showed three crowned hammers (see Figure 15-12). Later varieties dropped the stated value, relegating the Higley Copper coins to token status, but all are extremely rare today.

Because of their high value, many U.S. colonial coins, including the Higley Copper, were copied in subsequent years. Some copies were crudely made and easy to tell from the original; others were deceptive and will fool the unsuspecting collector.

Figure 15-12:
The 1737
Higley
Copper — a
later copy.

Distinguishing Quasi-Official Colonial Coins

As the insurgent colonies struggled to come together as one body, several attempts were made at a national coinage — one that would be universally accepted everywhere. One of the big problems with coins in the fledgling country was the discrepancy in the value of the same coin from colony to colony. Even as early as 1776, the year the colonies declared their independence, the goal was to create coins that would not only be accepted everywhere but that would also foster a new sense of nationalism and pride. After all, if the United States was going to be as cool a place as everyone thought it would be, Americans needed some cool coins of their own.

Continental Dollars

In 1776, the Continental Congress proposed a design for a new coin, roughly the size of the Silver Dollar later adopted in 1794. The 1776 Continental Dollar bears inscriptions and design elements attributed to Benjamin Franklin (see Figure 15-13). The word "Fugio" on the front of the coin is short for *time flies,* a reference to the sundial. Continental Dollars are known to exist in pewter, brass, and silver, and all are rare. This coin never seemed to have gotten past the testing phase, which is a shame, because this coin could easily have become the most popular of all colonial coins.

Figure 15-13:
1776
Continental
Dollar.

Fugio Cents

In 1787, Congress resurrected the idea of a national coinage, this time in a less ambitious, lowly copper coin. Congress reached back and borrowed heavily from the designs on the Continental Dollar. (Look at Figure 15-14 — they look awfully close when you put them side-by-side, don't they?) Congress hired this job out to James Jarvis, who embezzled much of the copper provided to him by the government. Nevertheless, enough Fugio Cents were made and enough have survived to make them an affordable colonial type. In 1856, a small keg containing thousands of Uncirculated examples was found at the Bank of New York. These account for most of the Fugio Cents collected today. Were it not for this hoard, an Uncirculated Fugio Cent would be a great treasure!

Figure 15-14:
1787 Fugio
Cent.

Nova Constellatio Coppers

In 1783, the Treaty of Paris ended the Revolutionary War, and the newly formed states were ready for their own coins, but many didn't have the facilities to make them, nor were facilities set up for a national coinage. So a man named Gouverneur Morris took some designs to Europe and had coins struck there. These are known as the *Nova Constellatio Copper* coins or *Novas* (see Figure 15-15).

Figure 15-15:
Nova Constellatio Coppers.

The front of the Novas show the letters "U.S." inside of a wreath, with the words "Libertas et Justitia" (Latin for "Liberty and Justice") around the outer edge. The back of the coin featured an all-seeing eye surrounded by rays, stars, and the words "Nova Constellatio" (meaning "New Constellation," which referred to the emerging U.S. nation).

Novas are important because of their intent. Despite the fact that they were made overseas, they actually represent one of the earliest attempts at a truly national U.S. coin.

Washingtoniana — America Goes Ape for Its First President

Wars make men famous, and the most famous person to come out of the Revolutionary War was George Washington. The man was a legend in his own time, worshipped by a nation he helped set free. Many Americans wanted to make George the American their new King, even though they had just kicked out George the Brit! Washington would have nothing of the sort, and he opposed having his portrait placed on coins. But that did not stop the U.S.

people, who loved him dearly, from creating all sorts of tokens, coins, and medals to commemorate their new hero and first president. Many of these pieces have become part of the colonial series. This section discusses some of the more popular ones.

Unity States Cent

The Unity States Cent got its name from the misspelling of "United" on the back of the coin (see Figure 15-16). The misspelling was probably deliberate to keep the minters from getting in trouble for counterfeiting U.S. coins. Although dated 1783, this coin was probably made later, because the design on the back of the coin is nearly identical to the backs of Large Cents produced from 1796 to 1807.

Figure 15-16:
Unity States
Cent.

1791 Washington Large Eagle Cent

When the United States began debating whether to open its own mint or hire someone else to make the coins, word got around quickly. In 1791, a British token maker created a Large Cent with the head of Washington on one side and a large eagle with a shield on its breast on the other (see Figure 15-17).

Figure 15-17:
The 1791
Washington
Large Eagle
Cent.

The token maker sent a quantity of these coins to the United States, where they were reviewed by the decision-makers, one of whom was George Washington. George pooh-poohed the coin for two reasons:

- He hated the idea of his picture on a coin because he refused to be treated like a King.

- He thought America should make its own coins.

The final decision: The United States decided to open a mint and make its own coins with a picture of a lady called Liberty instead of the head of a President.

1793 Ship Halfpenny

The British token manufacturer who made the 1791 Washington Large Eagle Cent didn't cry too much after losing the contract to make coins for America — he simply struck more tokens and sold them to collectors. The 1793 Ship Halfpenny (see Figure 15-18) was one such piece. The front of the coin is exactly like that on the 1791 Washington Large Eagle Cent except that it lacks a date. The back of the coin features a tall-masted sailing ship, a 1793 date, and a Halfpenny value. Even though this was a strictly British concoction, the Washington connection was a powerful draw, and the coin has made its way into listings of U.S. colonial coins.

Figure 15-18:
The 1793
Ship
Halfpenny.

1795 Grate Halfpenny

The 1795 Grate Halfpenny (see Figure 15-19) was another British token that worked its way into colonial collections because of the Washington connection. This coin got its name from the fireplace grate that appears on the back of the coin. The front of the coin bears the legend "Washington Firm Friend To Peace & Humanity." Apparently, by 1795 the British had already forgotten the death and destruction Washington and his armies wreaked on the British during the Revolutionary War!

Figure 15-19:
The 1795
Grate
Halfpenny.

Liberty and Security Penny

In 1795, another British token manufacturer made a series of Halfpennies and Pennies with the words "Liberty And Security" on the back. One of them was a large, Penny-sized, hunk of copper with Washington's head on the front (see Figure 15-20).

Don't confuse the old British Penny with America's modern Cent. The British version was much, much larger and much, much heavier. The Liberty & Security Penny is an impressive coin, indeed.

Figure 15-20:
Liberty And
Security
Penny.

Chapter 16

Copper and Nickel Coins: Made for the Masses

● ●

In This Chapter

▶ Finding out about copper and nickel coins

▶ Collecting Cents and Nickels

● ●

*A*fter you become a nation, you have the right to make your own coins. That's exactly what the United States government started doing in 1793, after they figured out what was needed to start a Mint. So what were the first coins struck by the U.S. Mint? Were they dazzling pieces of gold or shiny Silver Dollars? Nope — the first coins were lowly hunks of copper — Half Cents and Large Cents.

When the U.S. Mint started operations, the coins in circulation included money from other nations and various states. For example, you could pay for a sack of flour with a mix of British coins, French coins, Spanish coins, copper pieces from New Jersey, or coins from Massachusetts, not to mention a bunch of counterfeit or underweight coins. Different merchants took coins in at different values. If you traveled from Vermont to Pennsylvania with a pocket full of Vermont Coppers, you may have discovered that your money wasn't quite so valuable after all or that the storeowner would accept your money at a discount. Can you imagine going into a store today and offering a $20 bill in payment, only to have the cashier say to you, "Sorry, we'll only accept this bill for $15!" But, that's exactly what was happening every day, all through the new nation known as the United States of America.

Under this system, the public got poorer, the merchants got richer, government officials felt the heat, and a mint was established to produce a uniform coinage. The goal was to crank out coins to replace those already in circulation and to provide some relief for the poor public.

Back in 1793, the average employee worked from sunrise to sunset, six days a week for a dollar a day. You read it right — one dollar per day. So, if you wonder why the U.S. Mint made a coin with a value as low as a Half Cent, now you know.

Understanding numismatic terminology

As you read through this chapter (and Chapters 17 and 18), you may notice the following terms. You will find more terms in this book's glossary.

- **Common dates:** The dates in a series that have high mintages and that are easy to obtain

- **Date set:** A collection of all of the different dates in which a particular coin was issued

- **Mintages:** The number made of a particular coin

- **Mintmark set:** A collection of coins that includes one from each of the different mints around the country that produced a particular coin

- **Overdate:** A coin that shows two dates, usually one on top of another, the second being a correction of the first

- **Proofs:** Special coins of exceptional quality that were made for sale to collectors and not for general circulation

- **Type set:** A set of each of the different design types of a particular denomination

- **Upgrade:** The act of improving the coin in your collection, or a coin that is better than another example of the same type

- **Varieties:** Refers to either a minor change in the design on a coin or to *die variety*— a unique combination of obverse and reverse dies

I call Half Cents and Large Cents the *people's coins,* because they were never meant to be valued like the silver and gold coins. Their purpose in life was to get down and dirty with the people's business. Other people's coins include the Small Cent, the Three-Cent Nickel, and Five-Cent pieces made of nickel. These are the coins that greased the early U.S. economy and helped working people conduct their business in a fair and efficient manner. They were just what capitalism needed to thrive.

Today, we take these low denomination coins for granted. Some people call for the abolishment of the One Cent coin, claiming that nobody uses it anymore and that most Pennies end up in change jars. I say, "Keep the Cent!" A lot of people today still value the Cent just as much as the people valued their Half Cents back in 1793.

In this chapter, I introduce you to major types of copper and nickel U.S. coins. To help you make collecting decisions, I include the following information:

- Costs of completing different types of coins in various grades

- Rarities within each type

- Dos and don'ts to help maximize your collecting pleasure

Getting the Hang of Half Cents

Most non-numismatists are surprised to learn that the United States once made a coin with a value of only one-half of One Cent. However, Half Cents represented significant value when they first appeared, and they helped the average person conduct day-to-day business. By 1857, a rise in the value of copper and increases in prices and wages contributed to making the Half Cent and Large Cent obsolete, so both were discontinued in that year.

Although Half Cents were minted from 1793 to 1857, the U.S. Mint had a lot of gaps between production. For example, no Half Cents were made from 1812 to 1824 or from 1837 to 1839. Half Cents were made of pure copper and are roughly the size of a modern-day Quarter Dollar (see Chapter 17).

Most Half Cents have relatively low mintages and several rarities exist in the series. Nevertheless, prices for the common dates remain quite reasonable, which draws lots of collectors to the great values.

Major types of U.S. Half Cents

Half Cents appear in five major types, which are discussed in this section.

Liberty Cap, Head Facing Left (1793 only)

When Congress first considered designs for its new coins, it wanted to honor George Washington by placing his face on the front of America's money. Washington objected, however, so the Congressmen settled for some representation of liberty and freedom. But how do you display a concept like liberty or an idea like freedom? Mint officials chose to portray Liberty as a young female with flowing locks of hair. She carried a cap on a pole — not just any ordinary cap, but the cap of a freedman, someone formerly in bondage but finally free. For the back of the coin, the designer created a simple wreath design (see Figure 16-1).

Liberty Cap, Head Facing Right (1794–1797)

Liberty made a literal about-face beginning in 1794, when she began facing right instead of left (see Figure 16-2). In 1795, the weight of the Half Cent was reduced, so you find both heavy coins with lettered edges and lighter coins with plain edges in this year. The edges on later dates were supposed to be plain but in 1797, you have a choice between edges that are plain or *gripped* (featuring weird, irregular markings on the outer rim).

Figure 16-1:
The 1793
Half Cent.

Figure 16-2:
1794-1797
Half Cent.

Draped Bust (1800–1808)

In 1800, Half Cents finally picked up the Draped Bust design (see Figure 16-3), which had already been in use on other coins since 1796. Liberty seems to have grown up into quite a sophisticated young lady, with a new hairdo and a beautiful new dress.

Figure 16-3:
The Draped
Bust Half
Cent.

Capped Bust or Classic Head (1809–1836)

On this design, Liberty seems to have grown up even more — into a stern-looking, middle-aged *hausfrau* (see Figure 16-4). One of the more interesting coins in this series is the 1811 restrike, made many years later outside the U.S. Mint by combining an old, scrapped front from 1811 with a back from 1802. Most reference books include a privately issued 1837 Half Cent token just to give collectors something to own from that year, because no Half Cents were minted in 1837.

Figure 16-4:
The Classic
Head Half
Cent.

Braided Hair or Coronet Type (1840–1857)

In 1840, Liberty regained a more youthful appearance — her hair was done up in braids, and she wore a coronet instead of a headband (see Figure 16-5). Unfortunately, the public didn't get to see this design until 1849 — for the first nine years, coins bearing this design were struck only as Proofs and were made available only to a handful of lucky collectors who made a trip to the Mint. 1857 saw the end of this design type and (sadly) the end of all Half Cents, as well.

Figure 16-5:
The Braided
Hair Half
Cent.

Collecting U.S. Half Cents

Collecting U.S. Half Cents can present quite an enjoyable challenge, especially if you try to find them in high grades. For the most part, mintages were low and most examples spent a lot of time in circulation. Problem-free examples with smooth, glossy surfaces are highly prized by collectors. Here's what you can expect when collecting:

✔ **By type:** A set of the five major Half Cent types listed in the previous section makes a nice display that's affordable and easily completed. The only difficult coin to collect is the 1793.

  • **Difficulty rating:** Moderately difficult. You may find some Half Cent types at your local coin dealer, but your best bet for locating a 1793 Half Cent is at a major coin show, at an auction, or by mail order.

  • **Cost estimate:** Moderately expensive. In Fine condition, expect to spend upwards of $4,000 for a type set of U.S. Half Cents, with the 1793 accounting for most of the cost of the set. Spend $1,000 more and you can upgrade the later types to make the set even more attractive.

✔ **By date:** A date set of Half Cents is a real challenge. You're talking serious money when you get to the 1796, 1831, 1836, and the Proof-only dates from 1840–1849 and 1852.

- **Difficulty rating:** Very difficult. Be patient — it may be years before some of these dates appear on the market, especially in a grade you can afford!

- **Cost estimate:** Very expensive. Figure on spending at least $75,000 to put together a date set of U.S. Half Cents. You may get by with less, but you won't be happy with the quality of the coins. On the other hand, you can spend much, much more to get nicer coins.

✔ **By die variety:** Some collectors seek to acquire a coin from every combination of dies used to strike Half Cents (see Chapter 14 for a full explanation of die varieties).

- **Difficulty rating:** Extremely difficult to impossible. Many varieties are common or slightly scarce, but others are extremely rare. Most of the rare varieties are already held by advanced collectors, so figure on making this a lifetime project.

- **Cost estimate:** Unbelievably expensive. I won't even venture a guess here except to say that the amount of money required to complete a variety set of Half Cents (if it could be done) would run into the hundreds of thousands of dollars.

Living with Large Cents

Large Cents live up to their name. They are heavy chunks of copper about the size of a modern Half Dollar. Imagine lugging a dollar's worth of these coins around — you'd be lucky to have a pocket left.

Large Cents first appeared in 1793, about the same time as the Half Cents, with which they share the distinction of being the first coins issued by the United States government for regular circulation. For a coin of such low value, the Large Cent was considered to be an important coin. Large Cents were minted every year from 1793 to 1857, except 1815. Only the $5 gold piece comes close to such a near-perfect record!

Major types of U.S. Large Cents

Large Cents appear in seven major types, discussed in this section. Collectors also like to split them up into three major areas of interest — *Early Dates* (1793–1814), *Middle Dates* (1816–1839), and *Late Dates* (1840–1857).

Flowing Hair, Chain Cent reverse (1793 only)

The first Large Cent design of 1793 features a wild-eyed Liberty with even wilder hair (see Figure 16-6). The back of the coin features a chain of connected links around the words "One Cent" and the fraction "1/100." The chain was meant to suggest the unity of the States, but some nattering nabobs of negativity thought it looked more like the chains of slavery. Needless to say, the design didn't last long.

Figure 16-6:
The 1793
Chain Cent.

Flowing Hair, Wreath reverse (1793 only)

Later in 1793, the U.S. Mint replaced the chain on the back of the Large Cent with a wreath (see Figure 16-7). However, the other complaint, that of Liberty's wild hair, was not addressed, so this design was just as short-lived as the Chain Cent.

Figure 16-7:
The 1793
Wreath
Cent.

Liberty Cap (1793–1796)

At the end of 1793, U.S. Mint officials finally silenced the critics by adopting the Liberty Cap design that was to be used over the next four years (see Figure 16-8). After all, Freedom and Liberty were two of the reasons America fought the Revolutionary War. The Liberty Cap design was a modification of the designs used on the Half Cents of 1793 (refer to Figure 16-1). As lovely as this design was, it appeared only on U.S. copper coins. On Large Cents, the design lasted until mid-1796.

Figure 16-8:
The Liberty
Cap Large
Cent.

Draped Bust (1796–1807)

The Draped Bust design (see Figure 16-9) first appeared on U.S. Silver Dollars in 1795 (see Chapter 17). The design was rolled out in 1796, when it was placed on the Large Cent, Half Dime, Dime, Quarter Dollar, and Half Dollar. Finally, the U.S. Mint had a design it could sink its teeth into. The Draped Bust design mirrored women's fashion tastes and hairstyles of the early 1800s.

Capped Bust or Classic Head (1808–1814)

The Classic Head design portrays Liberty as a slightly older woman with hair held together by a headband that has the word "Liberty" upon it (see Figure 16-10). Thirteen stars, representing the original colonies, appear on either side of her head. The back of the coin shows the familiar Wreath design without the fraction "1/100."

Matron Head (1816–1839)

In 1816, Liberty became even older looking, her hair was tied up in a bun, and her headband became a coronet (see Figure 16-11). This is probably the least attractive presentation of Liberty in the entire Large Cent series (at least I think so), but many collectors have fallen in love with this type. Popularly known as the *Middle Dates,* the Large Cents from 1816-1839 enjoy lots of attention from variety collectors.

Figure 16-11:
The Matron
Head Large
Cent.

Braided Hair or Coronet Type (1839–1857)

Had the trend in aging Liberty continued, the next Liberty would have been called the "Old Hag" type. Thankfully, a fellow named Christian Gobrecht created a more youthful Liberty, this time braiding her hair around her face and giving her a thinner neck (see Figure 16-12). Known as the *Late Dates,* the Braided Hair type is also popular with variety collectors, but the differences can sometimes be frustratingly minute.

Figure 16-12:
The Braided
Hair Large
Cent.

Collecting U.S. Large Cents

Large Cent collecting has been an important part of U.S. numismatics for over 150 years, and it remains so today. A tremendous amount of information has been published about this interesting series, making it easy for you to jump right in with confidence and ease. Check out the following information to see if you, too, will be the next "victim" of the siren song of Large Cents.

✔ **By type:**

- **Difficulty rating:** Moderate. The 1793 Chain Cent is a *money coin;* that is, it's always available if you're willing to pay the price. The 1793 Wreath Cents are slightly less dear but not by much. The remaining types are all readily available in most grades, but only the Matron Head and Braided Hair types can be called inexpensive in high grades.

- **Cost estimate:** In Fine condition, a type set of Large Cents runs approximately $8,000, with the bulk of the money tied up in the Chain and Wreath types. In Very Fine, the cost jumps to roughly $15,000. Expect an even more dramatic increase if you attempt a type set in Extremely Fine condition.

✔ **By date:**

- **Difficulty rating:** Moderate. There are no stoppers in this series. Sure the 1793 Chain and Wreath Cents are expensive and the 1799 and 1804 Large Cents are rare, but you won't have to contend with any of the super-rarities that tend to take the fun out of collecting other series.

- **Cost estimate:** In Fine condition, expect an outlay of approximately $22,000–$23,000. Because of the difficult dates, be ready for dramatic price jumps as you move up even a single grade. If you're not too concerned about consistent quality, settle for lower grades in the early dates and better grades in the later dates. Many of the Uncirculated dates in the 1840s and 1850s are real bargains.

✔ **By die variety:**

- **Difficulty rating:** Extremely difficult to impossible. The Early Dates (1793–1814) contain hundreds of varieties, some of which are unique or nearly so, and many of which are extremely rare. The Middle Dates (1816–1839) allow for greater possibilities of completion, but be prepared to take out a second mortgage for some of the varieties. When collecting the Late Dates (1840–1857), the real challenge is telling the darn things apart. I admire anyone who collects these dates by die variety — it takes a keen eye and a lot of patience.

- **Cost estimate:** The moon! If you said to me, "Ron, here's a million bucks — go build me a variety set of Large Cents," I'd turn you down. That's how serious Large Cent varieties have become. Nevertheless, despite the costs and the obstacles to completion, thousands of collectors actively collect Large Cents by variety.

Seeking Out Small Cents

A strange thing happened in 1857. After over 60 years of making the clunky Large Cents, U.S. Mint officials discovered that the general public was perfectly willing to accept a smaller coin as One Cent. Perhaps the change to a smaller size coin could have been made years earlier, and the U.S. Mint may have saved itself millions of dollars — this we'll never know. But we do know that by 1857, the public accepted the change (pun intended) willingly and enthusiastically.

The first Small Cents were a mixture of Copper and Nickel that had a light color, earning them the nickname *White Cents*. In 1864, the weight of the Cent was reduced and the nickel removed, a new standard that lasted for nearly 120 years. Beginning in 1982, Cents were made of copper-plated zinc, as they still are today.

I must mention the Cents of 1943. The United States needed copper for World War II, so in 1943 the government used Steel as a substitute. The 1943 *Steelies* have a white color that is completely unlike any Copper Cent. Even today, coin dealers receive frequent phone calls asking about these unusual coins, usually from collectors who think they've discovered a great treasure.

Also known as Pennies, Small Cents are often a collector's first experience with numismatics. In low grades, they're so affordable that even a child can put together a nice collection on a tiny budget.

Major types of U.S. Small Cents

Small Cents appear in four major types, discussed in this section.

Flying Eagle (1856–1858)

The first Small Cent appeared in 1856 with a design completely unlike that of any of the Large Cents that came before. The front of the new Small Cent (see Figure 16-13) showed an American eagle flying to the left. This design was copied from the back of the Gobrecht Dollars created between 1836 and 1839 (see Chapter 17). The back of the coin showed a wreath made up of some interesting stuff that looks like corn and cotton. As beautiful as it was, this design lasted only three years.

Figure 16-13:
The Flying
Eagle Cent.

Indian Head (1859–1909)

The first Indian Head Cents appeared in 1859 (see Figure 16-14). One problem, though — that's not a Native American on the front of the coin. James Longacre, the fellow who designed the coin, stuck a Native American headdress on his daughter's head, then used her as a model. The design lasted for exactly fifty years and is one of the most popular series in U.S. numismatics.

Figure 16-14:
The Indian
Head Cent.

Lincoln Head, Wheat Ears reverse (1909–1958)

1909 was the 100th anniversary of the birth of Abraham Lincoln. What better way to honor this martyred President than to place his image on the most widely used coin in the United States (see Figure 16-15)? The Lincoln Cent marked the first appearance of a real person on an U.S. coin made for circulation, and this design will soon be 100 years old. (No other U.S. coin design has ever lasted this long.) Note that from 1909 to 1958, the back of the coin had a simple design consisting of two wheat ears on either side.

Figure 16-15:
The Lincoln
Head Cent.

Lincoln Head, Memorial reverse (1959–present)

In 1959, the back of the Lincoln Head Cent was changed to show the Lincoln Memorial (see Figure 16-16). If you look closely at the back of the coin, you can see Lincoln's statue inside the Memorial.

Figure 16-16:
The Lincoln
Memorial
Cent.

Collecting U.S. Small Cents

Most new collectors get their first introduction to numismatics by building a collection of Small Cents, particularly those of the Lincoln Head type made beginning in 1909. Most Small Cents are affordable, they're easy to find, and you'll meet plenty of other collectors who are eager to buy, sell, or trade with you and share their collecting stories. I can't think of a better place for the new collector to start.

✔ **By type:**

- **Difficulty rating:** Easy. You can find all four major design types of the Small Cent in any coin shop or at any show.

- **Cost estimate:** In Fine condition, a type set of Small Cents costs only $25. You can put together a nice set of Uncirculated examples of each type for around $250.

✔ **By date and mintmark:**

- **Difficulty rating:** Moderate. Rare dates include the 1856 (many collectors exclude this date because it's really a pattern that was meant to test the design but was never meant to enter circulation), 1877, 1909-S, 1914-D, and 1931-S. Even so, just about every date is available on the market at any given moment. No date, including the 1856, is outrageously expensive. Be careful not to get sidetracked, however, costs can go up dramatically if you decide to go after some of the major die varieties in these series.

- **Cost estimate:** In Fine condition, a date set of Flying Eagle Cents costs around $4,500, but you can whittle the cost down to $50 by excluding the 1856. Under the same terms, an Uncirculated date set runs either $7,500 or $500. A Fine set of Indian Head Cents costs roughly $2,000; an Uncirculated set requires an outlay of at least $8,000. A Fine set of Lincoln Head Cents (1909-Date) costs approximately $475 (and that's figuring in the later dates that come only in Proof condition). In Uncirculated condition, a complete date set of Lincoln Cents runs at least $4,000. Remember, major die varieties can add a lot to each of these sets.

✔ **By die variety:**

- **Difficulty rating:** Difficult. There are many die varieties in the Small Cent series — some that are obvious to the naked eye, and others that are more subtle but equally interesting. New die varieties are being discovered every year, and while some are extremely rare and popular, they are not necessarily expensive. Other varieties, like the 1873 Indian Head Cent with doubled Liberty on the Indian's headband, the 1909-S Lincoln Head Cent with the designer's initials on the back, and the 1955 Doubled Die Lincoln Head Cent, have been around for so many years that they have become integral parts of the date and mintmark sets, but it's up to you to decide what to include in your collection.

- **Cost estimate:** Inexpensive to expensive, depending on how involved you get in this area. Many die varieties cost less than $5; others can run into thousands of dollars.

Taking on Two-Cent Pieces

The law that changed the weight and metal composition of the Small Cent in 1864 also created a Two-Cent piece (see Figure 16-17), an odd denomination that really never caught on and that ended less than ten years later. The Two-Cent piece has the distinction of being the first United States coin to bear the inscription "In God We Trust." The front of the coin features a Union Shield, a popular, patriotic image during the Civil War Years. The caption that usually accompanied the Union Shield (but which did not appear on the coins) was "The Union — It Must And Shall Be Preserved."

Figure 16-17:
The Two-
Cent piece.

A collection of Two-Cent pieces makes a great conversation piece, especially when you show it to non-collectors, most of whom haven't the faintest clue that the United States made such a "funny" denomination. Of course, the fact that you have several of them will make you seem really cool.

✔ **By type:**

- **Difficulty rating:** Extremely easy. Two-Cent pieces were minted with only one design type.

- **Cost estimate**: Inexpensive. A Fine Two-Cent piece costs around $20; Uncirculated examples sell for less than a hundred Dollars.

✔ **By date:**

- **Difficulty rating:** Easy. Every date in this series is available and affordable. The 1872 can be tough to find, and you may have to hunt for the 1873 (which was struck only in Proof condition).

- **Cost estimate:** Moderately expensive. In Fine condition, a complete set of Two-Cent pieces costs approximately $1,250, although I've never seen or heard of a Fine 1873 (just buy a Proof for $100 or $200 more). A nice set of Uncirculated and Proof Two-Cent pieces can cost upwards of $3,000. Expect to pay a premium for coins that have a lot of their original red color.

✔ **By die variety:**

- **Difficulty rating:** Easy to moderately difficult. In 1864, "In God We Trust" appeared in two versions, one small and the other slightly larger. The Small Motto version is extremely popular and is a must-have variety. On the 1873 Two-Cent pieces, the "3" will either be *open* and look like a normal "3" or it will be *closed* and look more like an "8" at first glance. As in other series, minor varieties can add a nice diversion.

- **Cost estimate:** Expect to spend $100 for a Fine 1864 Small Motto and $1000 to $1500 for the extra 1873 variety.

Rounding Up the Three-Cent (Nickel)

In 1865, a new Three-Cent piece made of copper and nickel (75 percent and 25 percent, respectively, but they're called *Three-Cent Nickels* because they look more like nickel than they do copper) burst onto the scene. However, the U.S. had already been making a Three-Cent piece out of silver since 1851 (see Chapter 17). The problem with the old Three-Cent piece was that the coin was so tiny it was easy to lose (even back then, three cents' worth of silver was only a small amount). By using copper and nickel, the coins could be made larger and for less money. Three-Cent Nickels (see Figure 16-18) were made from 1865 to 1889.

Figure 16-18: The Three-Cent Nickel.

Three-Cent Nickels come in only one type, they were made over a period of slightly over 20 years, and all of the dates are within the means of most collectors. Add the curiosity factor of the odd denomination, and you have a winning collection.

- ✔ **By type:**

  - **Difficulty rating:** Extremely easy. Three-Cent Nickels were minted with only one design type.

  - **Cost estimate**: Inexpensive. Figure from $10 for a Fine example up to $100 for a nice Uncirculated piece.

- ✔ **By date:**

  - **Difficulty rating:** Easy. No super rarities in the series — the only challenge comes from the Proof-only 1877, 1878, and 1886.

  - **Cost estimate:** A complete set of Three-Cent Nickels in Very Fine condition runs approximately $3,500, while a set in Uncirculated and Proof condition starts at $7,500 and goes up from there.

- ✔ **By die variety:**

  - **Difficulty rating:** Easy to difficult. This series has only three major die varieties. Like the 1873 Two-Cent piece, the 1873 Three-Cent Nickel comes with the number "3" open and closed. 1887 boasts an overdate, where traces of a "6" can be seen underneath the "7" of the date. Researchers have uncovered lots of minor die varieties, but you'll need to have your eyes checked before you get into this area of minute differences.

  - **Cost estimate:** Inexpensive to moderately expensive. The 1873 die varieties are common and inexpensive, but the 1887/6 die variety runs $350 to $600, depending on condition. Minor die varieties can be expensive depending on how obvious and popular they are.

Firing Up for the Five Cents (or Nickels)

The U.S. started making Half Dimes (worth five cents each) in 1794, but they were small coins made out of silver, just like the first Three-Cent pieces. However, the silver shortages caused by the Civil War forced the government to come up with an alternative. That's where nickel came in — the metal, that is. Nickel is much harder than silver, which means two things: Nickel is more difficult than silver to strike into coins, but it's also cheaper, lasts longer, and wears better than silver. In 1866, the first Five-Cent piece struck in copper and nickel (75 percent and 25 percent, respectively) appeared on the market. They were larger and thicker than the Silver Half Dimes. Even though the government intended to replace the Half Dime with the new Nickels, they went back and forth between the two. For example, in 1871, over 2,000,000 silver

Half Dimes were struck, yet only 561,000 Nickels were made for circulation. Finally, 1873 saw the end of the Half Dime, and the Nickel has reigned supreme ever since.

Major types of U.S. Five-Cent pieces

Nickels appear in four major types, discussed in this section.

Shield (1866–1883)

The Shield Nickel War (see Figure 16-19) first appeared in 1866, following the end of the Civil War. The front of the coin copied the design of a shield from the Two-Cent piece and the reverse showed a large 5 within a circle of stars, with rays of light between the stars. (Later, the rays were dropped from the design.) This design type lasted until 1883, at which time the government felt secure enough to resurrect the head of Liberty.

Figure 16-19:
The Shield
Nickel.

Liberty Head or V Nickel (1883–1913)

In 1883, Liberty reappeared on the Five-Cent coins, this time as a head instead of a lady sitting on a rock (compare with the Half Dimes in Chapter 17). The back of the coin featured a large V (see Figure 16-20), the Roman numeral for "five." Through an oversight, the word "Cents" was left off the coin, creating an opportunity for con men to gold-plate the coins and pass them off as $5 gold pieces! Needless to say, this problem was fixed immediately, creating two major varieties for 1883. In 1913, the last year that V Nickels were made, only five examples were struck, creating one of the greatest rarities in the entire U.S. coin series.

Figure 16-20:
The Liberty
Head Nickel.

Indian Head or Buffalo Nickel (1913–1938)

As part of a major redesign of U.S. coins, the Nickel got a makeover in 1913 when Liberty was replaced with the head of a Native American chief, and the large V was replaced with an American bison (see Figure 16-21). This new design proved extremely popular and lasted until 1938. Even today, lots of collectors favor this purely American design.

Figure 16-21:
The Indian
Head Nickel.

Jefferson Head (1938–present)

The Nickel went Presidential in 1938, when Thomas Jefferson's image was placed on the front of the Five-Cent piece (see Figure 16-22) and his home (Monticello) was added to the back.

Clearly, the trend at the time was toward adding famous historical figures to coins. In 1909, Lincoln appeared on the Cent and in 1932, Washington made it onto the Quarter Dollar. The trend continued in 1946, when Franklin D. Roosevelt showed up on the Dime and in 1948, when Benjamin Franklin appeared on the Half Dollar. So it was no surprise when Jefferson appeared on the Nickel, where he and his house remain today.

Figure 16-22:
The Jefferson Head Nickel.

Collecting U.S. Five-Cent pieces

Nickels were made in four major types beginning in 1866. Collectors gravitate to this series because there are so many affordable dates and because of the draw of the purely American design on the Indian Head/Buffalo type. You can obtain many of the coins you need for your collection from circulation, which is a fun and easy way to start. When you're ready to get serious about this series, consider the following ways of collecting:

✔ **By type:**

- **Difficulty rating:** Easy. Finding all four types of Five-Cent pieces is a breeze.

- **Cost estimate**: Inexpensive. In Fine condition, a set of Nickel types runs less than $20. In Uncirculated condition, a nice type set of Nickels runs less that $200.

✔ **By date:**

- **Difficulty rating:** Impossible — the 1913 Liberty Nickel has already set two price records of over $1 million. However, if you stay within each type, or disregard the 1913 Nickel, the difficulty rating drops to easy. For example, the only scarce Shield Nickels are the dates from 1877 to 1881. The only tough "V" Nickels are the 1885 and 1912-S, and there are no rare dates in the Buffalo or Jefferson Nickel types.

- **Cost estimate:** A complete date set of Shield Nickels in Fine condition costs approximately $2,750. In Uncirculated condition, expect to pay $5,000 and up. If you exclude the 1913, a complete date and mintmark set of V Nickels in Fine condition will cost roughly $850; in Uncirculated condition, the potential cost jumps to at least $4,500. For $575, you can complete a date and mintmark set of Buffalo Nickels; in Uncirculated condition, expect to spend $28,000 for a Choice set (I told you they were popular)! Because they are so inexpensive, I recommend collecting Jefferson Head Nickels only in Uncirculated and/or Proof condition. A complete set of all dates and mintmarks should run approximately $200 to $250.

✔ **By die variety:**

- **Difficulty rating:** Moderately difficult to extremely difficult, depending on how far you go. Several design variations exist to tempt you and some are considered must-have varieties. The 1867 Nickel comes with and without rays on the back, the 1883 Nickel comes with and without the word "Cents," and the 1913 Buffalo Nickels come with the words "Five Cents" on a mound or in a recessed area. If overdates thrill you, choose between the 1883/2, the 1914/3, the 1918/7 from the Denver Mint, and the 1943/2. One of the most unusual varieties is the 1937-D Three-Legged Buffalo Nickel, an error created when some of the details were accidentally ground off the die used to strike the coins!

- **Cost estimate:** Moderately expensive to mega-expensive. Common varieties run $20 or less — others can run into the tens of thousands of dollars. I recommend staying within your budget — remember to collect what you like and stick with your long-range collecting plans.

Chapter 17

Silver Coins: Keeping Commerce Alive

. . . .

. . . .

Before the United States opened its first Mint, the country's forefathers knew that they needed three types of coins — coins for use by the public in everyday transactions, coins for bigger, merchant-to-merchant transactions, and coins for the very big, behind-the-scenes transactions (bank-to-bank and governmental deals). Copper coins (see Chapter 16) took care of the low end, gold coins (see Chapter 18) took care of the high end, and silver coins were perfect for the middle-of-the-road transactions. Goldilocks would have considered the copper coins too base, the gold coins too rich, and the silver coins "just right."

From 1792 to 1964, the United States issued a variety of different denominations of silver coins, ranging from the tiny Three-Cent Silver piece to the large, impressive Silver Dollar. Naturally, most of the silver coins were meant to be used in the United States, but one coin (the Trade Dollar) was actually meant to be shipped overseas to compete against other similarly sized silver coins from around the world and to promote our nation's interests wherever they were used.

1964 saw the end of silver coins in the United States. They were replaced by a *clad* coinage consisting of a middle layer of copper sandwiched between two layers of a copper and nickel alloy. I miss the luster of silver coins, the quick way they warmed up in your hands, and the huge size of the Silver Dollars I could buy from the local coin shops for $1.20 each. That was real money!

Keeping up with numismatic jargon

As you read through this chapter, the following terms appear frequently:

✔ **Common dates:** The dates in a series that have high mintages and that are easy to obtain

✔ **Date set:** A collection of all of the different dates in which a particular coin was issued

✔ **Mintages:** The number made of a particular coin

✔ **Mintmark set:** A collection of coins that includes one from each of the different mints around the country that produced a particular coin

✔ **Overdate:** A coin that shows two dates, usually one on top of another, the second being a correction of the first

✔ **Proofs:** Special coins of exceptional quality that were made for sale to collectors and not for general circulation

✔ **Type set:** A set of each of the different design types of a particular denomination

✔ **Upgrade:** The act of improving the coin in your collection, or a coin that is better than another example of the same type

✔ **Varieties:** Refers to either a minor change in the design on a coin or to *die variety* — a unique combination of obverse and reverse dies

Thrilling Yourself with Three-Cent Silvers

In 1851, a tiny silver coin was introduced with a value of three Cents. Why such an odd denomination? Because in 1851, it cost three Cents to mail a letter through the United States Post Office. To pay for such a letter, you had several possibilities, all cumbersome: You could pay with six Half Cents, three Large Cents, a Half Dime (from which you would receive four Half Cents or two Large Cents in change), a Dime (from which you would receive a handful of coins in change), and so on. A Three-Cent coin made it easy for the public to purchase postage stamps and reduced the need for other coins for change.

The new Three-Cent pieces were made of silver, but in a lower purity than other coins. It doesn't take much silver to make three Cents, so the coins were very small. At some point, they became known as *fishscales* because of their white appearance, thin metal, and tiny size. Later, they were called *Trimes* by U.S. Mint officials. Eventually, they were replaced by a copper-nickel version of the Three-Cent piece, and they gasped their last breath in 1873.

Today, most people are surprised to discover that the U.S. Mint issued a Three-Cent piece. However, if we used the same logic today that was used then, we'd have a Thirty-Four Cent coin with which to buy our stamps. Now, that would be weird!

Major types of U.S. Three-Cent Silvers

Three-Cent Silvers appeared in only one major design type (see Figure 17-1), but two minor changes in the design resulted in three different subtypes.

Figure 17-1:
Three-Cent
Silver.

✔ The first subtype has a plain star on the front of the coin and is known as the *Type 1* design.

✔ In 1854, two outlines were added to the star, creating what is known as the *Type 2* design.

✔ In 1859, one of the extra outlines was removed, resulting in the *Type 3 Trime*.

Collecting U.S. Three-Cent Silvers

A collection of Three-Cent Silvers is a real conversation piece, considering that most Americans have never seen even a single example. Many of the dates in the 1860s and 1870s are downright scarce, but you should be able to complete this series with a little effort (and money).

✔ **By type:**

• **Difficulty rating:** Easy, whether you collect just one type or all three sub-types.

• **Cost estimate**: If you just want one type, figure on spending $22 for a Fine example or $150 for an Uncirculated piece. All three sub-types run $70 in Fine and approximately $550–600 in Uncirculated condition.

✔ **By date/mintmark:**

- **Difficulty rating:** Moderately difficult. The one truly rare date in the series is the 1873, which was minted only in Proof condition. Even so, most of the dates from 1863 on had very low mintages, so finding them may present a bit of a challenge.

- **Cost estimate:** A complete date and mintmark set of Three-Cent Silvers in Fine condition costs approximately $5,000. A date set in Uncirculated condition runs roughly $10,000 and up. Even though an Uncirculated set costs more, your chances of success are greater than if you attempt a set in Fine condition because most of the later dates in this series exist only in high grade.

✔ **By die variety:**

- **Difficulty rating:** Moderately difficult. The four major die varieties include an 1862/1 overdate, an 1863/2 overdate, an 1873 Open 3 (which looks like a "3"), and an 1873 Closed 3 (which looks like an "8"). The 1862/1 is fairly common, the 1863/2 is very rare and available only in a Proof version, and both 1873s are expensive because they, too, are Proof-only issues.

- **Cost estimate:** The 1862/1 is inexpensive and affordable even in Uncirculated condition. The 1863/2 runs about $4,000 — if you can find one. The 1873s are *money coins* — easy to find but roughly $1,500 each.

Hunting Down Half Dimes

In 1794, the U.S. Mint began striking silver coins for circulation, focusing on what must have been thought to be the three most important denominations — Half Dimes, Half Dollars, and Silver Dollars. (Dimes and Quarters did not appear until 1796.) Half Dollars and Silver Dollars were big bucks in 1794, but Half Dimes were perfect for day-to-day transactions. Even today, a Five-Cent coin is considered an important part of the U.S. money system.

Half Dimes were discontinued in 1873, long after they had already started to be replaced in 1866 by the new copper-nickel Five-Cent pieces.

Major types of U.S. Half Dimes

Half Dimes appear in four major types, which are discussed in this section.

Flowing Hair (1794–1795)

Like the first Large Cents of 1793 (see Chapter 16), the first Half Dimes were mocked because of Liberty's wild hair and, in the case of the Half Dime, because of the scrawny eagle on the back of the coin (see Figure 17-2). It must have been terrible to have been an official at the first U.S. Mint, only to see your first products so roundly criticized in the media. I'm not sure whether it was the criticism or natural evolution that caused this design type to discontinue after only two years.

Figure 17-2:
Flowing Hair
Half Dime.

Draped Bust (1796–1805)

1796 saw a wholesale revision of U.S. coins, using the Draped Bust design (see Figure 17-3) that first appeared on Silver Dollars in 1795. The Half Dime features the smallest version of this design type, but it's just as beautiful on this coin as it is on the larger coins. In 1800, the still-scrawny eagle on the back of the coin was replaced with a larger eagle with outspread wings and a shield on its chest. This *Eagle and Shield* back was adapted from the Great Seal of the United States. The Draped Bust design lasted less than ten years on the Half Dime, but it includes the rare 1802, a classic U.S. rarity of which few were made and even fewer survive.

Capped Bust (1829–1837)

No Half Dimes were minted between 1805 and 1829, which represents a long time in coin years. When the Half Dime reappeared in 1829, it featured the Capped Bust design that had already been in use on other coins since 1807 (see Figure 17-4). This is a great series to collect because just nine dates are in the series, and all are equally common.

Figure 17-3:
Draped Bust
Half Dime.

Figure 17-4:
Capped
Bust Half
Dime.

Seated Liberty (1837–1873)

On this design type, Liberty sits in a large rock with her dress draped all around her. With her right hand, she holds a shield in front of her and, in her other arm, she cradles a staff with a plain freedman's cap stuck over the tip of the staff (see Figure 17-5). This series lasted nearly 40 years. Were it not for the 1870-S Half Dime (of which only a single example is known), you could expect to complete a date and mintmark set of these challenging coins.

From 1853 to1855, small arrowheads were added on either side of the date to let the public know that the weight of the Half Dimes was being reduced. This was important at a time when people were concerned that their money contained the full value in metal. In 1859, the words "United States Of America" were moved from the back of the coin to the front. A few prototype coins were made with an unusual combination of dies, neither of which had U.S.A. on them. Collectors eagerly seek after these coins without a country. Beginning in 1865, copper-nickel Five-Cent pieces began the slow process of replacing these tiny silver jewels — the death knell for the Half Dime sounded in 1873.

Collecting U.S. Half Dimes

Collecting U.S. Half Dimes is fun and challenging. Many rarities exist in the series, and a lot of coins are extremely scarce in high grade. You could spend literally a lifetime building, upgrading, and enjoying Half Dimes.

- **By type:**
  - **Difficulty rating:** Easy. None of the Half Dime types are rare, but you may have difficulty finding the Flowing Hair and Draped Bust types.
  - **Cost estimate**: Reasonable to expensive. In Fine condition, a type set of Half Dimes runs roughly $1,700 (add another $1,200 if you wish to include the Draped Bust/Plain Eagle subtype); in Uncirculated condition, figure on at least $10,000 or more.

- **By date:**
  - **Difficulty rating:** Easy to impossible. There are only two dates in the Flowing Hair series, both of which can be found with a little effort. The 1802 Draped Bust is a real stopper. Capped Bust makes for a nice, easy, and affordable collection. Forget Seated Liberty: There's only one 1870-S, and it's already spoken for.
  - **Cost estimate:** Reasonable to extremely expensive. A Fine set of Capped Bust Half Dimes runs $250 or so; in Uncirculated condition, the same set runs $2,750 and up. The two-coin Draped Bust set runs $2,000 or more in Fine condition and over $10,000 for the same pair in Uncirculated condition.

✔ **By die variety:**

- **Difficulty rating:** Easy to impossible. Each of the different types has its own interesting varieties, ranging from obvious and common to subtle and rare. The difficult part is in assembling a variety set of the 1794 to 1837 issues. This area is just now coming into its own, and you need a lot of luck (and money) to come anywhere close to a complete set of varieties.

- **Cost estimate:** Inexpensive to outrageously expensive. You can buy the 1861/0 overdate for as little as $20 or the 1802 Half Dime (yes, it's a die variety, too) for as much as $50,000!

Digging in for Dimes

Dimes and Quarter Dollars debuted in 1796, a full three years after the first copper coins appeared. Although they arrived late, Dimes have been an important denomination during their run from 1796 until today. With a few exceptions, Dimes have been minted almost continuously during that time in a variety of interesting types. Two great rarities exist in this series — the unique 1873-CC *No Arrows at Date* and the extremely rare 1894-S. While these two cost more than a house in southern California, you can collect plenty of other interesting and challenging dates that are much more affordable and approachable.

Major types of U.S. Dimes

Dimes appear in five major types, which are discussed in this section.

Draped Bust (1796–1807)

The very first Dimes bore the Draped Bust design that became the standard on all Silver coins in 1796 (see Figure 17-6). The first Dimes featured fifteen stars, one for each State of the Union. Initially, the plan was to include a new star for each state as they came on board. By 1798, the number of states (and stars) was up to 16, but this became so crowded on the coins that the number of stars was reduced to that of the thirteen original colonies. Imagine how the coins of today would look with fifty stars crowded onto such a tiny coin (reminds me of the candles on my birthday cakes).

Figure 17-6:
Draped Bust
Dime.

Capped Bust (1809–1837)

The Capped Bust design appeared in 1809 and ran until 1837 (see Figure 17-7). This series contains a number of interesting overdates and varieties, including 1814 and 1820 varieties, where the words "States of America" are spaced so closely together that they form a single word. No rare dates or stoppers exist in this series. A large number of collectors concentrate on the die varieties in this series, where they have a chance of cherry-picking a valuable variety for the price of a common type.

Figure 17-7:
Capped
Bust Dime.

Seated Liberty (1837–1891)

A larger version of the Half Dimes, the Seated Liberty Dime, ran from 1837 to 1891 (see Figure 17-8). Unlike the Three-Cent pieces and Half Dimes, Dimes were not replaced with other coins made of copper-nickel, so the year 1873 meant nothing to them — they just kept going and going. . . . Weight reductions in 1853 and 1873 saw the addition of arrowheads on either side of the date, signals to the public that lasted for three and two years, respectively. Plenty of challenging dates await the collector of this type, as well as some interesting varieties.

Figure 17-8:
Seated
Liberty
Dime.

Barber (1892–1916)

The new Dime that appeared in 1892 showed a head of Liberty (see Figure 17-9), but this time, she wore the cap she had on a pole on the last design. A headband with the word "Liberty" and a wreath hold her hat on her head. This type is known as the *Barber Dime* not because it had anything to do with the local haircutter, but because Charles Barber was the designer. Come to think about it, a haircut probably cost a Dime in 1892.

The Barber Dime series is home to the 1894-S, one of the rarest and most expensive United States coins.

Figure 17-9:
Barber
Dime.

Mercury Head (1916–1945)

In 1916, designer Adolph Weinman put wings on Liberty's cap, a classic design from ancient times that was quickly associated with the Roman god, Mercury (hence the nickname for this type).

Weinman placed a fasces on the back of the coin (see Figure 17-10). A *fasces* consists of a battle ax surrounded by a bundle of sticks, another design from the ancient Roman world that represented strength and unity. Unfortunately, the symbolism of the fasces received a bad name in World War II from Italy's Mussolini and his Fascist Party. Well-struck examples of this type have clearly defined and separated bands around the fasces. The most important area includes the bands in very center of the coin. If these horizontal bands are completely separated, the coin earns the coveted *Full Bands* designation and is therefore worth a premium. Some date/mintmark combinations with Full Bands are excessively rare.

Figure 17-10:
Mercury
Head Dime.

Roosevelt Head (1946–present)

The death of President Franklin Delano Roosevelt in 1945 prompted a quick design change for the Dime (see Figure 17-11). Roosevelt's head was placed on the front of the coin, and the fasces was replaced by a torch. The initials of the designer, John Sinnock were placed just beneath Roosevelt's head. Because of the anti-Communist sentiment that prevailed after World War II, some people thought the initial "JS" stood for Joseph Stalin and that some Communist operative had invaded the U.S. Mints and put the initials there as a secret signal to Communists worldwide. What will people think of next?

The Roosevelt Head Dime appeared in Silver through 1964, after which the coins were made of a *clad* metal of low value. Roosevelt Dimes are still being made today, 55 years after his death.

Figure 17-11:
Roosevelt
Dime.

Collecting U.S. Dimes

They're small and unassuming, but Dimes have been an important part of the U.S. money system since 1796. The Mercury Head and Roosevelt Dimes are extremely popular with new collectors, while the older (pre-1916) series offer plenty of challenges for the advanced collector. The following are some tips for collecting U.S. Dimes.

✔ **By type:**

- **Difficulty rating:** Moderately difficult. A type set of Dimes offers a wide range of interesting designs, each with its own story to tell. The Draped Bust type is scarce, but all of the later types are readily available.

- **Cost estimate**: For a type set of Dimes in Fine condition, expect to pay about $800 (add $2,000 more if you want the Draped Bust/Plain Eagle subtype). In Uncirculated condition, bring more money — at least $13,000.

✔ **By date/mintmark:**

- **Difficulty rating:** Difficult to nearly impossible. Draped Bust in every date is accessible but somewhat expensive. Capped Bust has no difficult dates. Seated Liberty has many common dates, many rare dates, and the unique 1873-CC No Arrows Dime. Barber has the scarce 1895-O, and the 1894-S is a classic rarity that always sets records when it appears on the market. Mercury Head has the key date of 1916-D, but all other dates are easy to find. Roosevelt Head in all dates and mintmarks are common.

- **Cost estimate:** Inexpensive to millions. For Draped Bust Dimes figure on spending $12,000 for a date set in Fine condition and at least $75,000 for a date set in Uncirculated condition — if you can find them. Capped Bust Dimes cost $1,800 for a set in Fine condition and roughly $30,000 for an Uncirculated set. Seated Liberty Dimes costs about $15,000 for a Fine set, but only if you exclude the 1873-CC No Arrows. I don't price an Uncirculated set because many of the coins are extremely rare in high grade, and the prices are speculative. Suffice it to say that you're talking six figures — and that's without the aforementioned 1873-CC No Arrows. For Barber Dimes the 1894-S takes all the fun out of putting together a date/mintmark set. If you exclude the 1894-S, a Fine set runs around $4,000; in Uncirculated condition, the price jumps to over $20,000. For Mercury Head Dimes, Fine sets cost around $1,500; Uncirculated sets cost at least $10,000 and substantially more if you add any Full Band examples. You can pick up a complete date/mintmark set of Uncirculated and Proof examples of Roosevelt Dimes for around $150. Buy yourself a nice set and stay away from the lower grades.

✔ **By die variety:**

- **Difficulty rating:** Easy to nearly impossible. Each type has its highlights. In the Draped Bust series, you can find several variations on the number of stars and berries on some dates. The Capped Bust series features two overdates. Because of its extended run, the Seated Liberty type has lots of interesting varieties, many of which are quite rare. Look for the 1893/2 overdate in the Barber series. Favorites in the Mercury Head series include the 1942/1 and 1942/1-D overdates. In the Roosevelt Dime series, the 1982 No Mintmark Dime is a perennial favorite.

- **Cost estimate:** All over the board. A 1945-S Micro-S Dime is just $20 in Uncirculated condition, whereas a 1905-O Micro O can run as much as $2,500. Collecting Draped Bust Dimes gets expensive because most of the dates are already valuable as type coins.

Touring around for Twenty-Cent Pieces

In one of the greatest numismatic debacles of all time, the U.S. government issued a Twenty-Cent piece from 1875 to 1878. The Twenty-Cent piece was only slightly smaller than a Quarter Dollar, and both coins shared a Seated Liberty design (see Figure 17-12). Because of the similarities in size and design, the public had great difficulty in telling the two coins apart. This lead to two losers in many transactions — the people who thought they were offering a Quarter when they really only had 20 Cents, and those who took the coin as a Quarter and immediately lost five Cents on the deal. As a result, the Twenty-Cent piece didn't last long. The last coins for circulation were made in 1876, and Proof examples were made only through 1878.

Figure 17-12:
The Twenty-
Cent piece.

The old adage "History repeats itself" came true in 1979, when the U.S. Government introduced the Susan B. Anthony Dollar (see the "Anthony Head (1979–1999)" section, near the end of this chapter).

Collecting Twenty-Cent pieces by type is easy because you have only one coin to buy!

- ✔ **By type:**
  - **Difficulty rating:** Easy — there's only one type.
  - **Cost estimate**: Affordable — $75 for a Fine example and $450 for one in Uncirculated condition.
- ✔ **By date:**
  - **Difficulty rating:** Extremely difficult. This series would be a piece of cake were it not for that darned 1876-CC, a classic U.S. rarity that will cost over $100,000.
  - **Cost estimate:** A complete set of Uncirculated and Proof Twenty-Cent pieces could run as high as $150,000. Knock off $125,000 if you can live without the 1876-CC.
- ✔ **By die variety:**
  - **Difficulty rating:** Easy to moderately difficult. Although minor die varieties exist in this series, I have never, ever met anyone who collects them.
  - **Cost estimate:** Who knows? Don't get carried away and pay big premiums for varieties in this series. You may have a hard time finding someone to sell them to in the future.

Calling all Quarter Dollars

The Quarter Dollar of 1796 was one of America's answers to the Spanish colonial coins that were important parts of the U.S. emerging economy. The main Spanish colonial coin was the *Eight Reales* (a large silver coin the size of a Silver Dollar) and the smaller One Real, Two Reales, and Four Reales). In some cases, the Eight Reales was actually cut up into eight pieces (hence the nickname *Piece of Eight*). Each piece was called a "bit" and had a value of 12½ Cents. Is this beginning to sound familiar yet? How about the high school cheer: "Two bits, four bits, six bits, a dollar — all for *Coin Collecting For Dummies* stand up and holler!" Two *bits* equal a Quarter Dollar; four bits, a Half Dollar; six bits, a nonexistent 75-Cent piece; and eight bits, a Dollar. Thus, the Quarter Dollar was created to replace the Two Bits and 2 Reales Spanish coins with America's own money. Think about it — as an American in 1796, wouldn't you have been proud to pay for something with a shiny new coin from your own country?

Major types of U.S. Quarter Dollars

Quarter Dollars came in six major design types during their long tenure from 1796 through today.

Draped Bust (1796–1807)

The Draped Bust Quarter first appeared in 1796 (see Figure 17-13), then promptly dropped off the scene, not to reappear until 1804. As result, there just aren't too many dates in this series, making it very easy for a collector to complete a date set. The 1796 is expensive, the 1804 is scarce, and the dates from 1805 to 1807 are easy to find.

Figure 17-13: Draped Bust Quarter.

Capped Bust (1815–1838)

John Reich's Capped Bust design appeared in 1807 on the Half Dollars, but because no Quarter Dollars were minted between 1807 and 1815, the design was several years late in coming to the Quarter Dollar (see Figure 17-14). Most dates in this series are common, but there is one standout — the 1827. This classic rarity was struck only in Proof, then was struck again many years later using an 1819 back!

Figure 17-14:
The Capped Bust Quarter.

Seated Liberty (1838–1891)

The Seated Liberty Quarter Dollar series is full of low-mintage dates, interesting varieties, and affordable dates (see Figure 17-15). Interesting coins in this series include the 1853 *Arrows and Rays,* the extremely rare 1873-CC, and varieties like the 1877-S (in which the mintmark was first punched into the coin sideways!). If you're looking for a fun, challenging series, give the Seated Liberty Quarters a try.

Figure 17-15:
Seated Liberty Quarter.

Barber (1892–1916)

In 1892, Charles Barber created a new Quarter Dollar (see Figure 17-16) using the same design that he also placed on the Dime and Half Dollar. The Barber Quarter series has three toughies to collect — the 1896-S, 1901-S, and 1913-S, but none of the three are beyond the means of most collectors. In fact, putting together a set of Barber Quarters in low grade is fairly easy, which is one of the reasons this series is so popular with collectors.

Figure 17-16: The Barber Quarter.

Standing Liberty (1916–1930)

In 1916, a new Quarter Dollar design by Hermon A. MacNeil hit the streets (see Figure 17-17). The front of the coin showed a bare-breasted Liberty in a flowing dress holding a shield and an olive branch and walking between two stone gates. The back of the coin showed an eagle in graceful flight. Why the officials at the U.S. Mint decided to make an R-rated coin is beyond me, especially when the lady was our own Liberty, the icon of freedom and liberty and everything that is good about the United States. In any event, a couple of design changes were made in 1917 to make the coin more acceptable from technical and aesthetic viewpoints. In the most obvious change, Liberty not only regained her modesty, but she began wearing a vest of chain mail, as well. On the back of the coin, the eagle was raised to a more central position, and three stars were moved underneath.

For years, experts believed that repressed prudes and their public outcry for decency were the reasons for covering up Liberty in 1917, but recent investigation has found little evidence to support such a claim.

Many collectors look for well-struck examples of this type that have full and complete detailing on Liberty's head. Those coins with a Full Head can be worth substantial premiums.

Figure 17-17:
The
Standing
Liberty
Quarter.

Washington Head (1932–present)

Had he lived that long, George Washington would have been two hundred years old in 1932, so Congress decided to celebrate with a new Quarter Dollar with George's head on the front (see Figure 17-18). The Washington Head Quarter Dollar was meant to be a commemorative coin, but it was so popular that it became a regular issue in 1934. Tough dates in the series include the 1932-D and 1932-S. All other dates are common. Like the Dimes and Half Dollars, the metal used to make the Quarter Dollars changed in 1965 from silver to a clad copper and nickel combination. Collectors love this series because it's easy and affordable to collect and because many of the later dates were minted only as beautiful, frosty Proof-only issues.

Figure 17-18:
The
Washington
Quarter.

Collecting U.S. Quarter Dollars

From the lovely Standing Liberty design to the popular Washington Head type to the challenging Seated Liberty series, U.S. Quarters present collectors with lots of choices and lots of fun. Read the following tips to choose the path that's right for you.

✔ **By type:**

- **Difficulty rating:** Easy. All of the main Quarter Dollar types are easily obtained.

- **Cost estimate:** A type set in Fine condition runs approximately $500 ($8,500 if you want to include the 1796 Draped Bust/Plain Eagle); in Uncirculated condition, expect to pay around $6,000 (or close to $30,000 if you include the 1796).

✔ **By date:**

- **Difficulty rating:** Easy to impossible. A date set of Draped Bust Quarters is possible but expensive. The 1827 makes completing a date set of Capped Bust Quarters expensive and unattractive. Same goes for the Liberty Seated Quarters, because only four of the 1873-CC No Arrows are known. In the Barber series, you find a couple of rare dates, but a complete set in circulated condition is still within the means of most collectors. Standing Liberty Quarters and Washington Quarters are no problem.

- **Cost estimate:** Figure on paying $12,000 for a date set of Draped Bust Quarters in Fine condition and leave it at that — the extreme rarity of the 1804 Quarter in high grade makes putting together an Uncirculated date set a dream. Likewise for the Capped Bust Quarters: The 1827 is known only in Proof condition and is always expensive. A Fine set of Seated Liberty Quarter Dollars runs more than $10,000, and that's without the 1873-CC No Arrows; an Uncirculated set would not only be expensive but impossible, because several dates are unknown or extremely rare in Uncirculated condition (then there's the 1873-CC No Arrows again). A Fine set of Barber Quarters runs $8,500, and an Uncirculated set costs at least $43,000. A date/mintmark set of Standing Liberty Quarter Dollars in Fine condition costs $3,750; an Uncirculated set runs at least $15,000 (figure multiples of that amount if you want Full Head examples).

Circulated sets of Washington Quarter Dollars are inexpensive, but because many of the later dates are Proof-only issues, I recommend attempting a set all in Uncirculated and Proof conditions — such a set starts at $3,000.

✔ **By die variety:**

- **Difficulty rating:** Easy to impossible. Draped Bust and Capped Bust Quarter Dollars are collected by die variety, but some are so rare as to be unobtainable. For example, a new variety of the 1837 was discovered recently, and only one lucky collector will have a chance to own it until another example is discovered. The Seated Liberty series contains numerous major and minor varieties, some of which are quite interesting. My favorites include the 1854-O Huge O, the Open and Closed 3 varieties of 1873, and the 1877-S S over Horizontal S. Surprisingly, no major varieties exist in the Barber series. Look for the 1918/7-S overdate in the Standing Liberty Quarter series. In the Washington Head series, highlights include doubled dies on some of the 1934, 1942-D, 1943, and 1943-S Quarters and over-mintmarks on the 1950-D and 1950-S issues.

- **Cost estimate:** Inexpensive to expensive, based on the difficulty ratings assigned in the previous bullet. I view varieties as a side-trip anyway — it's sometimes fun to get off the main road, but it's also easy to get lost. If you recognize hard-core die variety collecting as an expensive, life-long proposition, then I say, "More power to you." If you decide to collect some of the later date Quarters by variety, start with the obvious ones and work down to the less dramatic ones. (You're more likely to get your money back on the varieties everyone knows.)

Holding onto Half Dollars

The first United States Half Dollar appeared in 1794, one of only three Silver coins made that year. The Half Dollar has always been an important coin for commercial reasons, so in only a few years were none struck (1798–1800, 1804, and 1816). In the period from 1804 to 1840, when Silver Dollars effectively disappeared from the market, and gold coins were scarce, the Half Dollar became the coin of choice for large transactions. Today, Half Dollars are not nearly as important as they once were, and you won't see them that often — they seem to have lost ground to the Quarter Dollar. For example, in 1995, the Philadelphia Mint made over 1 billion Quarter Dollars and less than 27 million Half Dollars. Nevertheless, the Half Dollar series is a long and fascinating one, with lots of fans in numismatics.

Major types of U.S. Half Dollars

Half Dollars appear in eight major types, which are discussed in this section.

Flowing Hair (1794–1795)

The Half Dollars of 1794 and 1795 follows the design of the Half Dimes and Silver Dollars, showing Liberty as a woman with long flowing locks of hair (see Figure 17-19). The back of the coin features a scrawny-looking eagle within a wreath.

Most Half Dollars were made from silver deposited at the U.S. Mint at Philadelphia. A person with a bunch of raw silver or a pile of silver coins from other countries could take the silver to the Philadelphia Mint to have it melted down and refined, and then make new U.S. coins out of it. The person would then have shiny new coins to distribute to friends, customers, or the merchants with whom she did business. In fact, the U.S. government had little money with which to purchase silver, so it relied on people to bring the silver to it.

Figure 17-19:
Flowing Hair
Half Dollar.

Draped Bust (1796–1807)

The Draped Bust design (see Figure 17-20) debuted on Half Dollars in 1796, but silver deposits were so low that only 3,918 Half Dollars were struck in 1796 and 1797 combined. And none were made from 1797 to 1800. By 1801, mintages of the Half Dollar jumped until they nearly reached the one million mark in 1806. The only rare dates in this series are 1796 and 1797. A popular and challenging way to collect this series is by die variety.

Capped Bust (1807–1839)

In 1807, John Reich created a new design of Liberty for the Half Dollar. Liberty was older by then, so she was given a more mature appearance (see Figure 17-21). A freedman's cap was placed on her head, and a strip of cloth with the word "Liberty" on it was tied around her head. Because mintages were so high for this series, you can find many different die varieties. Collectors who pursue this avenue of collecting are known as *Bust Half Nuts,* and they belong to the *Bust Half Nut Club!*

Figure 17-20:
Draped Bust
Half Dollar.

The only real rarity in this series is the 1838-O, minted in the first year of production at the New Orleans, Louisiana Mint and now known by less than a dozen examples.

Figure 17-21:
Capped Bust
Half Dollar.

Seated Liberty (1839–1891)

The Seated Liberty design first appeared on U.S. Half Dollar in 1839 (see Figure 17-22). Mintages remained high for most dates but dropped off in 1878, when focus shifted to Silver Dollar production. Weight changes in 1853–1855 and 1873–1874 were indicated by the presence of arrowheads on either side of the date. The real mystery in this series is the 1873-S No Arrows Half Dollar. Mint records indicate that 5,000 were struck, but none has ever been seen. Rarities in this series include the 1853-O No Arrows and the 1878-S. Many of the 1861-O Half Dollars were struck by the Confederacy after it took over the New Orleans Mint.

Figure 17-22:
Seated
Liberty Half
Dollar.

Barber (1892–1915)

Charles Barber's version of Liberty appeared simultaneously on the Dime, Quarter, and Half Dollar in 1892 (see Figure 17-23). The Barber Half series has no rarities or stoppers to prevent you from completing a date and mintmark set. Nevertheless, finding nice high-grade examples is difficult because most coins in this series saw heavy circulation.

Figure 17-23:
Barber Half
Dollar.

Walking Liberty (1916–1947)

A.A. Weinman was responsible for creating new designs for the Dime and Half Dollar in 1916 (see Figure 17-24). Both designs represented major departures from Barber's staid head of Liberty (see the preceding section). On the Half Dollar, Liberty carries a huge olive branch and is wrapped in the American flag. The eagle on the back of the coin is one of my favorite renditions of this impressive bird.

You can find every date in this series with ease, even the scarcer 1921, but many of the early dates can get quite expensive in Uncirculated condition.

Figure 17-24:
The Walking
Liberty Half
Dollar.

Franklin Head (1948–1963)

Ben Franklin got a coin of his own in 1948 when John Sinnock created a new design for the Half Dollar (see Figure 17-25). As he did on the Roosevelt Dime, Sinnock placed his initials on the Half Dollar, where certain paranoid types immediately pronounced that they were those of Joseph Stalin. The back of the coin featured a large image of the Liberty Bell, a design allegedly lifted by Sinnock from the back of his commemorative Half Dollar of 1926. All Franklin Half Dollars are common, and a set of all 35 date and mintmark combinations is easy to complete. Collectors often pay big premiums for examples with Full Bell Lines on the Liberty Bell because only coins with full, complete strikes have them.

Figure 17-25:
The Franklin
Half Dollar.

Kennedy Head (1964–present)

Immediately after President John F. Kennedy was assassinated, plans were made to honor him on the Half Dollar. Engravers Gilroy Roberts and Frank Gasparro created an impressive design that remains extremely popular with collectors today (see Figure 17-26). Ninety percent pure silver coins were struck in 1964 only; from 1965 to 1970, the Half Dollars contained 40 percent silver, and thereafter, they were made of a sandwich of pure copper between layers of copper-nickel. All dates are common.

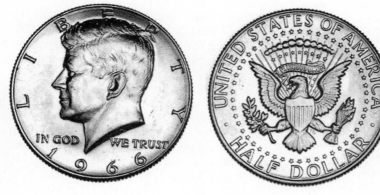

Figure 17-26: The Kennedy Half Dollar.

Collecting U.S. Half Dollars

Compared to other series, Half Dollars are a relative bargain. For example, you won't find any great rarities in the run from 1892 to present, making it easy and affordable for most collectors to obtain most, if not all dates, in the series. Their impressive size and attractive designs make Half Dollars a good collecting choice.

✔ **By Type:**

- **Difficulty rating:** Easy. Every type is readily available on the market.

- **Cost estimate:** Fine condition — $3,750. In Uncirculated condition, the rarity of Uncirculated Flowing Hair Half Dollars makes this pricing speculative, but figure on spending tens of thousands of dollars at least!

✔ **By date:**

- **Difficulty rating:** Easy to extremely difficult. Flowing Hair Half Dollars are easy to obtain, but expensive. For Draped Bust Half Dollars, the 1796 and 1797 are extremely rare. In Capped Bust Half Dollars, the 1815 is scarce, but the 1838-O is the real stopper. Seated Liberty Half Dollars are extremely difficult because of the 1853-O No Arrows and the 1878-S. All dates after 1891 are easy to find and collect.

- **Cost estimate:** A Fine condition set of Flowing Hair Half Dollars runs $5,000; an Uncirculated set is prohibitively expensive due to the rarity of high-grade coins. A set of Draped Bust Half Dollars in Fine condition runs $34,000, based largely on the 1796 and 1797 dates, both of which make an Uncirculated set extremely expensive. For Capped Bust Half Dollars, plan on spending $3,000 for a date/mintmark set in Fine condition (minus the 1838-O, of course) and $35,000 for an Uncirculated set. A Seated Liberty Half Dollars set in Fine condition approaches $20,000, and that's without the 1853-O No Arrows; several dates are unknown in Uncirculated condition, so I won't price an Uncirculated set, only dream about it! In the Barber series, a Fine condition date/mintmark set costs over $4,000, and an Uncirculated set costs over $45,000. Walking Liberty Half Dollars become a bit more reasonable, with a Fine condition set running $1,250 and an Uncirculated set costing at least $32,000. Franklin Half Dollars are so reasonable that I suggest an Uncirculated set at around $400. Same with the Kennedy Half Dollars, where you can buy a date/mintmark set all in Uncirculated and Proof condition for around $275.

✔ **By die variety:**

- **Difficulty rating:** Easy to extremely difficult. Just as in other denominations, the biggest challenges and difficulties come in trying to assemble die variety sets of the earliest dates and types. In many cases, the die varieties are unique or so rare as to be prohibitively expensive. In the Seated Liberty series, major varieties include the 1844-O Double Date, the 1847/6 overdate, and the With and Without Arrows varieties of 1873. Few people collect this series by die varieties because they are so difficult to tell apart. In the Barber series, you won't find any major varieties, but the 1892-O Microscopic O is a rare, minor variety.

- **Cost estimate:** Inexpensive to prohibitively expensive, ranging from $10 for a 1946 doubled die back to nearly $100,000 for an 1817/4 overdate.

Digging Around for Dollars

When Congress debated America's money system, the key denominations were the Silver Dollar and the Gold Eagle ($10). The purpose of the Silver Dollar was to compete with and replace the Spanish colonial Eight Reales, which was the most important, widely circulated silver coin in the Americas during the time. The United States was a new country and wanted coins of her own. The first Silver Dollars were impressive hunks of silver, each containing their full value in the semi-precious metal. Despite the theoretical importance of the Silver Dollar, none were minted between 1804 and 1836. In 1878, huge quantities of silver were found in the western states, and the floodgates opened: Millions upon millions of Silver Dollars were produced, and they became the darlings of collectors because of their rich, bright luster, their impressive size, and their availability.

I've included the Eisenhower, Susan B. Anthony, and Sacagawea Dollars in this section even though the majority of them no longer contain any silver. Of course, some of the Eisenhower Dollars were made of 40 percent Silver, so that has to count for something.

Major types of U.S. Dollars

Dollars appear in nine major types, which are discussed in this section.

Flowing Hair (1794–1795)

The first U.S. Silver Dollars bore Robert Scot's Flowing Hair design (see Figure 17-27). Because the U.S. Mint relied on depositors for its silver (see the "Flowing Hair (1794–1795)" section, earlier in this chapter), mintages are spotty. In fact, less than 2,000 1794 Silver Dollars were struck. Because of metallurgical problems, the director of the U.S. Mint altered the composition of the first Silver Dollars, illegally raising their silver content. While this wasn't enough of a crime to send him to jail, the change did cost the government over $2,000 at a time when $2,000 was a huge amount of money. As expected, the 1794 is rare, but the 1795 is affordable.

Figure 17-27:
Flowing Hair
Silver Dollar.

Draped Bust (1795–1804)

The Draped Bust Silver dollar (see Figure 17-28) comes in two subtypes, one with the plain eagle design of 1795 and a later version with an eagle with a shield. The rarest date in this series is the 1804, one of the greatest rarities in all of U.S. numismatics (holder of the record price of $4.14 million — see Chapter 24). Funny thing, though, the 1804 Dollar wasn't struck until at least 1834, when some were made as special presentation pieces for overseas VIPs. Several collectors are working on die variety sets from this type, but the high cost of the coins keeps most collectors out.

Figure 17-28:
The Draped
Bust Silver
Dollar.

Seated Liberty (1836–1873)

No Silver Dollars were struck for circulation between 1804 and 1836, which was an awfully long time to go without one of the bedrocks of the U.S. money system. In 1836, an employee of the U.S. Mint named Christian Gobrecht designed a new silver Dollar featuring a Seated Liberty design (see Figure 17-29) that was to become a standard on all silver coins just a few years later.

The back of the coin shows an eagle in flight amidst a field of stars (this beautiful Flying Eagle reverse was never adopted for use on Silver Dollars, but it did eventually appear on the new Small Cents of 1856–1858 — see Chapter 16). By the time Gobrecht's Silver Dollar made it into general circulation in 1840, the back of the coin was changed to a plain eagle with arrows with an olive branch in its talons.

Figure 17-29:
The Seated Liberty Silver Dollar.

The Seated Liberty Dollar series is replete with rarities. The 1858 was minted only in Proof, the 1870-S runs close to $100,000, and the 1873-S is unknown, even though U.S. Mint records indicate some were struck. Nevertheless, the Seated Liberty Dollar type continues to be a very popular series — just make sure you have a lot of money in the bank before you venture into this area.

Trade (1873–1885)

In 1873, the U.S. Mint began producing a special Silver Dollar to circulate in the Orient and compete with similar coins from other nations (see Figure 17-30). The new *Trade Dollar* bore a modified version of the Seated Liberty design — this time, Liberty is seated on a bale of cotton, and she offers an olive branch to an unknown recipient on the other side of the ocean. The Trade Dollar enjoyed some popularity in Asia, where merchants would punch their special marks into the coin to give it their stamp of approval. Even though the Trade Dollar was heavier than the regular U.S. Silver Dollars, it was good only for purchases up to $5 in the United States. After that, the Trade Dollar was worth only its bullion value, which was less than its face value. As a result, a lot of the coins found their way back into the United States, where they could be spent at a profit.

The appearance of the Morgan Dollar in 1878 spelled the end for the Trade Dollar, although Proof Trade Dollars continued to be struck through 1885. The last two years, 1884 and 1885, are extreme rarities in the series, with the 1885 being worth well over $1,000,000 for a nice example.

Figure 17-30:
Trade Dollar.

Morgan (1878–1921)

Little did George T. Morgan guess that his new Silver Dollar of 1878 would become the most important silver coin in the United States and the most widely collected coin in all of numismatics. Morgan's design is simple yet elegant, with a classic head of Liberty and an eagle with outstretched wings (see Figure 17-31). Thanks to large hoards of Silver Dollars uncovered over the years, sufficient quantities of Uncirculated coins exist to support the active collector market. Key dates in this series include the 1889-CC, 1892-S, 1893-S, and the Proof-only 1895. Certain Uncirculated Silver Dollars have mirrored surfaces ranging from partially mirrored to deeply mirrored. A *deep mirror Prooflike* is the collector's dream, and some dates are extremely rare in this format.

Figure 17-31:
The Morgan
Silver Dollar.

Peace (1921–1935)

Following World War I, everybody wanted peace. Some Americans wanted it so badly that they petitioned for a Peace Dollar (see Figure 17-32) and got it. Unfortunately, by the time the design was finished, Peace turned out to be nothing more than a small word on the back of the coin (maybe if the word "Peace" had been made bigger, we wouldn't have had World War II)! In a nod to classical ancient styling, the designer used a Roman spelling for the motto "In God We Trust," using a V instead of a U. This simple change accounts for a large portion of the phone calls received by dealers every day: New owners of Peace Dollars think they have a rare error. Peace Dollars were made from 1921 to 1935. The first year had an unusually high relief that was lowered in subsequent years. All dates are available and affordable, although the 1928 and 1934-S can be a challenge, especially in nice condition. After 1935, no more Silver Dollars were issued until 1971.

Figure 17-32:
The Peace
Dollar.

Eisenhower Head (1971–1978)

The Eisenhower Dollar was originally meant to honor the astronauts of Apollo XI for their historic landing on the moon. However, a portrait of Ike was placed on the front of the coin (see Figure 17-33) because he had died a few months before the lunar landing took place. The back of the coin shows an eagle landing on the moon with an olive branch in its talons. No mention is made of Apollo XI, so when the coin first appeared, the public immediately nicknamed it the *Eisenhower* (or *Ike*) *Dollar.* The Ike Dollars made for general circulation were made of the same copper-nickel-clad metal used on other U.S. coins beginning in 1965, but collectors were allowed to purchase specially packaged Uncirculated and Proof example in 40 percent silver. In 1975 and 1976, a special design was used to celebrate the U.S. bicentennial.

Figure 17-33:
The
Eisenhower
Dollar.

Anthony Head (1979–1999)

The Susan B. Anthony Dollar replaced the Eisenhower Dollar in 1979. Susan B. Anthony fought for women's rights, especially the right to vote, in the 1800s. When a new, smaller One Dollar coin was being considered, Suzie turned out to be one of the more popular subjects (see Figure 17-34). Mint officials thought a smaller Dollar would circulate better than the old 38 millimeter version, but the public absolutely hated the new coin because it was too easily confused with a Quarter Dollar (shades of the old Twenty-Cent piece all over again). Millions of the Anthony Dollars remained unissued in the government's vaults. A sudden demand for the coins depleted the supplies in the late 1990s, and in 1999 the design was resurrected for one more time. Yet people still get it confused with a Quarter!

Figure 17-34:
The Susan
B. Anthony
Dollar.

Sacagawea (2000–present)

Despite the failures of the Twenty-Cent piece and the Susan B. Anthony Dollars, and despite resistance from the general public, the government persists in developing small-sized Dollar coins. Their latest experiment, the Sacagawea Dollar, has met with some success. In my opinion, the *Sac Dollar* (as it is known) owes its success to two elements:

✔ Sacagawea is a more attractive subject than old Susan B. Anthony (see Figure 17-35), plus the addition of her little baby, Pomp, tugs at people's heartstrings.

✔ The golden color of the coin sets it apart from any other coin currently in circulation, and some people have hoarded the coin because they think it's made of real gold. While the jury is still out on whether the Sac Dollar will make it in this world, it has certainly created a storm of interest in coin collecting, which is just fine with me!

Figure 17-35: The Sacagawea Dollar.

Collecting U.S. Dollars

Silver Dollars are the largest silver coin produced by the U.S. Mint for general circulation, and they're beautiful and impressive. Is it any wonder that U.S. Silver Dollars are one of the world's most eagerly collected coins? The following are some ways for you to get in on the action.

✔ **By type:**

• **Difficulty rating:** Easy. All of the types listed in the preceding section are easy to find on the market, but the Flowing Hair and Draped Bust types are somewhat expensive.

• **Cost estimate**: A Silver Dollar type set in Fine condition runs $2,200; in Uncirculated condition, the price jumps to roughly $30,000.

✔ **By date/mintmark:**

- **Difficulty rating:** Easy to impossible. In the two-date Flowing Hair series, the 1794 is a rare coin. The huge price of the 1804 prevents 99.9 percent of the population from completing a set of Draped Bust Dollars. In the Seated Liberty series, the 1836–1839 Proofs are rare, the 1851, 1852, 1858, and all the Carson City issue are rare, the 1870-S is extremely rare, and the 1873-S is unknown in any collection. For Trade Dollars, the extreme rarity of the 1884 and 1885 Trade Dollars makes a date/mintmark set a nearly impossible task. Morgan Dollars are difficult because the 1895 is a stopper. Peace Dollars are a piece of cake, Eisenhower Dollars are easy, and Susan B. Anthony and Sacagawea Dollars are no problem.

- **Cost estimate:** In Fine condition, a set of Flowing Hair Dollars runs $22,000 (assuming you can find a Fine 1794), a set of Draped Bust Dollars costs $6,250 (no 1804 included), a set of Seated Liberty Dollars runs around $100,000, a set of Trade Dollars (minus the 1884 and 1885) costs roughly $6,500, a set of Morgan Dollars runs roughly $3,000 (not including the 1895), and a set of Peace Dollars runs $375. Unless you're extremely wealthy, don't even consider collecting the Flowing Hair, Draped Bust, or Seated Liberty types in Uncirculated condition. Even Trade Dollars and Morgan Dollars have enough rare coins in high grade to make their Uncirculated sets overly expensive. Only when you hit the Peace Dollar series does the price become manageable, and then you're looking at $2,500 for starters. The Eisenhower, Susan B. Anthony, and Sacagawea Dollars are all reasonably priced in Uncirculated and Proof grades.

✔ **By die variety:**

- **Difficulty rating:** Easy to impossible. The same comments apply here as they do for the Half Dollars (see the "Collecting U.S. Half Dollars" section, earlier in this chapter). Because of the extreme popularity of these series and the presence of many well-heeled collectors, prices for rare varieties often go through the roof.

- **Cost estimate:** Here are some examples of the huge price differences that variety collectors face: $10 for an 1878 Morgan Dollar with seven tail feathers on the eagle's tail versus $4.14 million for a Class I 1804 Silver Dollar.

Chapter 18

Gold Coins: Concentrated Wealth

• •

In This Chapter

▶ Introducing U.S. gold coins

▶ Examining the different types of U.S. gold coins

• •

*I*n this chapter, I introduce you to U.S. gold coins, those beautiful, yellow chunks of precious metal that are recognized throughout the world for their consistent quality, beauty, and value. I arrange this chapter according to the value of the coins, beginning with $1 coins and going through each denomination through $20.

Because of their high intrinsic value, gold coins possess a high numismatic value. Few collectors can afford more than one or two gold coins, and it is a wealthy collector indeed who can afford to collect gold coins by type. Only a few of the very wealthiest collectors have attempted to collect gold coins by date, but in the few cases where the attempt has been made, the results have been spectacular.

If you're not at the top of the economic food chain, you still have several collecting options available to you. A *denomination set* contains only six coins ($1, $2.50, $3, $5, $10, and $20), all of which are affordable in circulated grades. A *type set* contains examples of each of the different designs used on gold coins (for type sets you can stick with one denomination, several denominations or all of them — the choice is yours). You can always build a *partial type set* by foregoing the rare, early types and concentrating on the more modern, affordable gold coins. Also, you can collect coins with *mintmarks* from each of the different mints that produced gold coins in the United States (C for Charlotte, NC; D for Dahlonega, GA; another D for Denver, CO; O for New Orleans, LA; CC for Carson City, NV; S for San Francisco; and coins with no mintmark from Philadelphia, PA). *Proof coins* (those high-quality coins made expressly for sale to collectors) are extremely expensive, but you can find lots of interesting *die varieties* (coins with minor but often intriguing differences) and *overdates* (corrected dates stamped over incorrect dates). For a review of grading terms (like Uncirculated and Very Fine), see Chapter 9.

Beware of buying counterfeit gold coins. Buy only coins that have been certified by a reputable grading service or make sure you have your new purchases checked out by a competent expert.

$1 Gold Pieces

The smallest official U.S. gold coins are the Gold Dollars that debuted in 1849. Gold Dollars were not included in the numismatic lineup when the U.S. Mint first began producing coins in 1793, perhaps because of the competing Silver Dollar. However, when gold was discovered in California, Americans got a new coin to add to their change and collections. Most of the early dates in this series were made in large quantities, but beginning in 1857 (and with the exception of 1862), mintages dropped off, and the Gold Dollar was discontinued in 1889.

Liberty Head Gold Dollar (1849–1854)

With fresh supplies of gold coming in from California, the U.S. government found itself in the luxurious position of being able to add two new denominations — a $1 Gold piece and a $20 Gold piece (or Double Eagle). James Longacre created new designs for both coins that were unlike those already being used on other U.S. gold coins. Longacre stuck with a Liberty Head for the front (see Figure 18-1), but on the back, he chose a wreath to surround the denomination. This design lasted only five years. Although some dates in the series are rare, no stoppers prevent you from completing a set of all dates and mints.

Figure 18-1:
The Liberty
Head Gold
Dollar.

Perhaps the most interesting variation in the series is an 1849 Gold Dollar from the mint at Charlotte, North Carolina with a smaller-than-normal wreath on the back (collectors know of only four examples).

The history of gold coins in the United States

The first U.S. gold coins were made in 1795 and those first gold coins are all quite rare. Many were exported to other countries or melted down when their metal value exceeded their face value. Prior to the 1830s, gold was scarce in the United States, so most of the first gold coins were made for private individuals or banks who took their raw gold to the U.S. Mint where it was converted into coin form.

Many Americans believe the first big gold discoveries in the United States were made during the California Gold Rush that began in 1848. However, the first significant discoveries actually occurred in North Carolina and Georgia, which yielded a beautiful, greenish-yellow gold. Enough gold was found in the southeastern United States to support private mints and America's first two branch Mints at Dahlonega, Georgia and Charlotte, North Carolina. As a result, mintages of gold coins increased

dramatically after 1834, and the general public finally had a chance to see and use gold coins on a regular basis.

In 1848, James Marshall discovered gold in the area around Sacramento, California, touching off the famous California Gold Rush that brought riches to the United States — and thousands of emigrants to California. With huge quantities of gold ready to be made into coins, the U.S. Mint added two new denominations — the Gold Dollar and the large, heavy $20 gold piece (Double Eagle).

Production of gold coins continued at this pace until 1933, when President Franklin Roosevelt responded to the Great Depression by outlawing the ownership of all non-numismatic gold coins. Many of the older-date coins were recalled and melted down, turning some once common coins into great rarities.

Indian Princess Gold Dollar (1854–1889)

Beginning in 1854, James Longacre made the Gold Dollar larger and thinner, and he planted an Indian Headdress on Liberty's head (see Figure 18-2). Considering that Liberty had already worn everything from elegant turbans to coronets on earlier coins, a Native American headdress was not out of line, especially considering that many depictions of America during the Revolutionary War were as a Native American Princess. The earliest Indian Princess Gold Dollars have poorly defined hair details and are scarce in high grade. In 1856, Longacre made one final modification by improving the details and making the headdress a bit larger (many collectors consider this a separate and distinct type). Important dates in this series include the 1861-D (all were made by the Confederacy after it seized the mint at Dahlonega, Georgia) and 1875. (Only 420 were made.) The series ended in 1889.

Figure 18-2:
The Indian
Princess
Gold Dollar.

$2.50 Gold Pieces

The $2.50 Gold piece (or *Quarter Eagle*) first appeared in 1796 and remained an important part of the U.S. monetary system until the last year of issue in 1929. Nevertheless, most of the mintages are small compared to many of the larger denominations, resulting in many scarce or rare dates in this series.

What the heck is a Quarter Eagle? When the U.S. government created its first money system, the foundation of the silver coins was the Silver Dollar, and the foundation for the gold coins was a coin called the Eagle. The Eagle represented a value of $10; therefore, a Quarter Eagle was one-fourth of an Eagle, or $2.50. Likewise, a Half Eagle represents $5, and a Double Eagle represents $20. Collectors refer to U.S. gold coins both ways, so remember these names because you'll hear them again. The $3 Gold piece was not included in the original debate and didn't appear until 1854. Because of its odd value, you never hear the $3 Gold piece referred to as any fraction of an Eagle.

Turban Head $2.50 Gold piece (1796–1807)

The first U.S. Quarter Eagles depicted Liberty with a cap on her head that looks like a sophisticated turban (see Figure 18-3). Every date in this series started out with a low mintage, and most were destroyed when the value of their gold exceeded their face value. As rare as they are, there are no stoppers in this series, but you need a lot of money if your goal is to collect every date in this type.

Figure 18-3:
The Turban
Head
Quarter
Eagle.

Capped Bust $2.50 Gold piece (1808–1834)

In 1808, Liberty took on a more youthful appearance, she began facing left instead of right, and her turban became more like a beret with the word "Liberty" on the headband (see Figure 18-4). A big gap exists between 1808 and 1821, when no Quarter Eagles were produced. The 1808 Quarter Eagle almost deserves its own type listings because, by 1821, Liberty's head became smaller and some of her bustline was omitted. Every date in this type is scarce and valuable, but none is outrageously expensive.

Classic Head $2.50 Gold piece (1834–1839)

On this type, Liberty loses her hat but retains a "Liberty" ribbon to bind her curly hair (see Figure 18-5). The mintages for this type jumped following the discovery of gold in Georgia and North Carolina, so you can actually obtain every date in this type for a reasonable price. Even the difficult issues from the Charlotte, North Carolina and Dahlonega, Georgia Mints are affordable.

Liberty Head $2.50 Gold piece (1840–1907)

In 1840, Liberty received another hairdo, this time with her hair done up in a bun and the ribbon changed into a "Liberty" coronet (see Figure 18-6). This is a lengthy series, made for over 60 years, so expect a large number of low-mintage dates and expensive rarities in addition to the more common dates. One of the more interesting pieces is the 1848 Quarter Eagle with "Cal." punched into the back of the coin. These special pieces were made at Philadelphia from gold that had come all the way from California. Two dates (1841 and 1863) were made only as Proofs, and the 1854-S Quarter Eagle is one of the great rarities in U.S. numismatics.

Figure 18-4:
The Capped Bust Quarter Eagle.

Figure 18-5:
The Classic Head Quarter Eagle.

Indian Head $2.50 Gold piece (1908–1929)

One of President Theodore Roosevelt's legacies was the change he instituted on U.S. coins. Roosevelt loved the timeless designs of classical Greek and Roman coins, and he felt the U.S. designs failed to meet the standards of a great nation. Thus, in 1907, he instituted a wave of change that impacted all denominations of United States coins by 1916. One of the more interesting changes took place on the $2.50 (see Figure 18-7) and $5.00 gold coins, where the design was actually stamped into the metal of the coin (normally, the designs on coins are raised above the flat surfaces). The biggest complaint against this innovative design was that dirt would collect in the crevices on both sides, thereby transmitting all kinds of disease to anyone who handled the coin.

Figure 18-6:
The Liberty Head Quarter Eagle.

Figure 18-7:
The Indian Head Quarter Eagle.

A complete date and mint set of Indian Head Quarter Eagles contains only fifteen coins, all of which are within the means of most collectors. The only key date is the 1911-D.

$3 Gold Pieces

Yes, it's true — the United States made a $3 Gold coin from 1854 to 1889 (see Figure 18-8). At first glance, a $3 denomination seems a little unusual, especially because it didn't really fit into the coinage scheme used in the United States. So why a $3 coin? The answer lies in the postal rates at the time — the rate for First-Class mail delivery was a mere 3 Cents. Stamps could be bought singly (using a Three-Cent piece) or in sheets of 100 (using a $3 Gold piece). Unlike today, stamp prices remained stable for a long period of time; thus, the $3 Gold piece was a familiar sight until 1889, when the denomination ended.

Most $3 Gold pieces have low mintages. Three dates (1873, 1876, and 1876) were made only as Proofs. Then there's the unique 1870-S $3 Gold piece — one of the most valuable of all U.S. coins.

Figure 18-8:
Three-Dollar
Gold piece.

$4 Gold Pieces

The $4 Gold piece was nothing more than a proposed coin design (also known as a *pattern* — see Chapter 20) that never made it to the full production stage. $4 Gold pieces earned the nickname *Stellas* because of the large star that appears on the back of each coin (see Figure 18-9). Made only in 1879 and 1880, Stellas come in two types: Flowing hair, where Liberty's hair flows free, and Coiled Hair, where Liberty's hair sweeps up in a bun. Because they were patterns, Stellas are extremely rare and out of the reach of most collectors. However, I mention them here just because they are so beautiful and popular. Plus, even coin collectors can dream, right?

$5 Gold Pieces

The $5 Gold piece (or Half Eagle) shares with the $10 Gold piece (or Eagle) the distinction of being the first gold coin produced in the United States. Half Eagles were made almost uninterruptedly from 1795 to 1929 (but none were produced in 1801, 1803, 1816, 1817, and 1917 to 1928). Rare dates in the series include the 1815, 1822 (only three are known), 1825 (only two are known), the extremely rare 1854-S, the low mintage 1875, and the Proof-only 1887.

Figure 18-9: The $4 Gold piece.

Completing a set of the five major types listed in this section is easy, although the first two types tend to be a bit pricey. A meaningful collection of different dates can be built at reasonable prices, but you really need to be a multimillionaire before tackling a complete date set.

Turban Head $5 Gold piece (1795–1807)

This type is a larger version of the $2.50 Gold piece (see the "$2.50 Gold Pieces" section, earlier in this chapter) and also comes with either a Plain Eagle or an Eagle with Shield on the backs of the coins (see Figure 18-10). In fact, the backs (or *reverses*) of the coins cause some confusion unless you're familiar with some of the minting practices of the early Mint. For example, one of the rarest varieties of this type is the 1798 with a Plain Eagle reverse. Such a coin is not even supposed to exist, because the Plain Eagle reverse was last used in 1797. On the other hand, another puzzler is the 1795 with an Eagle and Shield reverse. This coin was two years ahead of its time — the Eagle and Shield reverse did not make its first regular appearance until 1797. Experts believe these unusual coins were made under emergency conditions with dies left over from earlier years.

Turban Head Half Eagles tend to be expensive because, like the Quarter Eagles, most were melted down for their metal value, which often exceeded the face value. Date sets can be built without much of a problem, but be aware that if you plan to build a set that includes major die varieties, the 1798 Plain Eagle reverse will stop you dead in your tracks.

Figure 18-10:
The Turban
Head Half
Eagle.

Capped Bust $5 Gold piece (1807–1834)

Don't let this relatively short series fool you — stuck in between many of the common dates (see Figure 18-11) are some of the most revered and valuable U.S. coins. Only three 1822 Half Eagles are known, and none are currently available for sale. The 1825/4 overdate is known by only two examples, but (thankfully) collectors have an alternative in the far less expensive 1825/1 overdate. The 1829 Large Date is extremely rare, the 1815 has an extremely low mintage, and for some reason, the higher-mintage 1819 is a rare coin, as well. Despite the daunting challenges, you can still purchase nice examples of this type for relatively reasonable prices.

Classic Head $5 Gold piece (1834–1838)

The design on this type (see Figure 18-12) matches that on the 1834 to 1839 Quarter Eagle, but the mintages are substantially higher, thus making a complete set both possible and affordable. Even the scarcer 1838 coins from the Charlotte, North Carolina and Dahlonega, Georgia Mints are affordable.

Liberty Head $5 Gold piece (1839–1908)

Struck over a 70-year period, the Liberty Head Half Eagle (see Figure 18-13) presents the challenge of a lifetime. Here are some of the highlights in this wonderful series:

- ✔ **1841-O:** Listed in U.S. Mint reports but none has ever been seen.

- ✔ **1854-S:** Only 268 were made, most of which have been destroyed.

- ✔ **1861-D:** Some were made after Confederate forces seized the Dahlonega, Georgia Mint in 1861.

- ✔ **1875:** Two hundred were made for circulation plus 20 Proofs, which makes them extremely rare.

- ✔ **1887:** Only 87 were made, all Proofs.

You face another challenge when trying to collect the highest possible condition. Many dates are extremely rare in Uncirculated condition, and some dates are rare above Very Fine. You could literally spend a lifetime (and the earnings of a lifetime) just upgrading and trying to complete this set, but you'd have an awful lot of fun.

Figure 18-11:
The Capped Bust Half Eagle.

Figure 18-12:
The Classic Head Half Eagle.

Figure 18-13:
The Liberty
Head Half
Eagle.

Indian Head $5 Gold piece (1908–1929)

This type (see Figure 18-14) is one of only two U.S. coins with an incuse design (the Indian Head Quarter Eagle is the other). The best way that I can think of to explain what *incuse* means is to compare it to belly buttons. Belly buttons that poke in are *innies* and those that poke out are *outies*. The designs on most coins are outies, but the design on this one is an innie.

Every date in this series is affordable, except for one. The 1929 is scarce, which means you can find it, but specimens start at several thousand dollars and go up from there.

Figure 18-14:
The Indian
Head Half
Eagle.

$10 Gold Pieces

The $10 Gold piece (or Eagle) is the bedrock of U.S. gold coins. When the government first devised a list of the different coins for production, the Eagle was chosen as the flagship for the gold coins, and most other gold coins were either fractional or multiple versions of the Eagle. For example, the $2.50 Gold piece was known as a Quarter Eagle, and later the $20 became known as the Double Eagle. However, even though it was considered an important coin, none were produced between 1804 and 1838. Many of the dates are downright scarce or rare because so few Eagles were made in some years.

Turban Head $10 Gold piece (1795–1804)

The $10 Gold piece was the highest-value coin made in the United States until the $20 Gold piece (Double Eagle) debuted decades later. The dates in the Turban Head Eagle series (see Figure 18-15) are all expensive, four- to five-figure coins. One important coin is the 1804 Eagle with a Plain 4 in the date — this rare coin was made around 1834 to go in the special Presentation sets that included the extremely rare 1804 Silver Dollars.

Figure 18-15:
The Turban Head Eagle.

Liberty Head $10 Gold piece (1838–1907)

Considering the number of decades over which the Liberty Head $10 (see Figure 18-16) was made, you may think a date set would be just as impossible to complete as a date set of Liberty Head Half Eagles. Surprisingly, such is not the case. First, you have fewer coins with which to contend, because no Eagles were produced at the Charlotte, North Carolina or Dahlonega, Georgia Mints. Second, the only super-expensive coin in this set is the 1875. There are no mega-rarities and no Proof-only issues, so the temptation is there. Hmm — should you go for it?

Indian Head $10 Gold piece (1907–1933)

As part of Theodore Roosevelt's campaign to beautify U.S. coins, he hired the renowned sculptor and artist Augustus Saint-Gaudens to revise the $10 and $20 designs. For the $10 Gold piece, Saint-Gaudens borrowed from the design on the then-current Cent and portrayed Liberty wearing an Indian headdress (see Figure 18-17). The back of the coin features a striking American Eagle perched atop a bundle of arrows. Although Saint-Gaudens is best known for his work on the $20 Gold piece (which also happens to be named after him), his Indian Head $10 design is a candidate for the most beautiful U.S. coin ever produced.

From a collecting standpoint, the 1933 is the only rare date. How rare, you ask? How about $50,000 to $100,000 rare!

$20 Gold Pieces

The $20 Gold piece (or Double Eagle) is a big chunk of gold. Each one contains nearly a full ounce of pure gold. Over the years, the U.S. Mints have made millions of Double Eagles, requiring a huge supply of gold. Fortunately, the United States has been blessed with an abundant supply of the beautiful yellow metal, but such has not always been the case. In fact, until gold was discovered in California, the Double Eagle was just a dream.

Today, the glittering golden Double Eagle is still a collector's dream.

Liberty Head $20 Gold piece (1849–1907)

The Liberty Head Double Eagle first appeared in 1849, following the discovery of gold in California. So much gold was found and the need for coins so great that the U.S. government decided to create two new denominations — a $1 Gold piece and a Double Eagle. The new Double Eagle features a head of Liberty on the front and a large eagle and shield on the reverse (see Figure 18-18). Many dates sell for only a slight premium over their metal value, so collectors find them appealing to collect. The following are some of the highlights and stoppers in the series:

- **1849:** Technically a pattern issue (see Chapter 20) and believed to be unique.

- **1861 Pacquet reverse:** An extremely rare coin with the designs on the back modified by a mint engraver named Anthony Pacquet.

- **1870-CC:** A monster rarity in any grade.

- **1882, 1883, and 1884:** Struck only in Proof condition.

Like most of the Liberty Head gold coins of other denominations, the Liberty Head Double Eagle series contains many rare dates and *condition rarities* (coins that are common in low grade but extremely rare in high grade).

Saint-Gaudens $20 Gold piece (1907–1933)

Beautiful, beautiful, beautiful. These are the words to describe the design on the Double Eagle created by Augustus Saint-Gaudens in 1907 (see Figure 18-19). In fact, I put this coin first on the list of my top ten coin designs in Chapter 25. Fortunately for collectors today, a high percentage of the original mintages still exist. Many Saint-Gaudens Double Eagles ended up in storage in European banks; over the years, they have filtered back to the United States. Thus, a common Saint-Gaudens Double Eagle can almost be considered a bullion coin, as the premium over the face value is small in many cases. However, other dates remain great rarities, despite high original mintages. Could they still exist hidden away in some bank vault somewhere?

Figure 18-18:
The Liberty Head $20 Gold piece.

Figure 18-19:
The Saint Gaudens $20 Gold piece.

The following highlights set the hearts of many collectors aflutter.

  ✔ **1907 Extremely High Relief:** The first design efforts by Saint-Gaudens featured an unusually high relief, meaning that the distance between the highest and lowest points of the coin was greater than usual. The result is stunning. However, because of the extra amount of time and effort required to make the coin, mint engravers lowered the relief before any were made for circulation, adding extreme rarity to these early versions.

✔ **1907 High Relief:** The modified version was nearly as impressive as the Extremely High Relief because the depth of the details was still greater than on any other coins struck for circulation. The U.S. Mint made slightly over 11,000 High Reliefs before throwing in the towel and flattening the design even further. As popular as the Saint-Gaudens Double Eagles are, collectors love the 1907 High Relief the best.

✔ **1927-D:** A big mintage, but hardly any are known to exist. Were they all melted down?

✔ **1933:** The 1933 Double Eagle was made in large quantities, but at the last minute, the government decided not to place the coins into circulation. Instead, they destroyed the entire production, except for a few pieces that either slipped out or were taken out illegally by U.S. Mint employees. Thus the 1933 Double Eagle has been illegal to own for many years. However, just recently, the U.S. government cleared the way for one (just one) example to be sold. I fully expect this to become the most valuable U.S. coin ever sold if and when it hits the market.

Chapter 19

Commemoratives: Raising Money with Money

• •

In This Chapter

▶ Commemorating events with coins

▶ Understanding commemoratives from the early years to modern times

▶ Taking a look at the 50 States Quarters Program

▶ Getting some tips for collecting commemoratives

• •

Commemorative coins are coins with stories. Stories keep a coin from becoming dull and boring, but they also tell the collector something about the United States and its history. Some of the best storytellers are commemorative coins because of their connection with famous people, places, and events. U.S. commemorative coins offer glimpses of history, fame, and positive virtues, shown by a variety of purely American images, icons, and designs. For collectors, commemoratives are some of the most appealing and popular coins around.

The big news for commemorative coin collectors in recent years is the 50 States Quarters Program begun by the U.S. Mint in 1999. Check out the "50 States Quarters Program" section, near the end of this chapter, for more information on this series and join the millions of new coin collectors who have discovered coin collecting because of this innovative program.

Commemorate This!

The basic reason for a commemorative coin's existence is to raise money for whatever purpose the coin commemorates. U.S. commemoratives have been used to raise money for expositions, monuments, Olympic contests, and other important issues. On the other hand, some quasi-commemorative coins, like the 1976 U.S. Bicentennial coins, were made for circulation and carried no premium whatsoever (except for the special collector sets sold by the government for a premium price). The same is true of the 50 States Quarters, which are basically circulating commemoratives.

Virtually all U.S. commemorative coins share the following characteristics, although plenty of exceptions exist:

- ✔ They are made to honor a person, place, organization, or event.
- ✔ They are made to raise money.
- ✔ They are short-lived, usually appearing only once.
- ✔ They are not meant to circulate as money, even if they have a stated value.

Although the United States has made commemorative coins since 1892, I segregate them into three fairly distinct time periods:

- ✔ **The early years:** 1892 to 1934
- ✔ **The age of abuse:** 1934 to 1954
- ✔ **Modern commemoratives:** 1982 to present

The Early Years: Commemoratives Under Control

The first U.S. commemorative coins were struck in conjunction with the World's Columbian Exposition in 1892 and 1893. The fundraising made possible by the early commemorative coins was fairly straightforward. An organization would estimate how many coins it could sell, the Mint would strike up the requested amount, and the organization would sell as many as possible, returning the coins it couldn't sell to the Mint to be destroyed. Little thought was given to creating artificial rarities, manipulating prices, or restricting the number of buyers. Rather, the early commemoratives served their fundraising purposes well, without the abuses that occurred later on (see the following section).

From 1892 to 1934, commemorative coins were issued sporadically, often with long gaps between issues. Great thought was given to proposals for commemorative coins during the early years and permission to produce the coins was given only in cases of great merit. The fact that four different commemorative coins were produced in 1925 is more a coincidence than an abuse of the system.

In this section, I introduce you to some of the more interesting commemorative coins issued during this period. These coins have, in my opinion, the best stories. The following list is by no means complete, however. Collectors recognize 50 different commemorative types comprising 144 different issues from 1892 to 1954. Any modern coin catalog or price guide contains a complete listing, plus all of the modern issues.

✔ **Isabella Quarter Dollar:** Issued in 1893 along with the Columbian Exposition Half Dollar for sale at the Exposition. The Isabella Quarter (see Figure 19-1) was a sop to women agitators, led by none other than Susan B. Anthony (see Chapter 17 for her special coin).

✔ **Lafayette Dollar:** The Marquis de Lafayette was a friend of George Washington's and an important supporter of America during the Revolutionary War. In 1900, a commemorative Silver Dollar was issued to help raise money for a proposed Lafayette statue that appears on the back of the coin.

✔ **Jefferson and McKinley Gold Dollars:** Gold dollars were struck in 1903 to raise funds for the Louisiana Exposition, celebrating the 100th anniversary of the Louisiana Purchase. I think the Exposition may have cost more than the entire Louisiana Purchase.

✔ **Lewis & Clark Exposition Gold Dollars:** These dollars were made in 1904 and 1905 to raise funds for the 1904 Lewis & Clark Exposition. Their guide, Sacagawea, did not get a coin of her own until 2000.

✔ **1915 Panama-Pacific Exposition coins:** This huge exposition celebrated the opening of the Panama Canal. A variety of different coins and sets were issued. You can choose between a Half Dollar, a Gold Dollar, a Quarter Eagle ($2.50), and two huge $50 gold pieces (one round, one octagonal). Because of their high face value, very few of the $50 gold pieces were sold, making them rarities today.

✔ **McKinley Gold Dollars:** Struck in 1916 (the fifteenth anniversary of William McKinley's assassination) and 1917 to raise money for his birthplace Memorial in Niles, Ohio.

✔ **Lincoln/Illinois Half Dollar:** Struck in 1918 to raise money for statewide celebrations of the 100th anniversary of Illinois statehood. Honest Abe Lincoln appears on the front of this coin.

✔ **Maine Half Dollar:** Struck in 1920 to raise funds for Maine Centennial celebrations.

✔ **Pilgrim Half Dollars:** Struck in 1920 and 1921 to celebrate the 300th Anniversary of the landing of the Pilgrims.

✔ **Missouri Half Dollars:** Struck in 1921 to honor Missouri's 100th Birthday (see Figure 19-2). The rarer of two types has a "2" and a "4" separated by a star on the left side of the front of the coin, symbolizing the admission of Missouri as the 24th State.

✔ **Alabama Half Dollars:** Struck in 1921 on the occasion of the 100th Anniversary of Alabama becoming a state. Some Alabama Half Dollars come with a small "2x2" in the right field on the front of the coin, recognizing Alabama as the 22nd State (the "x" was placed there as a meaningless spacer).

- **Grant Memorial coins:** Includes Half Dollars and Gold Dollars struck in 1922 to celebrate Grant's 100th birthday (had he been alive) and to raise money for various Grant-related projects. Some coins come with a small star on the front of the coin just above the word "Grant." What's it for? No one knows.

- **Monroe Doctrine Half Dollar:** Talk about scraping the bottom of the barrel for something to commemorate: 1923 was the 100th Anniversary of the Monroe Doctrine. Whoopee.

- **Huguenot-Walloon Half Dollar:** Struck in 1924, 300 years after a Dutch ship brought a group of Huguenots to the New World to escape religious persecution in Europe. Wow. Unless you're a Calvinist or were awake during history class, you've probably never heard of the Huguenots; which, if you think about it, proves the value of coins as records of history.

- **Stone Mountain Half Dollar:** Outside of Atlanta, Georgia is a mountain of granite that seems completely out of place. Known as Stone Mountain, this popular tourist spot bears a huge sculpture made by Gutzon Borglum, the same man who made the Mount Rushmore monument. In 1925, Half Dollars were made to publicize Borglum's Herculean effort.

- **Lexington-Concord Half Dollar:** On April 19, 1775, colonial Minutemen at Lexington and Concord, Massachusetts fired the "Shot Heard Round The World" and began the Revolutionary War. Struck in 1925, this coin commemorated the 150th anniversary of this historic event and helped to raise money for local celebrations.

- **Fort Vancouver Half Dollar:** In 1925, the fort that eventually became the city of Vancouver, Washington celebrated its Centennial, an event deemed significant enough to merit its own special coin. These were all minted at San Francisco, but for some reason, the mintmark was left off the coins.

- **California Half Dollar:** Struck in 1925 to commemorate the 75th Anniversary of California's statehood. The front of the coin shows a Forty-Niner panning for gold; the back of the coin shows an impressive Grizzly bear.

- **Sesquicentennial Half Dollar and Quarter Eagle:** Here's an event into which all Americans could sink their teeth: the 150th anniversary of the signing of the Declaration of Independence. The U.S. Mint celebrated the occasion with coins of silver and gold. The silver version features the Liberty Bell on the back; the Quarter Eagle displays Independence Hall.

- **Oregon Trail Half Dollars:** First struck in 1926 to raise money for the Oregon Trail Memorial Association. Although listed in the section of early commemoratives, Oregon Trail Half Dollars were made as late as 1939, at which time they were subjected to the same abuses as the other commemoratives of the period (see the following section).

✔ **Vermont Half Dollar:** Struck in 1927 on the 150th anniversary of the Battle of Bennington, Vermont to raise money for Vermont museums and celebrations. Collectors who like coins with animals love this coin because of the mountain lion on the back.

✔ **Hawaiian Half Dollar:** Struck in 1928, 150 years after Captain Cook "discovered" the Hawaiian Islands. The back of the coin has a neat depiction of a native Hawaiian chieftain (see Figure 19-3).

✔ **Maryland Half Dollar:** The first settlers arrived in Maryland in 1634, 300 years before this coin was issued in 1934. The front of the coin shows Cecil Calvert, the founder of Maryland. The back of the coin depicts his coat of arms.

Figure 19-1:
The Isabella Quarter.

Figure 19-2:
The Missouri Half Dollar.

Figure 19-3:
The
Hawaiian
Half Dollar.

The Age of Abuse: Commemoratives Out of Control

As fundraisers, commemorative coins were pretty straightforward. If you were a group trying to raise money, you could go to Congress with an idea for a commemorative coin. If Congress felt that your proposal had merit, it would approve a law directing the U.S. Mint to make the coins on your behalf. You could then pre-sell the coins by subscription, take delivery of the coins and begin marketing them to the general public, or sell the entire batch to a single dealer or distributor who would, in turn, sell them to the public. Your group's profit would be the difference between what the U.S. Mint charged you (usually face value) and what you sold the coin for. If, for example you sold a commemorative Half Dollar for $1.00, your profit would be $.50 on each coin.

However, if your group could convince Congress to do any of the following, you could vastly increase your profits:

✔ Allow coins to be made at all three Mints (Philadelphia, Denver, and San Francisco), creating three different coins to sell to collectors, potentially tripling your earnings.

✔ Continue making your commemorative coin year after year, increasing your profit potential dramatically.

✔ Create rarities by reducing the mintages to low levels, thus being able to charge more for the coins and increasing your profits dramatically. You could also create a rarity, and then sell the entire mintage to a single buyer, locking in a nice profit and leaving all the work to someone else. If the single buyer chose to, he could raise the price to whatever level the public would pay.

These scenarios actually happened, beginning with some of the 1934 commemorative issues. The abuses and manipulations led to a public outcry that stifled commemorative coin production for many years. Only in recent years has the commemorative spigot been opened again. The U.S. Mint now keeps a wary eye on the balance between creating enough commemorative coins and producing too many.

The following are some of the more interesting commemorative coins from the 1934 to 1954 period:

- **Oregon Trail Half Dollar** (see Figure 19-4): Wait a minute — wasn't this coin listed in the preceding section? Sure it was. I list this coin again here because it illustrates the abuses that entered the system. 1926 was the anniversary year, yet the Oregon Trail Memorial Association received permission to have coins made two years later in 1928, then again in 1933, 1934, 1936, 1937, 1938, and even as late as 1939. Come on. How much money did this group need? And 13 years after the first ones were struck? All of the later issues have very low mintages and almost all were bought up by speculators or sold at inflated prices.

- **Texas Centennial Half Dollar:** Struck from 1934 to 1938, with the mintages declining steadily and most of the coins going to speculators each year.

- **Arkansas Centennial Half Dollar:** Technically, a state can only have one Centennial celebration, but Arkansas milked it for all it was worth, issuing Half Dollars from 1935 to 1939. Even worse, the back of one of the 1936 issues shows the head of Senator Joseph Robinson, a violation of the tradition forbidding the image of a living person from appearing on a United States coin.

- **San Diego Half Dollar** (see Figure 19-5): I stuck this one in because this is the teeming metropolis where I currently live. Besides, the promoter tried to double the price of the 1936 version from $1.50 to $3.00 in just one year, so this coin fits the pattern of abuses of this time period.

Figure 19-4:
The Oregon Trail Half Dollar.

Figure 19-5:
The San
Diego Half
Dollar.

By 1939, the U.S. government had received so many complaints from dealers and collectors about the abuses in the commemorative coin program that it halted the production of all old and new commemorative coins. It wasn't until 1946 that the program was revived, when Half Dollars commemorating Iowa's statehood and Booker T. Washington were issued. The Iowa coin was made for only one year. The Booker T. Washington Half Dollar was made every year until 1951, when it morphed into the Booker T. Washington/George Washington Carver coin. This lasted until 1954, when the commemorative program was effectively laid to rest for nearly 30 years.

Modern Commemoratives: Money Coins

In 1982, George Washington would have been 250 years old, so it was time, once again, to strike up the band and strike up a new commemorative coin to honor the occasion. In reality, this was the Mint's toe-in-the-water test to see how the public would respond to a commemorative coin program. Except for 1985, the U.S. Mints have produced commemorative coins for collectors each year since. Mintages have increased, as have the number of different coins made each year, such that the average collector can hardly afford to collect every possible date set/mint set/type set option.

That's why I call modern commemoratives *money coins*. They are expensive compared to their face value, but if you have enough money, you can get all you want. The U.S. Mint has even reinstituted the practice of making gold commemorative coins, further adding to the collector's pain (in the wallet).

Some of the topics featured on modern commemorative coins include the following

- ✔ **Statue of Liberty:** The Statue appeared in 1986 on a Copper-Nickel Half Dollar, a silver One Dollar, and a $5 Gold piece.

- ✔ **200th anniversary of the U.S. Constitution:** This event was commemorated in 1987 on a Silver Dollar and a $5 Gold piece.

- ✔ **Dwight D. Eisenhower:** Ike appears twice on the front of his 1990 Silver Dollar.

- ✔ **Christopher Columbus:** Honored in 1992 on Copper-Nickel Half Dollars, Silver Dollars, and $5 Gold pieces.

- ✔ **Sports:** Several sports, including soccer, gymnastics, baseball, basketball, and swimming, are honored on modern U.S. commemorative coins.

- ✔ **War:** The Civil War, World War II, the Korean War, and the Vietnam War have all been subjects on modern U.S. commemoratives.

50 States Quarters Program

Commemorative coins usually have low mintages because they are made for sale at a premium to coin collectors. Thus, the general public remains unaware of the coin and whatever message it seeks to convey unless they spend the money to buy the coin.

Wouldn't it be wonderful if the United States came up with a circulating commemorative coin that everyone could see, one that could be purchased for its face value and one that anyone, even little kids, could afford to own? That way, everyone could get the message by actually seeing what the coin has to say.

Governments around the world come to understand the value of circulating commemorative coins. Even in ancient times, Romans used their coins as a way of celebrating military victories or announcing a new ruler (see Chapter 11). Germans produced many circulating commemorative coins, becoming especially prolific during the period from 1871 to 1939. However, the United States has rarely embraced the idea of a circulating commemorative coin. Until recently.

The greatest thing since sliced bread

In 1999, the U.S. government began the 50 States Quarters Program, an ambitious plan to issue five Quarter Dollars each year over a ten-year period. Each U.S. state has its own special Quarter Dollar, to be issued in the order in which the States were added to the Union. Eventually, all 50 States will be represented. The coins are made in large quantities and are placed into circulation at their face value, thus making them available to anyone in the general public. However, in keeping with traditional U.S. capitalism, the coins are also available in special collector sets in Uncirculated and Proof conditions, for sale at a premium (of course).

The U.S. Mint may have chosen the Quarter Dollar denomination for this program because of their experience with the Washington Quarter. First issued in 1932, the Washington Quarter was supposed to be a one-year commemorative coin to honor George's birthday. However, the Washington Quarter proved to be so popular that the U.S. Mint has made them every year since 1934. Also, in 1976, the U.S. Mint made a special Quarter to commemorate America's 200th birthday, so ample precedent exists in the Quarter series to justify the new program.

How has the 50 States Quarter Program been received? To put it mildly — enthusiastically. Millions of Americans eagerly await the introduction of each new Quarter Dollar. School kids have discovered the thrill of coin collecting for the first time, and it seems that everyone is building collections of these interesting Quarters. The United States is abuzz over the 50 States Quarter Program!

The 50 States Quarters schedule

The U.S. Mint gives each state the opportunity to design its own special Quarter, with the governor of each state determining the selection process. Artists submit their designs, from which finalists are chosen. The U.S. Mint reviews each finalist's design from a technical standpoint to see if the coins will strike properly. After a winning design is chosen, the coin is struck, and the public gets to see a new Quarter Dollar about every ten weeks.

Here's the timetable for 50 States Quarters:

- **1999:** Delaware, Pennsylvania, New Jersey, Georgia, and Connecticut
- **2000:** Massachusetts, Maryland, South Carolina, New Hampshire, and Virginia
- **2001:** New York, North Carolina, Rhode Island, Vermont, and Kentucky
- **2002:** Tennessee, Ohio, Louisiana, Indiana, and Mississippi
- **2003:** Illinois, Alabama, Maine, Missouri, and Arkansas
- **2004:** Michigan, Florida, Texas, Iowa, and Wisconsin
- **2005:** California, Minnesota, Oregon, Kansas, and West Virginia
- **2006:** Nevada, Nebraska, Colorado, North Dakota, and South Dakota
- **2007:** Montana, Washington, Idaho, Wyoming, and Utah
- **2008:** Oklahoma, New Mexico, Arizona, Alaska, and Hawaii

If you haven't discovered the 50 States Quarters yet, take a look at your pocket change or check with your local bank and start collecting them today. See if you can locate one of each of the designs illustrated here!

To find out more about the 50 States Quarter Dollars Program and to see new designs as they are developed, visit the U.S. Mint's Web site at www. usmint.gov.

Tips for Collecting Commemoratives

U.S. commemorative coins offer the collector a variety of interesting designs and stories. When you're ready to jump into this fascinating area of collecting commemoratives, remember the following tips:

- **Collect by type:** This is the least expensive way to collect commemorative coins. Basically, if you've seen one Oregon Trail Half Dollar, you've seen them all, so there's no real need to collect every different date and mintmark. Choose from the following type listings:

  - **Pre-modern Silver commemoratives (1892 to 1954):** One Quarter Dollar, 48 Half Dollars, and one Dollar. This set is reasonably priced; even a Choice Uncirculated set runs around $15,000.

  - **Early Gold commemoratives (1903 to 1926):** Five Gold Dollars, two Quarter Eagles, and two $50 Gold pieces. The two $50 Gold pieces are very rare and make this set an expensive proposition.

  - **Modern commemoratives (1982 to 2000):** Fourteen Half Dollars, 44 Dollars, 19 $5 Gold Coins, and two $10 Gold Coins (I don't include the 50 States Quarters — see the preceding section).

- **Collecting every issue:** Don't even consider going down this road unless you have lots of money. Or consider breaking out certain areas, such as the 144-piece set of pre-modern Silver commemoratives, the 11-piece set of early Gold commemoratives (without the two big Panama-Pacific $50 Gold pieces), or modern commemoratives. To keep collecting commemoratives fun and manageable, develop goals that are achievable and affordable.

- **Collecting by grade:** This refers only to the early commemorative coins. Quality was not a big issue, with either the U.S. Mint or with collectors, when these coins were made, so finding high-grade examples of many issues presents today's collector with an exciting challenge. Nevertheless, most are available in Gem Uncirculated condition (see Chapter 9 for help with grading terms) with some notable (and expensive) exceptions like the Lafayette Silver Dollar, the Grant with Star Half Dollar, both Missouri Half Dollars, and the Sesquicentennial Half Dollar.

✔ **Modern coin sets:** Many of the modern U.S. commemoratives are sold in multi-coin sets that have proved to be very popular with collectors. Be aware that the condition and the completeness of the packaging are often just as important as the condition of the coins. More modern commemoratives are coming.

If you're interested in obtaining modern U.S. commemorative coins, be sure to join the Mint's mailing list to receive advance notice of new issues. For information on U.S. Mint products, write to the U.S. Mint, Customer Care Center, Lanham, MD 20706-4331 or sign up for the "U.S. Mint Products Notification" e-mail service on their Web site at www.usmint.gov.

Expect the U.S. Mint to continue producing commemorative coins for many years to come. The number of new coin collectors has exploded dramatically in recent years, fueled in large part by the flood of new commemorative coins, not to mention the 50 States Quarters. Commemorative coins give these new collectors something interesting with which to begin their collections — a story!

Chapter 20

Advancing to Oddball Coins

● ●

In This Chapter

▶ Taking a look at pattern coins

▶ Collecting pioneer gold coins

▶ Understanding Proof coins

▶ Looking at coins from Hawaii

▶ Finding the unusual in error coins

● ●

After you get out of the mainstream of U.S. numismatics, you come across some interesting and unusual coins that are usually stuck in the backs of catalogs and price guides. Hidden among these treasures are some of the great rarities of U.S. numismatics, some of which are coins of incredible historical interest. There's something for everyone in these oddball coins, and in this chapter, I point out major items of interest in the hopes that you will discover and enjoy these numismatic oddities for yourself.

Oddball coins are definitely an acquired taste, which means that only serious collectors need apply. In this case, "serious" means one of two things:

✔ You have the time to find out enough about these coins to fully appreciate them.

✔ You have serious money to be able to afford them.

Understanding Pattern Coins

Before new coins are created, the U.S. Mint creates *patterns:* trial pieces (see Figure 20-1) that test how a particular design will appear in real life and whether any technical problems develop as the coin is struck.

Figure 20-1:
Pattern
coin.

Except in unusual instances, patterns always enjoy a low mintage, often less than a dozen pieces. As a result, patterns are not only hard to find, but they tend to be expensive. Multiply expensive by hundreds of different varieties, and the money required to put together a collection of pattern coins becomes substantial.

Even so, you may be interested in picking up a piece or two for your collection, in which case, I'd like to tell you about a few of my favorites:

- **1792 Silver-Center Cent:** The first U.S. One Cent pieces were big, heavy, and required a lot of scarce copper. As an alternative, smaller versions were made with a small plug of silver in the center that added value to make up for having less copper. They look neat and the idea had merit, but the coins were hard to produce and only a few were made.

- **1836 Gobrecht Silver Dollar:** Except for the 1804 Silver Dollar (which was actually made in 1834), no Silver Dollars were made between 1804 and 1836 (in 1804, several thousand silver dollars were made, but they were all dated 1803). In 1836, Christian Gobrecht created a new Silver Dollar with a figure of Liberty seated on the front and an eagle flying across the back. Because he placed his name on the dies, these are now known as Gobrecht Dollars. Over 1,000 examples were made, which is a lot by pattern standards. Today, they are among the most popular of all U.S. coins.

- **1856 Flying Eagle Cent:** In 1856, the U.S. Mint began experimenting with reducing the size of the Large Cent to a more manageable size that was easier and less expensive to produce. The result was a Small Cent (the size you're used to) that borrowed Christian Gobrecht's design of an eagle flying across the front of the coin. Like the Gobrecht Dollar, the 1856 Flying Eagle Cent is extremely popular. The mintage of over 1,000 pieces barely meets the huge demand for this pattern.

- **1882 Liberty Head Nickel:** I love this pattern for its shock value, because most collectors believe that the first Liberty Head Nickel appeared in 1883. Wrong. Remember — before the coin, there was a pattern!

- **1879 and 1880 Four Dollar Gold Stellas:** This odd denomination first appeared in 1879. Read more about them in Chapters 18 and 25 (where I include them among my ten favorite coin designs).

- **1849 $20 Gold piece:** This was the first $20 gold piece produced by the U.S. Government. The one example known to exist is a proud part of the National Numismatic Collection at the Smithsonian Institution. I wish it were a proud part of my collection!

- **1907 Indian Head $20 Gold piece:** Take an enlarged version of the Indian Head design from the $10 Gold piece (see Chapter 18) and stick it on the front of a $20 Gold piece. Sound impressive? It is, and it's unique.

Collecting Pioneer Gold

The first discoveries of gold in the United States were not in California, as you may have guessed, but in North Carolina and Georgia. Local minters turned this gold into coins to help alleviate the need for money in the region, especially because most of the output of gold coins from the U.S. Mint was melted for its bullion value as soon as the coins hit the streets.

When gold was discovered in California, new problems arose. Because California was so far removed from the Philadelphia Mint, there was no convenient way to turn gold dust and nuggets into usable coins, which were sorely needed to help regulate and facilitate business among the miners. To the rescue came private minters, who created a variety of different coins. Unfortunately, the temptation to cheat a little was too great, and many of the early *pioneer gold* coins (as they are known) fail to live up to the values or purity stated on them. Eventually, the federal government solved the problem by establishing an Assay Office in San Francisco, where raw gold was converted into $10, $20, and $50 gold pieces of standard, reliable weight and purity. When the official mint opened in San Francisco in 1854, most of the private minters went bye-bye, but not before leaving a lasting impression on numismatics. The following are some of the more important issuers of pioneer gold:

- **Templeton Reid:** Templeton Reid operated out of Georgia and made coins from native gold in 1830, becoming the first of our pioneer Mints (I guess you could call him a pioneer among pioneers). All of his coins are extremely rare.

- **The Bechtler Family:** The Bechtler Family operated a mint in North Carolina between 1834 and sometime in the 1840s. They have the distinction of having made the first Gold Dollars in the United States, beating the U.S. government by 15 years. The Bechtler coins were quaint pieces struck from handmade dies, but they served as important contributions to the economy of the region before the U.S. Mint opened its branches at Charlotte, North Carolina and Dahlonega, Georgia.

- **Moffat & Co.:** Beginning in 1849, the firm of Moffat & Company began producing high-quality ingots and $5 and $10 gold pieces in San Francisco from newly discovered California gold. Moffat & Co. made lots and lots of coins, but like most pioneer gold coins, they were later melted down. Thank goodness for coin collectors, or none might have been saved!

- **Clark, Gruber & Co.:** Clark, Gruber & Co. operated out of Denver, Colorado where the firm struck gold coins in 1860 and 1861. Its $10 and $20 gold coins have an interesting, stylized version of Pike's Peak on the back.

- **Wass, Molitor & Co.:** Wass, Molitor & Co. produced $5, $10, $20, and $50 Gold Coins in San Francisco between 1852 and 1855. Its most impressive piece of work was the huge $50 Gold piece struck in 1855 (see Figure 20-2). This massive piece of gold will set any coin collector's heart aflutter.

Figure 20-2:
The Wass, Molitor & Co. $50 Gold piece.

- **Kellogg & Company:** No, this group has nothing to do with breakfast cereal, but it has everything to do with big coins made out of California gold. Kellogg & Company operated out of San Francisco, where it produced high-quality $20 and $50 Gold coins in 1854 and 1855.

✔ **The Mormons:** In 1849, Brigham Young established a mint at Salt Lake City and oversaw the production of $2.50, $5, $10, and $20 Gold coins. Most of the coins had the inscription "G.S.L.C.P.G." that stood for "Great Salt Lake City Pure Gold." Unfortunately, the gold was neither pure nor from Salt Lake City (it came from California). The Mormons also made $5 Gold coins in 1850 and then again in 1860.

✔ **California Fractional Gold Coins:** California Fractional Gold Coins are actually mini-pioneer gold coins of low face value (25 Cents, 50 Cents, and One Dollar) that were made by local jewelers and merchants from 1852 to 1882. Hundreds of different varieties exist. Because they are relatively inexpensive compared to the higher denomination pioneer gold, collectors find them attractive and desirable.

To find out more about the California Gold Rush and pioneer gold, visit the CoinFacts Web site at www.CoinFacts.com or check out any of the general numismatic publications in the Cheat Sheet at the front of this book.

Finding Confederate Coins

In 1861, the Confederate States of America began making coins in two very different ways.

✔ The first way was to take over the U.S. Mints at Dahlonega (GA), Charlotte (NC), and New Orleans (LA), confiscate the gold or silver still remaining there, and strike coins using leftover Federal dies. In both instances, the coins struck by the Confederacy look exactly like those made by Federal employees, so the Confederate States of America still lacked a coin they could call their own.

✔ The second way was for the Confederacy to make coins of its own. Plans were made to have One Cent pieces designed in Philadelphia (quietly, of course, because this was Union territory) and Half Dollars struck at New Orleans.

For the Half Dollar, the back consisted of a totally new design with a Confederate shield in the center and a Liberty cap just above. A wreath and the words "Confederate States Of America" encircle the shield and cap. The front of the coin shows the normal Seated Liberty design of the period. The four known examples are all dated 1861. It's hard to say what one of these would be worth today, because every example is either in an institutional or private collection, with little chance of being released for sale in the foreseeable future.

I don't know why so few Confederate Half Dollars were made. The New Orleans Mint had plenty of silver on hand and even made over 2,000,000 regular Half Dollars, which could just as easily been made into Confederate Half Dollars.

Later, the Confederate die was used to make 500 *restrikes* (coins struck again in years later than the date shown on the coin, usually to satisfy collector demand) by grinding off the backs of normal 1861 Half Dollars and stamping them with the Confederate design. Even later, the Confederate die was used to make souvenir medals out of tin. Finally, the die was defaced with a chisel before being donated to the Louisiana Historical Society.

The Confederate Cent has an equally interesting story. The designer was a fellow by the name of Robert Lovett, Jr., who was probably chosen to make Cents for the Confederacy because of his previous experience in designing and making tokens. Only a few Cents were made before Lovett got cold feet and abandoned the project. Legend has it that Lovett carried one of the Confederate Cents with him and accidentally spent it one night in a local tavern. The story leaked out, and a prominent collector of the time hounded Lovett until he eventually sold the dies and the remaining Cents. The collector made restrikes in a variety of metals for sale to collectors. Later, the dies were defaced so that they couldn't be used again, but even more restrikes were made anyway. Ultimately, the dies ended up in the National Numismatic Collection at the Smithsonian Institution.

So where does that leave the collector who may be interested in these rare coins? The answer, as far as one of the four original Half Dollars goes, is out in the cold. Any of the 500 restrikes will cost from $3,000 to $7,000 each, depending on condition. Even the souvenir medals in tin (known as *Scott restrikes*) can run $2,000 to $3,000 in top condition. The Confederate Cent is worth in the $30,000 to $50,000 range, and a Copper restrike recently brought just over $12,000 at auction.

Appreciating Proof Coins

Proof describes a process for making coins specifically for sale to collectors. In modern usage, Proof coins are those struck using specially prepared blanks, highly polished dies, multiple strikes, and extreme pressure. The object of the Proofing process is to create a perfect coin, one with full details, mirrored fields, and no imperfections. Since 1858, the U.S. Mint has sold Proof coins to the public at a premium over their face value, often in partial or complete sets of all coins of the year. The "modern" Proof era began in 1936 (after a twenty-year hiatus during which no Proof coins were struck), and Proof set collecting is a preferred method, especially for beginning collectors.

What I am referring to in this section are the Proof coins issued from the early 1800s to 1916. Most of the Proofs from that time period are rare, with mintages ranging from just a handful to several thousand at most.

Proof versions exist of many of the coins I describe in Chapters 17, 18, and 19, but keep in mind that Proof coins are completely different animals from the coins made for regular circulation. They look different, they were made under different conditions and circumstances, and collectors approach them differently. Some dates, like the 1875 Three-Dollar Gold piece, were made only as Proofs.

Proof coins prior to 1858 are the rarest of the rare. Because they were created to satisfy collector inquiries, experts have no way of knowing how many of each were made. However, the number of examples that have survived indicate that the original mintages must have been extremely low, indeed. From this period, you can find Proof Half Cents, Large Cents, Three-Cent Silvers, Half Dimes, Dimes, Quarter Dollars, Half Dollars, and Silver Dollars (see Chapters 17 and 18 for explanations of these different denominations). A few Proof gold coins from this period are known, but they are extremely rare and valuable.

You can assemble a nice collection of Proof coins from the 1858–1916 time period, including many coins that are quite rare yet affordable. A denomination set containing a Small Cent, Two-Cent piece, Three-Cent Silver, Three-Cent Nickel, Half Dime, Dime, Twenty-Cent piece, Quarter Dollar, Half Dollar and Silver Dollar is relatively inexpensive, with only the Twenty-Cent piece and Silver Dollar costing in excess of $1,000 each. You can expand the set even further by including some of the different design types that were made during this period. As with the pre-1858 Proofs, gold Proof coins remain extremely scarce and expensive.

The key to collecting Proof coins is to find coins that are free of problems and that have never been cleaned. Some early collectors and curators had the nasty habit of dusting their coins from time to time, which left small, hairline scratches on the surfaces. Because Proof coins are supposed to represent perfection, this just won't do. However, some Proof coins are so rare that you simply have to take them as they come.

Some Proof coins, particularly the copper-nickel and silver coins of the 1880s, are hard to tell apart from the coins made for general circulation. Show any potential purchases to a competent expert or stick with certified coins.

Recognizing Hawaiian Coins

Once upon a time, Hawaii was an island nation ruled by a monarchy. Later, it became a U.S. territory and finally a state. Now, it's a favorite destination for tourists from around the world.

In 1847, copper coins the size of a U.S. Large Cent (roughly 27 millimeters) were made in the United States for King Kamehameha III. Unfortunately, the manufacturer messed up some of the spelling and the King hated his portrait on the front of the coin, so that was the end of any Hawaiian coinage projects for awhile.

In 1883, the new King, (David) Kalakaua I, promoted the idea of a national Hawaiian coinage. The coins, consisting of a Dime, ⅛ Dollar, Quarter Dollar, Half Dollar, and Dollar (see Figure 20-3), were all struck at the Philadelphia Mint. This is the tie-in that earns them a special place in U.S. numismatics and a listing in the back of the book along with the other oddball coins.

Figure 20-3:
The 1883
Hawaiian
Silver
Dollar.

Identifying Error Coins

To err is human. To err in numismatics means someone let a defective coin get out of the Mint. A defective coin is known as an *error coin,* and this area of collecting is becoming increasingly popular every day. Of course, the U.S. Mint released some pretty unusual and previously unknown error types in the past year or two, helping to fan the flames of desire among the millions of people who viewed the news reports and continue to scan their pocket change hoping they'll be the next lucky collector to find one!

The strangest error coin

Every once in a while, a coin comes along that defies explanation. My favorite is a 1970-S Proof Washington Head Quarter Dollar struck over a 1900 Barber Quarter. Obviously, this coin shouldn't even exist, yet it does.

The word "error" implies a mistake of some kind. In this case, there was no mistake. The only way for a 70-year old Silver coin from the opposite side of the country to find its way into a coining press making special Proof coins is if someone put it there deliberately. Make no mistake about it.

Error coins come in a wide variety of types, ranging from subtle mistakes to gross, obvious errors. Prices vary just as wildly, with some errors costing only a few dollars each, while others cost over $100,000.

Here are a few of the more dramatic and obvious errors, along with explanations of how they came about:

✔ **Off-center struck coins:** Sometimes *blanks* (disks of metal that are stamped to make coins) get stuck and don't feed properly into the coining machine. For example, if a blank is half-in and half-out of position when the die comes crashing down, the design will appear on only half the coin. The other half remains blank. This type of error is known as an *off-center strike* (see Figure 20-4). Off-center strikes are common but often dramatic, especially if only a tiny part of the design makes its way onto the coin.

Figure 20-4: Off-center strike.

✔ **Double and multiple struck coins:** Sometimes coins get stuck in the coining press and get stamped over and over. Double strikes are fairly common; any coin struck more than twice is rare. Occasionally, the second strike will be off-center or rotated slightly. In rare instances, a coin may even appear to have two dates.

✔ **Mated pairs:** *Mated pairs* occur when one coin overlaps another in the coin press and receives part of the design from the second coin. Mated pairs fit together perfectly, almost like two pieces of a locket. Because they are two separate coins and they usually get separated after they are struck, finding a mated pair is like finding a needle in a haystack. Mated pairs are among the most dramatic and desirable errors you can find.

✔ **Brockages:** In essence, a *brockage* is a true double-sided coin, except that one side appears normal, but the other side is a mirror image that is pressed into the coin. This happens when a blank slips over a coin that has already been struck; then this pair receives another strike from the dies. The blank ends up being the brockage and the other coin just ends up with a messed-up front.

✔ **Capped die:** A *capped die* occurs when a blank gets stuck on one of the dies. As the blank is hammered repeatedly into other coins, the metal flows around the die and forms a cup-shaped cap. The longer the blank stays attached to the die, the more dramatic and deeper the cap becomes. You could actually make a little tea set with these impressive errors.

✔ **Wrong metal/wrong planchet errors:** You may have heard of the 1943 Bronze Cent in the news media. If it doesn't ring a bell, here's the scoop: In 1943, Cents were made out of zinc-coated steel to preserve copper for the fighting during World War II. Somehow, a few leftover bronze blanks got stamped with the 1943 dies, thereby creating one of the most famous of all error coins. Some people think the 1943 Bronze Penny is worth $500,000, when, in fact, they usually sell from $30,000 to $100,000, depending on the condition.

✔ **Mules:** A *mule* occurs when two mismatched dies are placed together accidentally. Mules are generally very rare. In fact, you didn't hear too much about them until recently, when the U.S. Mint accidentally combined the front of a Washington Head 50 States Quarter Dollar with the back of the new Sacagawea Golden Dollar. This mistake caught the attention of the national news media, and millions of people began searching their pocket change for one of these valuable rarities. Have you looked in your pocket yet?

✔ **Struck fragment:** Sometimes a small fragment of metal gets fed into the coining press and receives an impression from the dies. These coins, called *struck fragments,* are really weird-looking because they are misshapen and the edges are really ragged. I recall seeing a picture of a nail with an impression of a Lincoln Cent smack-dab in the middle, which makes me think that some of these errors are deliberate instead of accidental.

Part V
Selling (Sob!) Your Numismatic Treasures

The 5th Wave   By Rich Tennant

"This is probably the rarest coin in my collection. It's the one that stayed in my pocket during a three-day slot machine competition in LasVegas."

In this part . . .

Sadly, the time will come when you may want to sell all or part of your collection. The reasons may be one of many: bad health, a home purchase, Suzy going off to college, or advancing age. Or you may simply have gotten tired of collecting coins. (Perish the thought!) Whatever the reason, approach the sale of your collection as diligently and as carefully as when you purchased your numismatic lovelies. Your new goal should be to get the most amount of money that you can for your coins, with the least amount of effort, as quickly as possible.

In this part, I explore various ways to sell your coins. You may settle on a single method that works best for you, or you may utilize one or more selling methods. Much depends on the amount of time you have and how much of your own effort you're willing to expend.

The greatest tragedies in numismatics — and ones I see repeated over and over again — are cases where collectors have died and their heirs have no clue as to the value of the coins or how to dispose of them. Rarely do the heirs obtain anywhere near the true value of their coins. Instead, they often get cheated. So take advantage of your knowledge of your own collection and save your heirs considerable grief and aggravation by controlling the sale of your coins while you're still alive.

Chapter 21

Selling Your Coins Yourself

• •

In This Chapter

▶ Knowing what to expect when you sell your own coins

▶ Getting ready and knowing where to sell your collection

▶ Becoming a master coin seller

• •

Selling your coins yourself can be a fun and rewarding experience. On the other hand, it can be a daunting, unpleasant task. A lot depends on your own personality, your abilities as a salesperson, and the way you handle acceptance and rejection. Consider carefully whether your time and efforts will net you more money than if you pay a commission to someone else who sells the coins on consignment and has better access to the coin market (see Chapter 22).

Your approach to selling your coins should be the exact opposite of how you purchased them. When you collected, you tried to buy the best coins for the lowest price; when selling, your goal should be to sell most of your coins for the best price, and the best coins for a stupendous price.

In this chapter, I give you detailed instructions on how best to market and sell your own coins. Try selling a coin or two this way to see if you enjoy the experience. If you have fun selling your own coins, go for it. If not, jump to Chapters 22 and 23.

Knowing What to Expect

To help you in your decision-making process, the following are a few of the realities that every seller faces, whether the product is a vacuum cleaner or one of your Silver Dollars:

✔ **Rejection:** Yes, people will turn down the chance to buy your coins. They may reject the price, the grade, or even you! And, they don't even need a reason to do so. You or your coin may be rejected ten times before you get a positive response. Can you handle rejection?

- **Lowball offers:** Some dealers will not work on less than a 100 percent profit, so you may receive an offer that is substantially below the market value of your coin. Can you handle a lowball offer without taking it personally and avoiding a big argument with the oaf who made it? Can you walk away from a fight?

- **Insults:** Sure, your coin is beautiful. The person who sold it to you thought so, and so do you. But what happens when you offer your coin to someone and he or she disputes the grade or insults the condition of the coin in an attempt to get a more advantageous price? Can you avoid taking it personally and trying to exact some sort of revenge?

- **Seller's remorse:** Seller's remorse ranges from a sad feeling you get when you sell something that has been near and dear to your heart to a sickening feeling you get when you discover that you sold something too cheap. If seller's remorse hits you, I offer the following advice: Get over it! Don't cry over spilled milk. Let bygones be bygones. *Que será será.*

  If you can't handle seller's remorse, let someone else sell your coins for you, or you'll go crazy every time you write an invoice.

- **Eager buyers:** Okay, I've given you the depressing aspects of selling your coins, so now it's time to give you a little hope. You will meet eager buyers who are willing to pay high prices for your coins. It's just a matter of finding them and holding yourself together until you do.

Deciding Whether to Sell Coins Yourself

In light of the issues raised in the preceding section, you have a decision to make about whether to sell your coins yourself, sell on consignment through a dealer (see Chapter 22), or sell your coins at auction (see Chapter 23). To make this decision, ask yourself the following questions:

- **Do I have the time?** Besides getting your coins ready to sell, do you have time to travel to coin shows in your area or around the country and present your coins to dealers and collectors? What is your time worth?297

- **Do I have the motivation?** Sales may not meet your expectations. Can you avoid becoming discouraged?

- **Do I have the desire?** Consider whether this is really what you want to do instead of, say, lounging in a hammock with a tall glass of iced tea.

- **Do I have the patience?** If your coins don't sell today, can you wait another week or month or year?

- **Do I have access to the market?** Consider whether you have contacts with the top collectors and buyers in your area of interest.

Be honest as you answer each question, then let your answers be your guide. If you feel weak or inadequate in any area, perhaps you should forsake this idea and start negotiating terms with a dealer or auction house. On the other hand, if everything looks positive, get busy!

Getting Ready to Sell Your Collection

Whenever you sell something, prepare for the sale by making the item as close to new and as attractive as possible. After all, when you sell your house, you don't leave it unpainted, dirty, and unkempt. When you sell your car, you don't leave it unwashed and unwaxed, with empty fast-food bags in the back seat. Coins are the same way. You want your presentation to be professional and attractive.

Knowing what you have

This may sound obvious, but make sure you know exactly what you have before you try to sell it. In order to price your coins properly, you must know what they are. That means you must carefully evaluate and classify each coin. For example, some of the gold coins that were issued by the Charlotte, North Carolina Mint in the 1800s have weak *mintmarks* (a small letter C that identifies the coin as coming from the Charlotte Mint). Do you have the more common coin without the mintmark, or do you have the rare coin with a weak mintmark? Have you checked your coin to see whether it is a rare die variety that may be worth many multiples of the price of a common coin?

Doing this sort of research before you begin selling ensures that you won't give anything away.

Understanding that looks are everything

A dirty holder can make a nice coin look bad or make it difficult to even see the coin. Spend the money for new holders for your entire collection. Placing your coins in new holders allows potential buyers to see your coins at their best and gives your collection a consistent, attractive appearance — one that shows you appreciate and care for your coins.

Getting the grading done beforehand

Take a careful look at your coins and decide which ones are candidates for third-party grading (see Chapter 10). If you need help, seek the advice of a competent professional (see Chapter 2). Get any rare or valuable (over $200) coins graded so that you can eliminate arguments over grading with your buyer. Rest assured that if you don't have the coins graded, the new buyer will. Dealers know the value of certification, and you should take advantage of it for your own benefit.

After your coins come back from the grading service, carefully evaluate the coins to see whether you agree with the grades. Try resubmitting any coins that appear to be conservatively graded — you may be rewarded with a higher grade.

Pricing properly

Use price guides to determine the latest wholesale and retail prices for your coins. If a particular coin is so rare that it has not appeared on the market for several years, be aware that some guides base their pricing on auction records that may be five to ten years old. In such cases, determining a price is pure speculation, so err in your favor.

As far as pricing goes, remember the old saying: "You can always go down, but you can't go up." Try for a high price initially. If you don't have any success, you can always lower the price later.

Before you show a single coin to the first potential buyer, be sure you have everything neatly organized, properly priced, and ready to go. Coin dealers, especially those at coin shows, have little patience for a seller who fumbles around looking for price guides or has no clue as to what price she has or wants. Be prepared so that you and the buyer can make quick, informed decisions.

Knowing Where to Sell Your Coins

Who knows your market better than you do? If you've spent any amount of time at all acquiring your own coins, you already know the best contacts in the business. Most likely the people you've dealt with in the past are the same people who are interested in purchasing your coins today. Here's where you may find them:

Coin dealers

If you have a good relationship with a local dealer, try a sample sale to see the levels at which he or she is willing to buy your coins. Be aware that dealers have a lot of overhead (rent, utilities, salaries, and so on) so in order to stay in business, they must make a profit on the coins they sell. Your goal is to find the dealer who is willing to work on the lowest profit margin because that means more money in your pocket.

You can sell your coins to dealers in one of two ways:

- ✔ **As a complete deal:** You may not receive as much money per coin by selling your collection in one fell swoop, but at least every coin will be sold.

- ✔ **One coin at a time:** You may make more money per coin, but you'll probably end up with some unsold coins.

Either way, compare the amount of money you receive under each method and balance that against the time and effort you spend preparing and marketing the coins.

Selling your entire collection

Selling your entire collection is perhaps the easiest, least time-consuming, least labor-intensive way of selling your coins. If you desire, you simply pile your coins into a big box, cart them down to the local coin shop, and say, "Figure out what you can pay me for these." Of course, I suggest being a little more prepared than that — have an inventory list made up so that all the dealer has to do is check to be sure that all of the coins are present and accounted for, then write his offer down beside each one.

Just as you compare prices when you purchase coins, obtain at least three bids for your collection, just to be sure that the offers you receive are fair. However, you may have difficulty finding dealers to make bids on your material. Many dealers refuse to make offers because of the time involved and the possibility of rejection. Don't let this discourage or prevent you from getting at least three bids — the third bid may be the highest and best.

Before selling your collection, have a rough idea of what it's worth. That way, when you receive an offer, you know if it is in the ballpark or way out in left field. Keep in mind that the opportunity to sell your collection intact is worth something over having to break it up. So even if an offer is below what you want or expect, keep in mind the work ahead of you if you pass the offer up (see the following section).

Selling your collection one coin at a time

Selling your collection one coin at a time involves much more effort than selling your collection intact. Theoretically, the time you spend selling your collection increases its value, but in reality, does it?

Assume that you have a $20,000 coin collection that you're trying to sell. Dealer A has already looked at the collection and offered $16,000. However, you think you can get close to $20,000 if you split the collection up and offer the coins on an individual basis. After spending a total of 35 hours marketing your collection, you sell $17,000 worth of coins and you believe you can sell the rest for an additional $500. On the surface, it looks like you came out $1,500 ahead by marketing your coins yourself. But did you really?

To make a proper comparison, you must factor in a value for your time. One way to determine a proper value for your time is to simply multiply the number of hours you spent marketing the coins times your hourly wage. In this example, if you make $10 an hour at your regular job, your time was worth $350 (35 hours × $10), so you still come out ahead by breaking up the deal. The break-even point is actually $42.86 per hour ($1,500 divided by 35 hours). Thus, if you make over $40 an hour as a wage-earner, reconsider trying to market your own coins and let a dealer handle the sale.

Don't discount or underestimate the value of your time. The time you spend selling your coins could be spent doing something else, including working and earning money or taking it easy. In life, to do one thing you must give up another. This is known as an *opportunity cost.*

Don't lower your prices until you're satisfied that no one in the world will pay what you're asking. As you sell your coins one at a time, you invariably end up with leftovers. By hanging tough on prices and rationing out your best and most valuable coins, you won't end up with a bunch of junk coins when all is said and done. See the "Mastering the Art of Selling" section, later in this chapter, for tips on becoming a master salesperson.

Junk coins will always be junk coins. Your best potential resides in your best coins, so concentrate on getting the best prices for them.

Coin shows

Coin shows are great places to sell coins. You have a roomful of dealers competing against each other, plus you have specialists who are strong in certain areas and who are often willing to pay big premiums for the right coins. Also, many dealers at shows are weekend warriors who do business only at shows and who don't have offices (thus eliminating their overhead). This arrangement gives them a competitive advantage over other dealers because they can pay higher prices for your coins.

If you have coins to sell, there's no better place than a coin show. If you're breaking up your collection and offering your coins on an individual basis, a coin show is the perfect venue for you. Unfortunately, if you have a big collection (called a *deal*) to sell, a trip to a coin show may not do you much good. That's because coin dealers are simply too busy at the shows to stop and figure a bulky or extensive collection. Nevertheless, you can sow the seeds of interest by discussing your sale with the attending dealers. From your discussions, you can determine which dealers merit a follow-up call after the show concludes.

Coin shows are often beehives of activity. At a good show, the crush of the crowd makes movement through the aisles difficult. Many of the dealers are occupied with clients, showing them coins, and doing deals. There you are with your box of coins, wondering what to do next. Where do you start? How do you start? Adherence to a set of basic, common-sense rules will make everyone's experience a lot better:

- **Be polite.** People respond favorably to a friendly smile. So smile!

- **Wait your turn.** If several people are waiting to speak with a dealer, wait your turn. There is no such thing as an emergency in the coin business.

- **Don't look over someone's shoulder while he is working on a deal.** Because coin shows are such open affairs, corporate spies can find out a lot about who is dealing with whom just by craning their necks here and there and observing. For this reason, plus the fact that it's nobody else's business anyway, dealers are sensitive when people start looking over their client's shoulders while in the middle of a deal.

- **Don't interrupt a deal.** The customer you interrupt may be deep in thought while considering a potential purchase. I would not want to be in your shoes if you ruin a sale by rudely interrupting.

- **Never make offers in front of a dealer's table.** If you see someone offer a coin worth $200 to a dealer for $100, restrain yourself from blurting out, "I'll pay $120!" You may need a doctor to set your nose.

- **Don't sell coins to someone else in front of a dealer's table.** Likewise, if you see a client considering the purchase of a $500 coin at a dealer's table, don't interrupt and offer an identical coin for $450. I made this mistake early in my numismatic career. The response reminded me of when I've tried to take food away from a hungry dog.

- **Keep the area open and clear.** When you view the coins at a dealer's table, keep your stuff off the display cases so that other people can view the merchandise. Don't hog the table.

- **Leave food or drinks at the door.** Imagine a dealer's coin worth $10,000 soaked in coffee. Imagine you are the person who spilled the coffee. 'Nuff said!

Direct marketing via publications or online services

You may choose to go directly to the collectors. This may work if you have a specialized collection, such as a collection of die varieties of U.S. Half Cents (see Chapter 16) or Half Dollars (see Chapter 17).

Through specialty clubs

Specialty clubs are groups of people who focus on a particular area of numismatics, such as pre-1840 Half Dollars or U.S. colonial coins. Most specialty clubs (listed in the Cheat Sheet at the front of this book) allow their members to publish price lists in their publications. You'll have to pay something for this privilege, but it costs far less to advertise in a specialty publication than it does in any of the large, national numismatic publications. The audience will not be as large, but you can bet the collectors you meet will be as serious about their collecting and as eager to buy as anyone you'll ever meet. Be sure to target the right audience: Don't attempt to sell a silver Dollar to the collectors in the Early American Coppers Club.

Through trade papers

An alternative — and it's not a pretty one — is to advertise your collection in numismatic periodicals like *Coin World* or *Numismatic News*. Think of the last time you sold a household item or a car through the classified ads. Remember all the phone calls and the amount of time you spent showing the item to each potential buyer? Remember all the tire-kickers? This is what you'll be facing if you try to market your collection directly to collectors. So ask yourself, "Do I really want to be a coin dealer?"

Through online auctions

Online auctions simplify the buying and selling process, but you have to have a computer and, preferably, a high-speed connection. I like online auctions for coins that range in value from $1 to $500. Above $500, the buyers thin out, and their bids don't seem to be as strong as they are at lower levels. Online auctions take a certain amount of effort, charge a fee, and require you to ship your own packages, but you may find the process to be fun and rewarding. I know I do!

Consider the following advantages of online auctions:

- ✔ Online auctions are fun.
- ✔ Commissions are very low.
- ✔ You meet new collectors from all around the world.
- ✔ Feedback ratings help keep the bad guys at bay.
- ✔ Your coin may sell for much more than it is worth.
- ✔ The results are almost immediate compared to mainstream auctions (see Chapter 23).

Consider the following disadvantages:

- ✔ Online auctions are time-consuming and labor intensive.
- ✔ You have no clue who your bidders are.

✔ The best bidders may not even be online when your auctions close.

✔ You are responsible for all correspondence, accounting, collection of money, and shipping of the coins.

If you want to try your hand at being a mini auction company, try listing some coins on eBay at www.ebay.com. In my opinion, eBay has the biggest audience and the best buyers of any online auction service. Listing is easy — all you need to do is follow the instructions on the site, and you can have your first auction up and running in no time.

Be sure to add pictures to your auctions — they really help sell your coins for more money.

Mastering the Art of Selling

Selling is truly an art form. The best sellers have outgoing personalities, a love of banter, and self-confidence. However, the best sellers didn't get to the top overnight. Like you, they had to start somewhere. This section gives you some tips on improving your selling skills.

Being assertive

Many people are afraid to approach coin dealers at shows, especially the biggest dealers with the cases full of rare and exotic coins. In reality, those dealers may be your best buyers. Don't automatically assume that a dealer will reject your coins without giving him or her a chance to say "no" (you may be surprised to hear a "yes").

Coin dealers have an old saying: "You can't sell from an empty wagon." What this means is that dealers must maintain a certain level of inventory so that customers have something to choose from when they come in to buy coins. The only way to keep the wagon full is to buy coins from collectors like you!

Talking 'em up

Remember back when you bought your coins? Remember how the seller pointed out how lustrous, how well struck, how perfectly centered, and how well preserved they were? They haven't changed, have they? So use the same descriptions when you sell your coins. Accentuate the positive and minimize the negative. There's nothing wrong with talking up your coins, just be sure you're truthful and accurate.

Appealing to a need

In truth, no one "needs" a coin. Coins are luxury items that come after the basic needs of food, clothing, and housing are satisfied. However, after a person becomes a collector, they "need" all kinds of coins: coins that fill holes in their albums, coins that are upgrades for coins they already own, or coins that they don't even know they want yet. Appeal to those needs, and your coins will fly from you.

Conveying a sense of urgency

Buyers hate to think that they may be missing out on something, so it's always a good idea to convey a sense of urgency. Let the buyer know that other parties are interested in your coins (which will be true if you're marketing your coins properly) or that the price you are asking is only good for a limited amount of time. This excites the buyer and forces a quick decision.

Sticking to your pricing

If you offer a coin to a potential buyer for $1,000 and they politely decline to purchase your coin, don't blurt out, "How about $900." All you're doing is telling the buyer that your prices are meaningless and that all they have to do is wait for a pregnant pause and you'll lower your price. Show some backbone.

By the same token, a buyer may make a counteroffer. For example, she may offer you $950 for the coin you're pricing at $1,000. In this case, consider the offer seriously and accept it if you agree that it is a fair one.

Be aware that if you walk away from a counteroffer, you're rejecting an offer that, once rejected, will disappear. Many dealers take great offense when they make an offer to a seller, who then shops the coin around to other dealers and comes back to see whether the offer still stands. The nicer dealers will honor their offer even though they aren't obligated to do so. The nastier dealers will tell you to get lost.

Selling from the bottom

The biggest mistake made by both collectors and dealers alike (yes, I've made the same mistake myself) is that they allow someone to cherry-pick their collection. *Cherry-picking* means that a buyer is allowed to come in and buy the best and most valuable coins, leaving the undesirable coins for the owner to contend with later. Invariably, the coins that remain are hard to sell.

The best possible deal for you is to sell your collection intact, even if it means taking a discount to do so. That way, you don't have to worry over many of the issues addressed in this chapter, or at least you only have to worry about them afterward.

If you can't strike a deal to sell your collection intact, you can avoid cherry-picking by *selling from the bottom*. This means focusing your energies on selling the lowest quality, least valuable coins first and saving the best and most valuable coins for last.

The practice you get selling from the bottom will serve you well when the time comes to sell your best coins. By then, you'll have the experience of a seasoned veteran, and no one will be able to stand against you in a negotiation.

The 20/50/30 rule

You may have already heard claims about how coins are as liquid as stocks and bonds — in other words, how they sell quickly at full market prices. Don't believe it! That may be true for certain generic coins that enjoy close buy and sell prices, but most coins take time to sell. In some cases, it may be months or years before you find the right buyer.

I came up with the 20/50/30 rule to illustrate the liquidity of most coin collections. Here's how the rule works:

✔ Twenty percent of the collection will sell right away, either because you under-graded or underpriced the coins, or because the coins are rarities or in-demand coins. Selling these coins requires little or no work.

✔ Fifty percent of the collection will take a little bit longer to sell. These are the coins that are right on the money and grade, but you have to wait for the right buyer. You may have to put the coins on a price list, walk the collection around to dealers at shows, telephone certain customers, or run the coins

through an online auction. Selling these coins requires a fair amount of time and effort.

✔ Thirty percent of the collection will languish and be very difficult to sell. These are the problem coins, the cheap junk, the odd and unusual stuff for which there is no demand, or stuff that is so common that every collector already has what you're offering (dealers call these types of coins *spillage*). Selling these coins requires a lot of time or a willingness to reduce the price enough to attract wholesale dealers. In most cases, the profit of a deal is tied up in these types of coins, so you have a desire to sell the coins as quickly as possible balanced against a need to get the best possible price.

You can't figure the profit on a collection until every coin is sold. Until then, you don't have real profits; you have paper profits. If you're familiar with the stock market, you know that paper profits mean nothing until you finally sell the stock.

Remaining patient

Patience is indeed a virtue when selling your coins. Sometimes, coins simply take time to sell. Many factors affect how quickly (or slowly) you can sell your coins: market condition, dealers' inventory levels, dealers' and collectors' cash positions, the state of the general economy, and so on. Even after you strike a deal to sell your coins, you may have to finance the deal to make it work, adding more time to the day that you finally get your money.

Keeping Good Records

Under our current U.S. tax code, you're required to pay a tax on the difference between what you paid for your coin and the selling price. This is a complicated area of the tax law, and my purpose is not to teach you how to calculate how much tax you owe, but to remind you to keep accurate records when you buy a coin and again when you sell it.

- ✔ On the buying side, keep a record of the purchase date, the purchase price, how you paid for the coin (cash, check, credit card, and so on) and from whom you purchased the coin.

- ✔ On the selling side, keep a record of the sale date, the sale price, and to whom you sold the coin. Be sure to record all transactions — losses can be offset against gains to reduce your total income.

If you don't have such records, you may be assessed a higher tax, penalties, and interest if your income tax return is audited.

A competent tax expert or financial planner can help you in this area, not only with tax advice, but timing advice, as well. Depending on your financial and tax situations, you may have to choose between selling your collection now or later.

Donating the Rest

If, despite all my advice, you end up with a bunch of coins that you can't sell, consider donating them to a charitable organization (specifically, a numismatic charitable organization). A charitable donation accomplishes three things:

✔ You get rid of all your coins.

✔ The charitable organization gets something to display or sell.

✔ You get a nice tax deduction.

Depending on the value of the coins you're donating, you may have to obtain an independent appraisal to support your deduction. For more details, contact a tax professional or contact the Internal Revenue Service and ask for Publication 526 — "Charitable Contributions."

Chapter 22

Selling on Consignment

● ●

In This Chapter

▶ Selling through dealers on consignment

▶ Choosing a dealer

● ●

*I*f you decide against selling your coins by yourself (see Chapter 21), you still have two options: having a dealer sell your collection on consignment or selling your coins at public auction (see Chapter 23). In this chapter, I offer guidance on selling your collection on consignment.

Selling your collection through a dealer can save you a lot of time and trouble, especially if you can find a dealer who is well-connected in the market and who has a large stable of wealthy clients. Perhaps that sounds mercenary, but if ever there was a time to be mercenary, this is it.

You want a dealer who is both a good marketer and who has a good market. If a dealer is weak in either or both of those areas, find another.

Understanding the Consignment Arrangement

Wouldn't it be great if you could find someone to sell your coins for you? Someone who would contact people, display your coins in a shop or office setting, take your collection to coin shows, handle all the sales and record-keeping, consult with you on a regular basis, and do all of this for a small commission?

This ideal scenario is called *selling on consignment,* a popular and oft-used method that, when handled properly, gives you almost complete control over the sale of your coins. You set the prices, you determine what counteroffers to accept, and you decide the pace at which the coins are sold. Selling on consignment gives you flexibility, the opportunity to adjust your strategy as time goes by, and access to the expert advice of a numismatic professional.

Dealers like selling on consignment because it expands their inventory with no investment or cash layout, they incur no risk (other than the risk of loss), and they have a chance to make some extra money with little extra effort. The opportunity cost to a dealer is minimal — they already have an established business, they already spend most of their time dealing in coins, and coin shows are already a part of their normal schedules.

Agreeing on a Commission

What ends up going into or coming out of your pockets is the most important number in any consignment arrangement. Another word for this number is *commission,* or the fee that is paid for the successful sale of any coin. A commission can be a flat fee or a percentage of the selling price. Either way, the commission is worked out in advance between the buyer and the seller. The commission should reflect the value of the services provided by the dealer balanced against the needs of the seller. Naturally, dealers try to negotiate the highest possible commission (increasing what ends up going into their pockets) and collectors try to negotiate the lowest possible commission (decreasing what ends up coming out of their pockets).

Finding a fair commission

Fairness is in the eye of the beholder, so to speak. Fairness has more to do with perception than it has to do with money. For example, if you enter into a one-sided deal that favors the other party, you will never be happy no matter how much money is involved. The same thing is true for the dealer. The commission level must be set high enough so that dealer has an incentive to actively promote your collection. Otherwise, the dealer directs all of her energies into selling other coins, relegating yours to the background. The perfect commission is one that the dealer is happy to accept and you're happy to pay.

Looking at typical commissions

Consignment selling is nothing new, so what does a typical commission look like? The answer depends on what type of coins you have for sale. Some coins, by their very nature, require great effort to sell while others require little or no effort. Obviously, the harder-to-sell coins command a higher fee, while the easy stuff deserves a lower commission.

A good, across-the-board commission rate, and one that I've used successfully in many consignment arrangements, is ten percent of the selling price. For the odd, slow-moving stuff, I normally charge 15 to 20 percent, and for fast-moving, easy-to-sell, high dollar coins, I charge five percent. But, that's me — you and your dealer must work out your own arrangement.

Choosing a Dealer

Selling on consignment isn't just about money; it's about finding someone who will work hard to sell your coins. A good dealer is interested in maximizing the total value of your collection. After all, if you're paying the dealer a percentage of sales, the higher the value, the more money the dealer makes.

When selecting a dealer, look for someone who can advise on grading issues and who can help you set prices. You may already have established a good relationship over the years with a coin dealer as you built your collection. However, now that you're selling, ask yourself the following questions:

- ✔ Is this the person I want to handle my collection?
- ✔ Can I trust this person to work in my best interests?
- ✔ Will this person market my collection aggressively?
- ✔ Does this person have access to retail markets in addition to wholesale markets?
- ✔ Is this person respected in the marketplace?
- ✔ Is this person or company financially strong and stable?
- ✔ Will this person provide references from other collectors whom he or she has helped in the past with similar situations?
- ✔ Does this person or company have adequate insurance to protect my collection against theft or loss?

Many coin dealers carry little or no insurance to protect against loss. When you ask about insurance, don't just accept the answer; insist on seeing the policy and verify with the insurance company that the policy is valid and current. Determine what losses and thefts are covered — often, the coverage for coins during transport to and from coin shows is reduced or requires special measures. If your dealer doesn't have adequate insurance to protect your coins, look elsewhere.

Selling your coins via consignment is an easy, no-hands approach, but it still requires some effort on your part. You need to find a dealer you can trust and who will go the extra mile to sell your coins for you. If you do your homework properly, the rest of the process is a piece of cake. Just sit back, relax, and wait for the money to come rolling in.

Chapter 23

Auctioning Off Your Coins

• •

In This Chapter

▶ Deciding whether auctions are right for you

▶ Choosing a numismatic auction house

▶ Negotiating auction terms and signing the contract

▶ Giving your coins a hand

• •

Are rare-coin auctions the best way to sell your collection? I suspect that if you asked that question of famous collectors, they'd all extol the virtues of selling their respective collections at auction. Each year hundreds of less famous collectors sell their coins at public auction, indicating the high level of faith in this age-old selling method. A quick glance at numismatic history reveals that most of the great collections of the past were sold at auction and that most price records have been set at auction (see Chapter 24).

In this chapter, I steer you through the process of deciding whether auctions are right for you; and if they are, I let you know what to expect.

Selling your coins at auction can be an exciting and profitable experience. Just having someone else do all the work makes the commissions worth every penny!

Deciding Whether Auctions Are Right for You

Auction houses lure consignors with the potential for runaway prices. That's why the headline of every post-auction press release points out the extraordinary and unexpected prices that were realized in the sale. That's why you often see comparisons between pre-sale estimates and the final selling price, always showcasing the coins that realized the biggest premiums.

Clearly, some coins and some collections are perfect candidates for selling at auction. Others are not. How can you tell the difference? This section can help.

Do you have the right stuff?

The key is in the word "potential." A coin with potential is one that, for reasons of value or condition, has a chance at achieving a premium price at auction. Table 23-1 illustrates what I mean.

Table 23-1		The Potential for Runaway Prices	
Coin	**Grade**	**Value**	**Potential at Auction**
1914-D Lincoln Cent	Very Fine	$250	None. This is a popular coin that's easy to sell for close to its full value
1914-D Lincoln Cent	Gem Red Uncirculated	$11,000	Lots. If this coin has any chance of being an MS-66, the price will triple!
1953-S Franklin Half Dollar	Extremely Fine	$3.75	None. The value is too low.
1953-S Franklin Half Dollar	MS-65 Full Bell Lines	$10,000	Lots. An MS-66 example with Full Bell Lines recently sold for $69,000.
1905 $20 Gold piece	Extremely Fine	$475	None. Take away the auction commission, and you probably end up with less than if you sold it yourself.
1905 $20 Gold piece	Choice Uncirculated	$13,000	Lots. This is a scarce date that becomes very rare in high grade. One additional grade point makes this coin worth over $20,000

Not every coin in your collection has the potential to excel at auction, so you have to look at your collection as a whole. Ask yourself, "Does the potential benefit of selling my coins at auction exceed the commissions on my collection?" If the answer is no, see Chapters 21 and 22. If the answer is yes, consider selling your coins at auction.

Do you have a timeline long enough?

By their very nature, auctions take longer than other methods of selling. Here's a rough timeline:

- **Sixty days before the auction:** A deadline is set for consignments.
- **Forty-five days before the auction:** The catalog is completed and sent to the printer.

- ✔ **Thirty-five days before the auction:** The finished catalog is mailed to potential bidders.

- ✔ **Zero to 30 days before the auction:** Absentee bids are received.

- ✔ **Day of the auction:** Your coins sell for fabulous prices!

- ✔ **Thirty days after the auction:** All bidders must have paid for their purchases.

- ✔ **Forty-five days after the auction:** You receive payment, less commission. Any unsold items are returned at this time.

Based on this timeline, it takes 105 days from the time you consign your coins until you receive the final settlement check. Can you wait that long?

Choosing a Numismatic Auction House

After you decide to sell your coins at auction, the next step is to choose an auction house. Take great care in choosing a firm to sell your coins. After all, this is your legacy — the collection you've spent years building, improving, and protecting. But how do you choose? What should you look for? What's important? What's not? This section spills the beans.

Auction house, auction firm, and *auction company* — they all describe the same thing.

- ✔ **Relationships:** An auction firm, no matter how large, is made up of individuals. Know with whom you're dealing and whether you feel comfortable working with them. Who are the principals of the firm? Consider whether you've dealt with this firm before, either as a buyer and a seller? If so, how was the experience?

  As the process moves along, you may be dealing with cataloguers, photographers, marketers, and accountants. Do you know who they are? Can you work with them?

- ✔ **Name recognition:** Has anyone heard of this company before? Chances are that if you haven't heard of them before, neither has anyone else, so who is going to be bidding on your coins?

  The buzz in the business can tell you a lot about a company. Don't be afraid to ask around for people's opinions. This is the kind of information you won't get from any promotional brochure, and it's the information you need.

- ✔ **Longevity:** How long has the company been around? I don't care what anyone tells you, it takes a long time to build up a steady clientele of loyal, sophisticated, and aggressive buyers. Longevity in the auction business means the company must be doing something right.

✔ **Orientation toward numismatics:** This probably sounds obvious, but does the auction company you're considering specialize in numismatics or will your collection appear along with Persian rugs, estate jewelry, or an old toy collection? Of course, it's nice when buyers cross over into numismatics from other collectibles areas, but you're better off dealing with a company whose sole focus is on coins.

✔ **Numismatic expertise:** The quality of the descriptions of your coins depends entirely upon the expertise of the people who catalog them. Who will be describing your coins? What are his credentials? What experience does the company have in writing up coins? Can or will the company make the effort to determine whether your coins are *rare varieties* (slight differences between coins of the same type that can often be quite valuable), and does the company have the numismatic library to research the coins in your collection?

✔ **Presentation:** Each auction firm employs its own special ways of presenting your collection to its buyers. In other words, the catalog of your collection could end up being a bunch of mimeographed pages stapled together or a thick, glossy, professionally prepared book. Most likely, the end result will be somewhere in between. Your goal should be to get as close to the high-end presentation as possible. A quick look at the company's previous catalogs should give you a good idea of how your collection will be presented.

✔ **Financial stability:** After your coins are sold, will you get paid? Has the company ever been late paying consignors? Has the company ever declared bankruptcy? Discreet inquiries can alert you to any recent developments on the financial front, especially those that may prevent you from getting paid.

✔ **Internet presence:** Does the auction company have a presence on the Web? Will your collection be marketed on the company's Web site as well as in print form? What interface does the company use to capture bids over the Internet? Is the site user-friendly? How many visitors visit the site each month? Will other auctions be presented on the Web site that may detract from your sale?

✔ **Where your coins will be sold:** A barn auction in Lancaster County, Pennsylvania is not likely to attract the kind of attention and buyers you desire. The ultimate location for a coin auction is one where there are already a lot of potential buyers (at a coin show, for example) or where it is convenient for buyers to travel to and from (any major city). "If you build it, they will come" may work for ball fields in the middle of Iowa, but you want to make it as easy and as convenient as possible for buyers to attend your sale.

✔ **When your coins will be sold:** Most auction firms hold several sales a year. In which sale will your coins appear? Will they be sold in the next available sale, or will your coins be placed in a holding pattern while other people's collections are sold first? Will your collection be split up over two or more sales? At what time of day will your coins be sold? Will your coins be sold during the day, when dealers are busy at the coin show, at night when they are most likely to be at the sale, or on a Saturday when many dealers are already on their way home?

✔ **Insurance:** What happens if your coins are lost or stolen while in the auction company's possession? Will they be insured? If so, for what value: wholesale, retail, the stated value on your contract, or some other value? Who gets paid if the coins are lost — you or the auction company? Be sure to raise these issues and be satisfied that you and your coins are protected before you sign any contract. Ask to see a copy of the company's insurance policy to see whether it exists and to see whether the company maintains adequate levels of protection.

Negotiating Auction Terms

Auction companies make their money by charging commissions. In Chapter 8, I introduce you to buyer's fees, which are the commissions charged to the buyer at auction. In this section, I explain the fees that are charged to the *consignor* (the person whose items are being sold at auction; that is, you!).

Seller's fees

Most auction houses charge consignors a flat fee, called a *seller's fee* that's usually a small percentage of what the items actually bring at the sale. Suppose the consignor agrees to pay a ten percent commission to the auction house. If the auctioneer hammers down the coin for $250, the consignor gets $225 ($250 less 10 percent of $250).

Always try to negotiate for the lowest possible seller's fee, understanding that the auction company may tie its cataloging and marketing efforts to the amount of commissions it receives. In other words, don't shoot yourself in the foot by cutting the commission so close to the bone that the auction house has little incentive to promote your coins.

Seller's fees depend, in large part, on the value of individual coins and on the value of your collection as a whole. A $20,000 collection consisting of five coins may qualify for a lower commission than a $20,000 collection of thirty coins, because less work is involved with the first collection. You can generally expect to pay a lower commission for a $100,000 collection than for either of the $20,000 collections.

Some of the more aggressive companies have been known to pay a *negative seller's fee* (instead of charging you a commission, they actually pay you a commission to sell your coins). For example, the seller may receive 105 percent of the hammer price. Essentially, the auction house is giving a part of the buyer's fee back to you. Auction houses do this to attract more and bigger consignments.

While auction companies would like you to think their commission structures are set in stone, you can bet they'll negotiate the seller's fees, especially if more than one company is involved or if you have a substantial collection.

Reserve bids and buy-back fees

I recommend placing reserve bids on any of your coins that have significant value. A *reserve bid* represents the least amount of money you are willing to accept for a particular coin. Reserve bids ensure that your coins don't sell for less than they're worth. A *buy-back fee* is the commission (often reduced) that you pay if you buy your own coin back.

By exercising a reserve bid, you prevent someone else from buying the coin, and you prevent the auction company from making its normal commission. On the other hand, if you buy back your own coin, you should not be responsible for both the buyer's fee and the seller's fee, especially if the auction company fails to get a reasonable price for your coin.

To compromise, auction houses offer reduced buyback fees that give you the opportunity to protect your coins at a rate that discourages you from setting the reserve price too high.

The goal is to sell your coin, not buy it back. Set your reserve bids at a reasonable level so that your coin is sold. Here's an example: Your contract calls for a ten percent seller's fee, with a buy-back rate of a flat eight percent. Your coin has a retail value of $200, the coin has a presale estimate of $180 to $200, and you set a reserve price of $160 because you've already been offered that much for the coin by another dealer. Table 23-2 gives you a look at how the fees work at various levels:

Table 23-2	Your Profit After Fees Are Paid			
Hammer Price	**Seller's Fee (10 Percent)**	**Buyback Fee (8 Percent)**	**Resale Price**	**Net**
$125	$0	$10	$160	$150
$150	$0	$12	$160	$148
$160 (reserve)	$16	$0	—	$144

Hammer Price	Seller's Fee (10 Percent)	Buyback Fee (8 Percent)	Resale Price	Net
$170	$17	$0	—	$153
$180	$18	$0	—	$162
$200	$20	$0	—	$180

Notice that when a bidder hits your reserve price, the coin is considered sold and the full seller's fee kicks in. As you can see, the fees really impact the end result. To equal the previous offer of $160, your coin has to sell for just under $180 at auction, plus you have to wait all that extra time.

Table 23-2 reinforces my earlier points:

✔ Not all coins are suitable for auction.

✔ Try to get the lowest possible seller's fees and buy-back fees.

✔ Set reasonable reserve bids.

Hidden fees

Watch out for hidden fees that can stack up against you. For example, some companies charge small fees for photography, *page space* (the amount of space devoted to each coin's description), and insurance. You may be asked to pay a *lotting* (a flat fee for each individual listing in the sale catalog).

Don't pay 'em. Most or all of these fees should be covered by the seller's fee. If not, shop around for another company. You can find enough good numismatic auction houses that don't charge these types of fees.

Signing a Contract

The law in most states requires the auction company to provide a written agreement or contract specifying the terms and conditions negotiated between you and the company. Be sure to read the contract carefully. Read every section. Look for hidden fees. If you don't understand a provision of the contract, ask the auction company to explain it to you. If you still don't understand what you're signing, consult an attorney. If you need to make adjustments or changes to the contract, make them before you sign it.

After you sign the contract, you're bound by its terms and conditions.

Giving Your Coins a Helping Hand

After you sign the contract and your coins are safe in the hands of the auction company, your job is far from over. After all, you have a vested interest in seeing that your coins do well. The following are a couple of tips that help promote the sale of your coins:

✔ **Share your knowledge.** While the sale catalog is being produced, offer the auction company anecdotal information that may make your coins more valuable. For example, you may have pedigree information that links your coin to a famous collection or a sale in which you paid a record price for your coin. Old sale envelopes or contemporary documents help create a story that may excite a potential buyer. If you have technical information about your coins, provide it to the auction house. Anything like die variety information, weights, or unusual characteristics may make a big difference in the final selling price.

✔ **Shout from the mountaintops.** "Hey, those are my coins coming up for sale!" Let all your family, friends, members of your coin club, and other numismatic buddies know that your coins will be sold at auction. If you know some serious bidders who are likely to be interested in buying your coins, arrange for them to get an auction catalog. Often, the auction company will provide you with a small number of extra catalogs that you can mail yourself. For security reasons, I don't recommend giving your friends' names and addresses to the auction company unless you obtain their prior permission.

Online Auctions

I list online auctions here simply because they have "auction" in their name. Technically, online auctions are just another form of direct marketing, so I cover them in Chapter 21.

Part VI
The Part of Tens

The 5th Wave   By Rich Tennant

"Check it out, Wendel — six Liberty Nickels! I found them behind the cushion when I was having the furniture wrapped in plastic covering."

In this part . . .

*E*veryone has his or her favorite something or other, but in this part, I get to tell you mine. Although short and sweet, the three chapters in this section contain some of the most fun material in this book.

I start off by introducing the ten most valuable U.S. coins. You may be surprised at how valuable rare coins have become in recent years! (Hint: The most valuable U.S. coin is worth well over $1 million.)

Next, I list my ten favorite U.S. coin designs. These are some of the prettiest and most intriguing designs ever to appear on any coins ever made anywhere in the world. That's quite a statement, isn't it? Check 'em out for yourself and see whether you agree.

Finally, I offer my ten favorite Web sites for your Internet surfing enjoyment. Every time I visit one of these sites, I discover something new — you will, too!

Chapter 24

The Ten Most Valuable U.S. Coins

*B*ack when I was a youngster, only a few coins sold for over $10,000, and it was rare indeed for a coin to bring over $50,000 at auction. Not so anymore! Blame it on inflation, an influx of investors, or plain old excitement about coins, but prices for rare coins have gone through the roof.

I've limited this chapter to coins sold at public auction. Admittedly, some coins that were sold privately may have made this list (or at least they may have moved up a notch or two), but there is simply no way to verify the accuracy or the terms of such sales. For example, how should I treat the 1885 Trade Dollar from the Eliasberg sale? Reportedly trading hands in 1999 for a cool $1.5 million, this coin would have moved to the fifth position on this list if the transaction had been at public auction.

The great thing about numismatics is that it never stays the same. By the time you read this list, there may already have been changes in the rankings and/or the prices realized. Right now, 1804 Silver Dollars dominate the list simply because several have appeared on the market in the past few years. But what would the unique 1870-S $3 gold piece (see Chapter 18) be worth today? As I write this, the U.S. government just legitimized one of the 1933 Double Eagles, finally allowing a collector to legally own this ultra-rarity. If the coin is sold at auction, it could set a new price record. What if the Smithsonian Institution decided to sell its unique 1849 Liberty Head $20 gold piece? What if Bill Gates decided to collect U.S. coins? (Call me if you need an advisor, Bill.)

What I'm trying to say is that the fireworks in U.S. numismatics are far from over.

The Ten Most Valuable United States Coins

Here then, without fanfare, are the top ten most valuable U.S. coins that have sold at auction. I've included specific information about the sales in which they appeared (the auction company, sale name, sale date, and/or lot number in the catalog) just in case you want find out more about each coin. If you're patient, you can probably find many of these auction catalogs on eBay — just be warned that some of these catalogs are collector items themselves. See Chapter 23 for more information on auctions.

1804 Silver Dollar ($4,140,000)

Sold by Auctions by Bowers & Merena, Inc. as part of the Childs collection in August 1999 (Lot 458). Graded Proof-68 (on a scale of 1 to 70) by the Professional Coin Grading Service.

In 1999, a phenomenal coin known as the Childs 1804 Silver Dollar (after the family that owned it) came on the market. Up to that time, only three United States coins had ever sold for over $1,000,000 at auction. Because the Childs example was the finest 1804 Silver Dollar in existence, there was considerable speculation as to what it may bring. At the time, the Eliasberg 1804 Silver Dollar was the top record-setter at $1,815,000, so the buzz was that the Childs 1804 Silver Dollar would bring at least $2,000,000 and possibly as much as $2.5 to $3 million. When the coin came up at auction, I was in the Professional Coin Grading Service's grading room listening to a live simulcast along with the graders and staff. The coin quickly broke through $2,000,000, then $3,000,000 and in less than two minutes sold for $3,600,000. With the additional buyer's fee of 15 percent, the total price came to $4,140,000 — a new record that more than doubled the previous record.

1804 Silver Dollar ($1,840,000)

Sold by Stack's of New York on October 18, 2000. This was a reappearance of the Dexter-Dunham example.

1913 Liberty Head Nickel ($1,840,000)

Sold by Superior Galleries on March 9, 2001 in their ANA 2001 National Money Show Auction (Lot 728). Graded Proof-66 by the Numismatic Guaranty Corporation of America. This was a reappearance of the Eliasberg specimen.

I was the auctioneer at this sale, and the thrill of selling a 1913 Liberty Head Nickel (a coin tied for the second most valuable U.S. coins of all time) was an experience I will long remember. Just before this lot came up, the room filled to capacity, camera crews from local networks and the Discovery Channel readied their equipment, and an air of excitement filled the room. The coin was placed on an easel at the front of the room so that everyone could see it. I asked the armed, off-duty policeman who was standing next to the coin if he had ever been hired to guard a Nickel before. He laughed.

In less than a minute, the coin sold for $1,600,000 to Martin Paul of the Rarities Group, who was acting as agent for Dwight Manley, a sports agent and major player in numismatics. With the 15 percent buyer's fee, the total price came to $1,840,000. Reportedly, Manley offered $2,000,000 for this coin prior to the sale, but was turned down, a rejection that appears to have saved him $160,000!

1804 Silver Dollar ($1,815,000)

Sold by Auctions by Bowers & Merena, Inc. as part of the Louis Eliasberg, Sr. collection in 1997 (Lot 2199).

1913 Liberty Head Nickel ($1,485,000)

Sold by Auctions by Bowers & Merena, Inc. as part of the Louis Eliasberg, Sr. collection in 1996 (Lot 807). In 2001, this lot reappeared on the market and sold for $1,840,000.

1907 $20 Saint Gaudens Ultra-High Relief ($1,210,000)

Sold by Ira & Larry Goldberg Coins & Collectibles, Inc. on May 31, 1999 (Lot 885).

1804 Silver Dollar ($990,000)

Sold by Rarcoa in Auction '89 (Lot 247). This was the Dexter-Dunham example. In 2000, this lot reappeared on the market and sold for $1,840,000.

1913 Liberty Head Nickel ($962,500)

Sold by Stack's of New York as part of the Reed Hawn collection in 1993 (Lot 245).

1885 Trade Dollar ($907,500)

Sold by Auctions by Bowers & Merena, Inc. as part of the Louis Eliasberg, Sr. collection in 1997 (Lot 2350). In late 1999, Legend Numismatics reportedly paid $1,500,000 for this coin in a private transaction.

1907 $20 Saint Gaudens Ultra-High Relief ($825,000)

Sold by Sotheby's of New York in the Bloomfield sale, December 16, 1996 (Lot 60).

Honorable Mentions

In this section, I've added some honorable mentions: Coins that were previously at or near the top of the list. None of these coins, however, has appeared on the market since 1982, which, at least in numismatics, is ancient history. Any one of the coins in this section could set a world record price if it appeared on the market today. As with the previous section, I've listed specific information about the sales in which they appeared.

1787 Brasher Doubloon ($725,000)

Sold by Bowers & Ruddy in its first installment of the Garrett collection in 1979 (Lot 607).

1870-S $3 Gold coin ($687,500)

Sold by Bowers & Ruddy in its U.S. Gold Coin Collection sale, 1982 (Lot 296). This complete collection of U.S. gold coins was formed by Louis Eliasberg, Sr., a fact hidden at the time but revealed later.

1822 $5 Gold coin ($687,500)

Sold by Bowers & Ruddy in its U.S. Gold Coin Collection sale, 1982 (Lot 378).

Chapter 25

Ten Favorite U.S. Coin Designs

*B*eautiful designs can be found throughout the U.S. coin series. Although I have trouble playing favorites, this chapter lists the ten designs that I like the most. You may choose completely different designs, and that's okay. After all, beauty is in the eye of the beholder.

Saint-Gaudens' $20 Gold Piece

After a few years in office, President Theodore Roosevelt enlisted the services of Augustus Saint-Gaudens, one of America's most famous sculptors, to come up with new designs for the $10 and $20 U.S. Gold coins. For the $10 Gold piece, Saint-Gaudens chose a head of Liberty wearing a Native American headdress — certainly impressive, but not impressive enough (in my opinion) to make this list. For the $20 Gold piece, Saint-Gaudens chose a full figure of Liberty, walking toward the viewer, holding a torch aloft in one hand and an olive branch in the other. In the background, the rays of a rising sun blast forth. At lower left, you can see a tiny U.S. Capitol building. This beautiful design lasted until 1933. In 1986, the U.S. Mint used this design again when it began issuing official gold bullion coins. Find out more about this coin in Chapter 18.

Buffalo (or Indian Head) Nickel

A new Five Cents (Nickel) design appeared in 1913 to replace the 30-year-old Liberty Head design with the large V on the reverse (read more about this coin in Chapter 16). James Earle Fraser wanted purely American elements for his new design, so he settled on the head of a Native American for the front and an American bison for the reverse. The new coin was an immediate success and has since become one of the most widely-collected of all U.S. coins. How popular is it? In 2001, the U.S. Mint issued a new commemorative Silver Dollar based on these very same designs.

Oregon Trail Commemorative Half Dollar

In 1926, the U.S. Mint struck a new Half Dollar to commemorate the Oregon Trail, which was used by Pioneers as they settled the West. James Earl Fraser and his wife, Laura Gardin Fraser, created a stunning design that deserves inclusion in my Top Ten U.S. Coin Designs list. James drew again on his popular Native American motif, this time featuring an outline of a map of the United States behind a Native American chief with a nearly full-length headdress, loincloth, bow, and blanket. The reverse of the coin features a Conestoga wagon being drawn by a team of oxen, heading into a large, setting sun. Most commemorative coins were struck for one or two years, after which the dies were retired. In the case of the Oregon Trail commemorative, however, the issue appeared in most of the years all the way up to 1939. Find out more about this coin in Chapter 19.

$4 Gold Stella

In 1879 and 1880, the U.S. Mint toyed with the idea of a $4 Gold coin. Two different designs were used for the front of the coin and because each is beautiful, I include both of them here in a sort of tie. One design shows a head of Liberty facing left, with her hair loose except for a coronet that has "Liberty" written on it. The other design shows a head of Liberty facing left, this time with her hair in a neat bun. The back of the coin features a large star in the center. Not only are these two coins beautiful, but they are rare and valuable. Visit Chapter 20 to find out more about this and other pattern coins.

Massachusetts Pine Tree Shillings

In 1652, John Hull of the Massachusetts Bay Colony began striking silver coins. His first coins were plain blanks of silver, up to the size of a Quarter Dollar, with a small "NE" stamped on one side and the denomination (III, VI, or XII) on the other. Then came his Willow Tree coins, but they were really crude-looking pieces. Next came his Oak Tree pieces, somewhat of an improvement, except the trees have no leaves and look pretty bare. Finally, Hull came up with his Pine Tree coins, with trees that actually look like trees. The reverse has the date 1652 and the denomination (III, VI, or XIII); both sides have *legends* (words or inscriptions) surrounding the centers. I discuss this and other colonial coins in Chapter 15.

1776 Continental Dollar

In 1776, the American colonies itched to be free. The Revolutionary War was in full swing, the colonies declared their independence from Great Britain, and the Continental Congress considered the idea of issuing coins and currency. One idea was to issue a Silver Dollar-sized coin, which the Congress did. Except for some brass or silver pieces, most Continental Dollars were struck in Pewter. The obverse has a neat sundial design and on high-grade examples, you can even see a face on Mr. Sun. The reverse has a chain of linked rings, each with the name of one of the thirteen colonies. Find out more about Continental Dollars and U.S. colonial coins in Chapter 15.

Gobrecht Dollar

Between 1804 to 1836, no Silver Dollars were struck in the United States except for the rare 1804 Silver Dollar (actually struck in 1834)! In 1836, the U.S. Mint asked a man named Christian Gobrecht to design a new Silver Dollar, and he created two stunning new designs. The first design showed Liberty in a flowing gown, seated on a rock, holding a staff and cap in one hand and a shield in the other. With few exceptions, this design appeared on most U.S. Silver coins from 1838 to 1891. The back of the coin showed the second impressive design — a flying eagle. This reverse design was used only between 1836 and 1839, but later appeared in a modified version on the 1856-1858 One Cent. Find out more about Gobrecht Dollars and other U.S. pattern coins in Chapter 20.

Walking Liberty Half Dollar

In 1916, A.A. Weinman came up with a new design for the Half Dollar, showing Lady Liberty in a long, striped gown walking toward the left. Weinman borrowed some of Saint-Gaudens' design elements (see the "Saint-Gaudens' $20 Gold" section, earlier in this chapter), including a rising sun, a long flowing gown, and a large olive branch. However, Weinman did add a touch of his own — a billowing flag draped around Liberty's shoulders. The reverse of the Walking Liberty Half Dollar features an eagle with its wings spread, either landing or taking off from a pine branch. This obverse design was such a favorite that in 1986, it was chosen for the new silver bullion coin that the U.S. Mint has issued every year since. I tell the story of U.S. Half Dollars in Chapter 17.

Standing Liberty Quarter Dollar

Like the Half Dollar, 1916 saw the unveiling (literally and figuratively) of a new design for the Quarter Dollar. When the changes were revealed, the public gasped in shock. Herman MacNeil's design featured a bare-breasted, full-length figure of Liberty in a flowing gown walking through a stone gate. In one hand she carried an olive branch; in the other, a protective shield. The partially nude design was changed right away — in 1917, Liberty was covered up with a coat of chain-mail armor! Look for more information on Standing Liberty Quarter Dollars in Chapter 17.

Panama-Pacific Commemorative $50 Gold

In 1915, San Francisco held a grand exposition to celebrate the opening of the Panama Canal, one of the greatest engineering feats of all time. The U.S. Mint issued a series of special coins to commemorate the event. Included were Half Dollars and $1, $2.50, and $50 Gold coins. The $50 Gold coins were massive chunks of gold in both octagonal and round shapes. Because of their high value, few collectors could afford to purchase one, so they are rare and valuable today. The obverse features a head of Minerva wearing a plumed helmet. A large owl appears on the reverse, perched on a pine branch loaded with cones and needles. Dolphins swim around the outer edges on the Octagonal version. I discuss commemoratives in greater detail in Chapter 19.

You can see illustrations of all top 10 U.S. coin designs at my Web site at www.CoinFacts.com. Have fun!

Chapter 26

Ten Great Numismatic Web Sites

In This Chapter

▶ Surfing for numismatic stuff

▶ Finding the best coin-related sites

Ten years ago, the Internet was virtually unknown except to military and academic types. Today, it pervades our lives and has become an important tool for everything from researching homework projects to making travel arrangements and buying books, groceries, and anything else that can be packaged up and shipped. For the numismatist, the Internet has created a vast new world of opportunities to buy, sell, and get more information. The Web sites listed in this chapter are the ones that I find to be extremely useful — they're the ones I keep visiting over and over again. Check 'em out for yourself!

CoinFacts (www.coinfacts.com)

Called "The Internet Encyclopedia and Price Guide of United States Coins" and "The Ultimate Coin Book," this site offers free, in-depth information for all collectors of U.S. coins, from beginners to advanced collectors. Thousands of color images await you, including pictures of some of the most rare and valuable U.S. coins. Special sections for hard-core numismatists contain die variety and rarity information to determine whether a coin is common, scarce, or extremely rare. You would need a complete numismatic library to match the information included here! Navigation is easy and intuitive. I'm sort of biased towards this site because I built it!

American Numismatic Association (www.money.org)

Hosted by the largest organization for collectors of U.S. coins, this site provides information about the American Numismatic Association and its programs and benefits. I like the "Museum Exhibits" section, which includes highlights from the museum's collection. The Frederick Mayer collection of Colorado Pioneer gold features coins you won't find anywhere else, and the collection of Vermont Copper coins is particularly impressive. Although the A.N.A. operates an online store, this site remains essentially non-commercial, so you can enjoy your visit without suffering the buy, buy, buy mentality of most commercial numismatic Web sites.

United States Mint (www.usmint.gov)

The U.S. Mint discovered the Internet in a big way, creating one of the most successful coin-selling sites on the Web. Years ago, the U.S. Mint sold Proof sets and Mint sets only through the mail. Today, collectors may purchase them over the Internet along with bags of coins, new sets, 50 States Quarters, bullion coins, display holders, supplies, and even special spoons — all online and from the convenience of their homes. Kids have their own special section, with plenty of neat information to excite the collectors of tomorrow.

Numismatic News (www.krause. com/coins/nn)

Krause Publications (KP) produces the weekly numismatic newspaper, *Numismatic News,* as well as the *Bank Note Reporter, World Coin News, Coins Magazine, Coin Prices,* and a host of superb numismatic reference books. The KP site offers a nice "Question and Answer" section, an "Item of the Week," and a classified ad section that allows collectors to search for particular items.

Numismatic Bibliomania Society (www.coinbooks.org)

The Numismatic Bibliomania Society is a not-for-profit organization comprised of collectors and dealers in numismatic literature, which includes any literature relating to coins, medals, tokens, and paper money. The society's Web site is extremely informative and often includes biographical information about numismatic authors, research into classic numismatic literature, results of book auctions, and interesting anecdotes related to numismatics.

If you want to find out about coin books old and new, this is the site to visit. Check out the Information Section to learn more about "Types of Numismatic Literature," "Bibliography," "Exhibits," and "Libraries."

eBay (www.ebay.com)

As the largest person-to-person online auction company, eBay offers millions of items each and every day, including thousands of coin auctions. You'll find colonial coins, common coins, rare coins, medals, tokens, paper money, world coins, error coins, numismatic publications, and much more.

You never know what will show up on eBay. Bidding is easy, fun, and (be careful!) addictive.

University of Notre Dame (www.coins.nd.edu)

With the Robert H. Gore, Jr. collection as a foundation, the Department of Special Collections at the University of Notre Dame produced what I think is the premier Web site for U.S. colonial coins. By associating themselves with the Colonial Newsletter Foundation, this Web site now includes some of the best-researched information by the best names in the field. If you've never tasted colonial coins, sample them here and prepare to be hooked for life.

CoinLink (www.coinlink.com)

With its self-explanatory name, CoinLink provides easy access to anyone and anything associated with numismatics. I use this site frequently and recommend it as a jumping-off point to the world of coin collecting.

How To Grade U.S. Coins (www.coingrading.com)

In 1990, Jim Halperin wrote a book entitled *How To Grade U.S. Coins,* explaining in detail the sometimes arcane methods used to determine the condition of a coin. Halperin relies on illustrations to show where damage to a coin is most likely to impact the grade and to show where friction is most likely to occur. Halperin explains the process of weighting surface preservation, luster, strike, and eye appeal to determine an accurate grade for the coin you hold in your hands. Other sections include "Prooflike Coins," "Computer Grading," "Grading Other Series," how grading services evaluate problem coins, and more. Here's the deal: You can buy the book for $14.95 or read the entire book free on this Web site.

Coin Clubs (www.coinclubs.com)

Looking for a coin club in your area? Check out this site. Additional features include "Info-Links," "How To Promote A Coin Show," and "Virtual Collections."

Appendix

Coining a Phrase

*N*umismatics has a specialized language all its own — this appendix helps you understand the jargon.

About Good: a grading term for a coin that is so badly worn that you can barely recognize the type and date.

About Uncirculated (AU): a grading term used to describe a coin that is nearly new. Also referred to as Almost Uncirculated.

ancient: a coin struck before Medieval times.

artificial toning: fake colors on a coin that usually hide flaws.

bagmarks: the nicks and dings caused when coins smack into each other.

blank: the disk of metal that is stamped to make a coin.

blemishes: any defects on the surface of a coin.

bourse: a coin show where dealers buy and sell among themselves and with the general public.

branch mint: any U.S. Mint other than the Philadelphia Mint.

BU rolls: set quantities of coins that are Brilliant Uncirculated. For example, a BU roll of Morgan Dollars has 20 coins, none of which have been circulated.

C: the mintmark of the U.S. Mint at Charlotte, North Carolina.

Cameo Proof: a coin that has frosty devices and brilliant fields.

catalogs: the printed listings offered by coin dealers at auction or showing fixed prices. Catalogs are often great sources of information and illustrations.

CC: the mintmark of the U.S. Mint at Carson City, Nevada.

certified: authenticated and graded by any of the independent, third-party grading services.

choice: a nice coin. Usually used with other grading terms, for example, Choice Very Fine or Choice Uncirculated.

Choice Uncirculated (CU): equal to Mint State 63 on a scale of 1 to 70.

circulated: a coin that is worn through use.

circulation strike: a coin that was made to be used and spent. The opposite are Proof coins that are made specially for collectors and are not meant to be spent.

clad: coins made of layers of metal. Examples include modern U.S. Dimes, Quarters, Half Dollars, and Dollars that have centers of copper and outer layers of a copper-nickel alloy.

cleaned: a coin that has had dirt or toning removed with a cleaning agent. Cleaning ranges from light to severe, depending on what is used to clean the coin. Cleaning may disqualify a coin from being certified.

coin doctorer: someone who attempts to improve the appearance of a coin through cleaning, repairing, plugging and/or any other deliberate alteration.

coin show: a gathering of coin dealers in a public place for the purpose of meeting and trading with collectors and other dealers.

colonial: a coin issued by, or used in, any of the American colonies. Includes some foreign coins.

commemorative: a coin struck specifically to honor a place, event, or person. Commemorative coins are generally sold at a premium and are not meant to circulate.

common: a coin that is readily available and inexpensive.

condition: the grade of a coin.

Condition Census: a listing of the top examples known of a given coin. For instance, the Condition Census for Large Cents includes the best examples known of a particular variety.

consignment: the coins that are given to an auction house or dealer to sell.

contact marks: any marks on a coin that occur from contact with another coin or foreign object.

D: the mintmark of the U.S. Mints at Denver, Colorado and Dahlonega, Georgia.

design type: the name given to the design on a particular U.S. coin.

device: any of the design elements on a coin.

die: the steel cylinder with a design on it used to strike one side of a coin.

die variety: every die is unique, especially early U.S. dies engraved by hand. A die variety is a unique combination of obverse and reverse dies. Some die varieties can be extremely rare.

dip: to clean a coin in a chemical bath to remove toning.

doctored: a coin that has been cleaned, altered, repaired, or otherwise "improved" to make it more valuable.

double-struck: a coin that has been struck twice from the dies.

edge: known as the third side of a coin, the edge is the surface that encircles a coin.

elements: the various designs, lettering, and markings on a coin.

encapsulated: placed in a sealed plastic holder by any of the independent, third-party grading services.

error: a coin that results from a mistake in the coining process.

estimate: a guess as to what a coin will sell for at auction, usually based on price guides and comparable sales.

Extra Fine (EF or XF): a well-preserved coin with a grade range from 40 to 49 on a grading scale of 1 to 70. Also called Extremely Fine.

eye appeal: the visual aspects of a coin. Coins with nice eye appeal are worth a premium.

face value: the value that is stated on a coin. For example, the face value of a Dime is ten cents. The collector value of the same coins may be substantially higher.

Fair: a grading term for a coin that is so worn that the type is barely identifiable.

Fine: a grade range from 11 to 19 on a grading scale of 1 to 70.

Finest Known: the coin ranked as the best example known of a denomination, type, date, or variety.

first strike: the first coin, or one of the earliest coins, struck from a pair of dies. These are usually Prooflike, well struck and nearly perfect.

full strike: a coin that has complete details thanks to a crisp, bold stamp from the dies.

Gem Uncirculated: a grade range of 65 to 66 on a scale of 1 to 70.

Good: a grading term for a coin that is very worn but has most of the devices outlined.

grade: the determination of the degree of wear (or lack thereof) on a coin.

grading: the art or skill of determining the condition of a coin.

incomplete strike: a coin in which parts of the design are missing or weak. This can be caused by poor pressure, misaligned dies, or foreign matter on the dies.

intrinsic value: the metal or bullion value of a coin, regardless of the face or collector value.

legend: any of the wording or lettering on a coin. A motto, such as, "In God We Trust," can be a legend.

luster: the shiny quality of new metal. Luster decreases as wear increases.

mintage: the quantity of a particular coin struck by the U.S. Mint.

Mint set: a specially packaged set of Uncirculated coins produced and sold by the U.S. Mint.

Mint State (MS): Uncirculated coins that range from 60 to 70 on a grading scale of 1 to 70.

mintmark: the small letter (or letters) on a coin that identify the mint where the coin was struck.

multiple-struck: a coin that was struck more than once.

numismatics: the study of coins and coin collecting.

O: the mintmark of the U.S. Mint at New Orleans, Louisiana that struck coins from 1838 to 1909.

obverse: the front of a coin, usually the side with the date or head. When you flip a coin and call "heads," this is the side you want.

off-center: a coin that was not perfectly centered when it was struck. Off-center strikes can range from minor to extreme.

original: a coin that has never been cleaned or impaired in any way.

original roll: a roll of coins that remains as fresh as the day the coins were first struck.

original toning: the natural color on a coin, as opposed to artificial toning.

overdipped: a coin that has received one too many chemical baths in a misguided attempt to clean it.

overdate: a coin with two dates (or parts of dates), one on top of the other.

overgrading: the deliberate or unintentional grading of a coin above its true grade. This practice is sometimes used to sell coins for more than they are worth.

P: the mintmark of the U.S. Mint at Philadelphia, Pennsylvania, the mother of all U.S. Mints. Early coins from Philadelphia had no mintmark; more modern issues bear the letter P.

pattern: a coin that tests a design to see how it appears in coin form and to determine whether it strikes properly. By definition, a pattern is a design type that was never accepted for regular use.

pioneer gold: privately issued gold coins struck by a variety of minters anywhere in the United States where gold was discovered.

Poor: a grading term for a coin that is so badly worn that you can barely recognize the type and date. *See* "About Good."

plugged: a coin that once had a hole drilled through it, but now the hole has been filled to bring the coin back to its original appearance and full value.

Prestige set: a special set of Proof U.S. coins that includes the normal denominations, plus one or more of the Proof commemorative coins issued that year.

price guide: any number of publications that list wholesale and/or resale prices for coins, often in a number of different grades or categories.

price list: a published listing of a dealer's inventory, priced for sale.

Proof: a special process for producing coins of exceptional quality and brilliance. Proof coins exhibit a full strike, mirrored surfaces, and sometimes a cameo effect.

Proof set: the specially packaged set of Proof coins produced and sold by the U.S. Mint each year.

Prooflike: a circulation strike that mimics the deeply reflective appearance of a Proof coin.

restrike: a coin from genuine dies, struck later than the year indicated on the coin, usually to satisfy collectors.

reverse: the back of a coin, usually the side without a date or a head. When you flip a coin and call "tails," this is the side you want.

S: the mintmark of the U.S. Mint at San Francisco, California.

seller's fee: the commission charged to the consignors in an auction.

series: the complete listing of all dates and mints of a denomination or design type that were struck.

set: a complete collection of all the dates and mints of a denomination or design type that were struck.

Sheldon scale: the grading scale developed by Dr. William Sheldon that ranks coins on a scale of 1 to 70, with 70 representing perfection.

strike: the degree to which metal flows into the recesses of the dies when a coin is struck. The strike of a coin is usually referred to as weak, soft, bold, or full.

struck: a coin created in a press by stamping a blank piece of metal with a pair of dies.

successful bidder: the winner in an auction.

surface: the outer layers of metal on all sides of a coin.

token: a small coin with no stated value. These are usually made for commemorative or advertising purposes.

toning: the color changes that occur on coins as a result of oxidation or contamination. Sometimes toning can be ugly; often it can be quite beautiful. Beware of artificial toning.

type: any particular design or denomination.

undergrading: the grading of a coin below its true grade. This practice is sometimes used to purchase coins below what they are really worth.

Very Fine (VF): a grade range of 20 to 39 on a grading scale of 1 to 70.

Very Good (VG): a grade range of 7 to 11 on a grading scale of 1 to 70.

wear: friction on the surface of a coin.

world coins: any coin issued by countries other than the United States.

year set: a collection of all denominations produced in a given year.

Index

• Y •

Notes

FOR

DUMMIES®

The easy way to get more done and have more fun

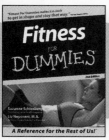

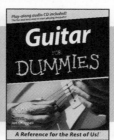

FOR DUMMIES®

A world of resources to help you grow

 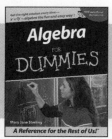 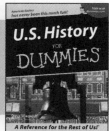
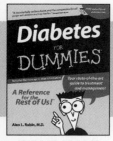